D1209892

The Centre of the World at the Edge of :

The
Centre
of the
World
at the
Edge of A
Continent

Carol Corbin and Judith A. Rolls

University College of Cape Breton Press

©Carol Corbin, Judith A. Rolls, 1996.

All rights reserved. No part of this work may be reproduced or used in any form or by any means, electronic or mechanical, including photocopying, recording, or any information storage or retrieval system, without the prior written permission of the publisher.

The University College of Cape Breton acknowledges the support received for its publishing program from the Canada Council's Block Grants program.

"Music as a Living Tradition" was previously published in the *Proceedings from the Conference "Cape Breton in Transition: Economic Diversification and Prospects for Tourism,"* Sydney, N.S.: Louisbourg Institute, 1995.

A preliminary version of "The Use of Nicknames in Cape Breton" was presented to the *Canadian Society for the Study of Names* at the Learned Societies Conference at the University of Windsor, June 1988.

"The World Which Is At Us" was previously published as "Re-Gaeling Cape Breton," in *Canadian Geographic,* Jan/Feb 1996.

Cover design by Brenda Berry, Goose Lane Editions
Printed and bound by Tribune Printing.
10 9 8 7 6 5 4 3 2

Canadian Cataloguing in Publication Data
  The centre of the world at the edge of a continent
  ISBN 0-920336-82-5

1. Cape Breton Island (N.S.) – Social life and customs.
2. Cape Breton Island (N.S.) – Civilization.
3. Popular culture – Nova Scotia – Cape Breton Island.
I. Corbin, Carol, 1951- II. Rolls, Judith A. (Judith Ann). III. Title.

FC2343.4 C46 1996   971.69   C96-950047-5
F1039.CZC46 1996

University College of Cape Breton Press
Box 5300
Sydney, Nova Scotia
CANADA B1P 6L2

TABLE OF CONTENTS

III. Community and Family Life

IV. Culture and Identity

Foreword

We called this book *The Centre of the World at the Edge of a Continent* because the play of contrasts it inspires seems apt for Cape Breton. How can an edge be a centre? Indeed, how can Cape Breton be the centre of the world? But that is exactly what it is — to us. In these studies, we do not look at centres of power — Ottawa or Washington; we look at ourselves and we know that this place is very much the centre of our world, even as this island rests on the edge of the North American continent.

I am one of those "Come From Away" people, lucky enough to be able to live here. My first few weeks on the Island of Cape Breton, late August and early September, 1991, were blueberry picking time. Because I grew up in cities in the United States, picking blueberries was something I had never done before. My neighbours in Marion Bridge, Maureen and Sonny MacLeod, took me to the Marion Bridge Blueberry Festival at the community pasture. It was a brilliant sunny day, the kind that for some reason seems exclusive to Cape Breton. The fields were golden with early autumn grass, and people were scattered about in clusters, stooped picking berries. I ate blueberry cake, I rode on a horse-drawn haywagon, I listened to fiddle music and watched stepdancing.

To most Cape Bretoners, this festival is a typical one, replicated in different forms across the island almost every weekend. But for me it was altogether new and fascinating. I felt like I had stepped into a world out of time, out of the stream of the ordinary urban existence that I had known. Even after four years here (and the questionable assertion that I now am a Cape Bretoner), I am still often surprised by an unexpected experience – Newfoundland potato cakes at Christmas time, extravagant Halloween decorations, the consistent and steadfast community attendance at a wake, a novel wedding dance, a gift, a visit, and the interminable beauty of this island.

Cape Breton begs to be written about, and, of course, it is written about. A joke among my friends in Louisbourg is that I'm here just to write a book and then I'll leave. Maybe I am seen as an American anthropologist seeking vestiges of a simpler life on this island. Or maybe they think that I need the stimulation of a gorgeous natural environment and a rich cultural life to use as a setting for a romance novel. I don't know. But all I have to do is leave the island and I know, without a doubt, that it is a special place.

CAROL CORBIN
Louisbourg, Nova Scotia
March 17, 1996

Clearly, Cape Breton and its culture is special. I was among the fortunate to grow up listening to the strains of fiddle music and *Put a Nickel in the Parking Meter* on CJCB radio. And I waited anxiously to see my Aunt Mary Denny's round and square group on Cape Breton Barn Dance or to hear my grandmother, Eunice Pickup's version of "Annie Laurie" being featured on Lloyd MacInnis' People and Things. These and other events, like wonderful Sunday picnics and having to wait for Ross' ferry or rainy camping trips in the days before floored tents, served as the building blocks for the values that I have embraced throughout my life – humour, practicality, honesty, family traditions, appreciation for the arts, and so forth. And although the myriad experiences one encounters along the road to adulthood both temper and embellish our early beliefs, these "tools" have continued to give meaning to my life.

Working on this book has given me an opportunity to examine closely the culture and values from which I come and to understand how they manifest themselves in our day-to-day lives. I have had to identify, analyze, and rectify my own basic assump-

8

tions about Cape Breton and it has not been easy. However, through this process I have acquired a grander appreciation for the island and I have been reminded how "small" things give life big meaning.

JUDY ROLLS
Sydney, Nova Scotia
March 17, 1996

We are grateful for funding from the Aid to Small Universities Program which partially assisted in the research for this book. We also wish to thank David Schmidt, Laura Peverill, Kate Currie, Michelle MacDonald, Gail Jones, and Robert Morgan for their help and encouragement with this project.

Introduction:
Communication, Culture, and Cape Breton Island

CAROL CORBIN

Why are two communication scholars editing a book about Cape
Breton culture? Besides our individual appreciation for Cape
Breton and the people and traditions, why are we connecting
communication with culture? Communication theorists like
James W. Carey believe that communication and culture are in-
separably linked.[1] Communication has two important cultural
aspects. First, it is the act of transmitting messages, and messages
are always culturally bound in both the language and the customs
of a people. Second, communication is ritual, repetition, and symbolism. It is the metacommunication that informs and guides the
message dimension of communication. The very act of greeting
("Hi, how are you?" "Good dear, good.") is more ritual than message. We learn little information about the person we greet, yet
we solidify the connection between people each time we engage
in ritual communicative acts. Culture, then, is the guiding and
binding aspect of communication. All cultures are constructed
communicatively, and they are re-constructed every day as we re-
peat the rituals of our relationships within our societies.

Communication is the basis of human fellowship, and is a
word closely connected to "community." It produces, creates, sus-
tains, and changes the interpersonal links that make us social
beings. It is within the social structure and these myriad social
networks that culture exists.[2]

Of course, the word "culture" can be an elusive term. According to Raymond Williams, it is one of the most complex words in
the English language and has evolved to have three distinct us-
ages in English. First is the reference to a general human "process
of intellectual, spiritual and aesthetic development."[3] The second

usage "describes the works and practices of intellectual and especially artistic activity."[4] And the third usage "indicates a particular way of life, whether of a people, a period, a group, or humanity in general." This third definition – a way of life – is closely related to the German use of the word Kultur. Elias Norbert investigates this aspect of culture in his various books about manners and social control in the Middle Ages. He defines culture as the everyday expressions of a people: "They take form on the basis of common experiences. They grow and change with the group whose expression they are. The situation and history of the group are mirrored in them."[5]

It is primarily Norbert's definition of culture that informs the essays in this volume. Culture, from this perspective, is multi-layered and fluid. It is constructed both vertically and horizontally, with all sorts of variations in between. Vertically, culture moves from top to bottom and bottom to top between the class strata of any society. For example, high culture, or "Culture" with a capital "C", is often the purview of the upper classes. During the Middle Ages, manners and civility (civilité) were fostered among the elite as a way of separating themselves from the peasants and lower classes. As royal courtiers cultivated the affectations of the ruling class, the aspiring wealthy – the bourgeoisie – imitated the court style of dress, speech, table manners, and so forth, in order to move effortlessly into elite circles. But courtly style was mercurial. Just as the bourgeoisie mastered the court's table manners, the manners would change, ever so subtly, but just enough to expose the odd faux pas and hence distinguish the "ins" of the upper classes from the "outs" of the lower ones. Attributes of high culture, then, often are cultivated at the top and aspired to (often poorly) from the bottom.

Yet high culture, today as in the past, it isn't simply a top down model with the elites determining fashion trends and leading the way in refined dining manners. Consider blue jeans. What began as a working person's trousers were co-opted by the elite who incorporated them into their casually elegant couture, and soon designer names distinguished the "better" jeans from the "cheap" ones. Or take jazz. Once a resistance form of music among black Americans, it lost its power as a counter cultural musical symbol when predominantly white audiences embraced it and turned it into a high art form. Now Ivy League universities offer music appreciation courses in the history and significance of jazz.

Cultural forms and systems cross class borders effortlessly because they are constructed in symbols. They are fluid and ethe-real artifacts of human communication. Not only do the symbolic manifestations of culture move between and among the classes of a people, they also move across and between peoples geographi-cally, transported by messengers, troubadours, and, eventually, through media. In this way culture is constructed horizontally. For most of human history we were bound by geography, either in nomadic territories or in agrarian tribes, to the place where we were born. Few people travelled more than a few miles from their homes. But even before mass transportation and mass communi-cation, even before the printing press and worldwide web sites, information and ideas were exchanged between people and across cultures, clan to clan, village to village, and tribe to tribe. In this respect all cultures are hybrids, constellations of attributes that fit particular people at particular times in particular places.

Technologies of mass communication contribute greatly to cultural hybridization by making expressions of culture readily available to vast audiences. Vertical and horizontal distinctions are levelled with a flick of the ON switch. What was once the bailiwick of the upper class now can be broadcast to the masses, and subjects germaine to one particular region now reach far be-yond any geographical boundary. Mass communication creates popular culture – a classless, borderless blanket of "I Love Lucy," McDonald's hamburger chains, and Shakespearean plays on PBS. (You will notice that all three of these examples originated in the United States, even the Scottish-sounding fast food con-glomerate.) Distinctions of class, traditions, and language are blurred. Today's Asian farmers have more knowledge of and ac-cess to global events and information than any European king or queen did 150 years ago – that's a mere five generations.

The cultures created by mass communication cannot replicate the authenticity, the aura, of engaging with living human beings. The one-of-a-kind artifact, the kitchen parties, the personal cup of tea can never be replicated in mass media. Everyday or "folk" culture has in its very make-up a certain resistance to commodifi-cation and quantification. "Folk," as in the German Volk and its Teutonic precursor folc,[6] means 'people', or the 'people's culture.' Folk is not necessarily some quaint anachronism, like a Grandma Moses painting – which, by the way, is no longer deemed folk, but now high art – but a truly people-generated way of doing things. While we may value folk culture, the authentic and the "real" of any culture, we know that it can slip effortlessly, imperceptibly, beyond its vertical and horizontal borders. A recording of Cape Breton's Jo-Anne Rolls is heard across Canada on the CBC and gives new lyrical ideas to a Saskatchewan musician. We switch on the TV in Cheticamp and watch Hmong tribes in Thailand making quilts, and we think of a new pattern for our next hooked rug.

The quest, therefore, cannot be to find the "true" or "real" culture of a place. Indeed, it may be futile to attempt to uncover the roots of traditions, since their seeds are spread like wild flowers, growing and maturing where we least expect them, and dying off in the place they originated. There is often no logical direction of influence: the edge of the world becomes the centre, and the centre, the edge. (How else can one explain why Celtic fiddlers from Ireland and Scotland come to Cape Breton to learn "traditional" Celtic fiddling?) But the medium of influence is clear: human communication. Whether we are praying together at a wake, swapping stories over steaming cups of tea, or wooing a skating partner at Centre 200, it is in our everyday conversations that Cape Breton's communities are renewed and sustained.

Even as we engage in personal interactions, we cannot help but recognize the powerful influence of mass-mediated messages. We live in an age when a vast array of messages is beamed endlessly, tirelessly, to every corner of the globe, creating what feels like one big, unified, homogenous culture. But somehow differences remain. Indeed, it is possible that these differences are increasing, as both refreshing alternatives to mass society and as markers of resistance to homogeneity in a post-colonial world.[7] One might travel to the Hebrides or Okinawa to learn about another culture, not because it is less developed or more developed, but because we have learned to value and respect differences, indeed to revel in difference. In a trans-cultural exchange it is easy to pick out the sameness of peoples as well as their differences. How the Other eats, sleeps, entertains, worships, and communicates are all noted in the postcards we send home or in academic studies of the subtleties of gesture and customs in a different society.

To cross the causeway to Cape Breton is to discover this sense of difference, and this collection of essays about everyday life on the Island celebrates the crossing. To most Cape Bretoners, each essay reflects one story of who we are. To others, they attempt to describe and explain what we do or did, and why we do or did it. The contributing authors attempt to turn Cape Breton culture inside out and look underneath its surface for the meanings embedded beneath. Not every ritual or cultural practice has been included, not every ethnicity or subculture has a story here, and not every voice has been recorded. In this respect, these essays are abstractions of the real life adventures of people living, working, and playing on Cape Breton Island.

Certain themes run through many of the essays which, when taken together, may help give meaning to some of the experiences of Cape Bretoners. One theme is the quality of social interaction that people of Cape Breton have. Getting together, whether over tea or over tarabish, is an essential part of the culture. By extension, another theme emerges as we recognize the importance of orality. Not only is there a lot of "just plain talk" going on in Cape Breton – in Gaelic, Mi'kmaq, Acadian French, Ukrainian, English, Italian, and other languages – we also realize the importance of the oral transmission of traditions, life stories, and fiddle tunes. Most of us on Cape Breton have an exceptional sense of humour, a characteristic that not only appreciates a good joke but exhibits the self-assurance to laugh at ourselves. This humour endures despite the economic hardships that currently bedevil our Island. Hence, many of the essays contain a hint of bittersweet nostalgia, of a loss of innocence in the face of modern media, modern technologies, and a rapidly changing quality of life. As we open our homes, our cultures, and our pristine shores to ever more people, we lament the changes these outsiders bring to our way of life and the uncertainty of the future. Nevertheless, these essays engender a sense of optimism and a belief that the tenacious Cape Breton character can weather these storms and adapt to, even be strengthened by, the global cultural changes going on around us.

Writing about Cape Breton culture is a new way of writing our history. Every cultural feature we document crystallizes some part of our present and past. This new kind of history emphasizes the activities of everyday life, of bingo and stepdancing, of sidewalk conversations and watering holes, and does so in the words of the people themselves. The shift from "Great Man" historiography (with its focus on generals, kings, and presidents) to cultural history has come about for a number of reasons. Some would say it is in response to the feminist revolution in which women are demanding a voice, a presence, in the great recording of humanity. Others would say the shift is part of a larger social phenomenon of the second half of the twentieth century, one that privileges the expressions of once-silenced groups; the invisible communities of working class, native, elderly, and other previously marginalized people all have gained voices. Sam Migliore's essay in this collection is an example of the type of cultural study that allows the informants – those who are being studied – to speak for themselves. Sam interprets and frames their words, but for the most part the cultural "experts" have yielded their vaunted positions. Now the informants, the ordinary people, are the experts and the scholars act as facilitators to allow them to speak.

The authors of the essays have varied backgrounds and interests. They are students and scholars, some from Cape Breton and some from away. They have finely tuned their ears to the Cape Breton conversations and customs all around them. Of course, like a fish describing water, the culture in which we were born and in which we live is, for the most part, invisible to us. It simply is the way it is, and to a certain extent the way it always has been. It is commonsensical, normal, usual, and everyday. And to many it seems unimportant – certainly not noteworthy. But as we encounter more cultures and recognize the distinctiveness of each, we come to appreciate that which is our own. We reflect upon the qualities of our everyday lives and record their nuances, knowing that they are ever changing, ever receiving influences from around the globe, and ever more various and multifaceted than we could possibly capture in a lifetime, let alone in a single volume.

References

1. Carey, James W. *Communication as Culture.* Boston: Unwin Hyman, 1989.

2. Carey, 22-23.

3. Williams, Raymond. *Keywords.* (Second Edition) New York: Oxford, 1983: 90. Clifford Geertz, on the other hand, works with 11 different definitions of culture based on Clyde Kluckhohn's *Mirror for Man* covered in 27 pages of Kluckhohn's book. (Geertz, Clifford. *The Interpretation of Cultures.* New York: Basic Book, 1973: 4-5.) For our purposes, Raymond Williams's three definitions ought to do.

4. Williams, 90.

5. Elias, Norbert. *History of Manners.* New York: Pantheon, 1978:6.

6. Williams, 136.

7. See for example *The Politics of Difference,* Edwin N. Wilmsen and Patrick McAllister, forthcoming from the University of Chicago, 1996.

I. Pastimes

'See You at the Forum':
Pleasure Skating The Cape Breton Way

COLEEN MOORE-HAYES

The smell of wet, woollen mittens wafting from the warm-morning heater, Foster Hewett announcing, "It's hockey night in Canada," and Faron Young crooning "On the Wings of a Snow White Dove." These are but three of the symbols that have become synonymous with my first memories of skating. Throughout this essay, I will share with you the memories and reflections of generations of Cape Bretoners for whom pleasure skating is as much a part of the culture as is tartan and fiddle music.

Skating at the forum.
Beaton Institute Eachdraidh Archives
– University College of Cape Breaton

Nova Scotia Leads the Way

John Quinpool (1936) wrote in Halifax's *First Thing Publishers* that the earliest record of skating in America was DeMont's expedition to Acadia in 1604. Young Acadian men stationed at St. Croix,

New Brunswick, hunted rabbits by skating across frozen ponds and brought their quarry down with snowballs. When the settlement was transferred to Port Royal, Nova Scotia, a year later, that community was credited with establishing the first permanent skating rink in Canada.

It is not surprising, considering Canadian winters, that ice-skates, along with snowshoes, would be among explorers' and fur traders' equipment for winter travel. It wasn't, however, until the middle of the nineteenth century that ice skates became associated with leisure time activity.

Initially, skates were made with a wooden frame that was screwed into the heel of a boot. Leather straps were used to secure the wooden frame to the foot. The result was a cumbersome and not very effective skate. This predicament became the catalyst for what would be one of the many times that Maritimers took the lead in advancing the sport of skating.

In 1861, the first metal skates were produced in Halifax, (Eitzen & Sage, 1986). Not only did this initiative put Nova Scotia in the forefront as the originator of metal-spring skates, but it also became a lucrative business that attracted an international clientele. Skates made in Nova Scotia were shipped across Canada, the United States, and throughout Europe. British and French soldiers stationed in Canada took enthusiastically to ice-skating, and when they returned to Europe, the Nova Scotia-made skates went with them (Eitzen & Sage, 1986).

There was, however, one major barrier to enjoying the sport of skating. Despite a growing desire on the part of skaters to participate in this new-found pastime, the heavy snow fall frequently covered skating surfaces, ruining the ice. Often, for days or even weeks at a time, poor ice conditions made it impossible to skate comfortably or safely. To remedy this situation communities started constructing sheds large enough for people to skate inside. Although the first indoor ice-rink was built in Quebec in 1859, the Maritimes did not lag far behind. In 1863, the first covered rink in Halifax was opened at the Horticultural Gardens (Howell & Howell, 1969, p 23).

Skating rinks continued to grow in popularity and became the centres of social activity after Confederation. In the late 1800s party-goers dressed in formal attire would attend costume balls and carnivals in skating rinks. Platforms and chairs were built at the edge of the ice surface and patrons would be treated to games, music and entertainment (Quinpool, 1936).

Perhaps one of the reasons for the popularity of recreational skating was that it is an activity that can be enjoyed by women and men of all ages. In Cape Breton, where sports were usually deemed male activities, girls were taught, and indeed encouraged, to skate as early as boys. Pleasure skating was safe, healthy, inexpensive, and easily accessible throughout the long winter months. It was also one of the few sports that was considered to be "ladylike."

I have been a regular skater for over 30 years and my interest in skating prompts me to believe that pleasure skating is an excellent example of a cultural practice in Cape Breton. To investigate skating in Cape Breton, I conducted a series of interviews with skaters and compared their interpretations of skating with my personal experience. The demographics of the skaters I interviewed varied in age, background, and marital status. One of the people I spoke to was a teenage boy who had recently started skating, while many of the others had more than a half century experience on the ice. In one case, a woman invited me to go through her skating scrapbook of pictures and articles about Sydney skating and skaters since the early days of the Sydney Forum. Two of the skaters were in their late eighties and were still enjoying the sport. But regardless of their demographic differences, the reasons why each one skated were fairly consistent: it is a great form of exercise; it is a good way to meet new friends or renew old acquaintances; the cost of skating is relatively inexpensive ($0.10 in the 1920s, $2.00 today); and it is an activity the whole family can enjoy. But the most common response was that they skate because it makes them feel good. Nothing, not even advanced age, has diminished their enjoyment of the sport.

The early skating rinks in Cape Breton were, for the most part, owned and operated by churches. In Sydney, St. Theresa's Parish rented a plot of land from the Dominion Steel and Coal Corporation and, in 1936, it was turned into an open air rink. Hockey teams, coached by the men of the Parish, played there, and skating parties were held every Saturday night, weather permitting (St. Theresa's Parish 1934-1984, 1984). Although hosted by the Parish, the whole community was welcome to attend these events.

Perhaps because of the festive origin of the early skating parties, it became popular to play music during pleasure skating. At outdoor skating rinks in Sydney, 78 r.p.m. records were played on a gramophone and a horn was used to amplify the sound. Aggie Lake, a long-time Sydney skater, said that while the scratchy sound of the music may be considered poor quality by today's standards, "on a cold clear night, skating with your beau, it was beautiful music" (Lake, 1995).

The Arena Rink on Inglis Street was the first indoor rink in Sydney. It was built in the early 1900s and, like the outdoor rinks, was used for both hockey games and pleasure skating. It was replaced in the 1930s by the Sydney Forum which would become "the" skating place in Sydney for the next 55 years.

Skaters came to the Sydney Forum from all over Industrial Cape Breton. Like the patrons of the 1800s, some came just to watch and they were usually treated to quite a show. Men and women, alone or in pairs, skated as if they were dancing, while records or a local band played music in 1/16th time. An evening of skating in Cape Breton consisted of 15 musical pieces, called "bands," four of which were designated as left bands. These bands are skated in a clock-wise direction, with the woman skating on the outside. To skate a left band, the woman would have to skate with as much strength as her partner so as not to lag behind or lose the beat. Subsequently, young girls became as proficient at the sport as their male counterparts. In a 1976 Cape Breton Post article, Romeo MacNeil, a life-long skater and 35-year employee of the Sydney Forum, described Sydney's skaters as the best pleasure skaters in the world. He said having observed skating for over 50 years that he had never seen more "powerful and beautiful couples skating" (MacNeil, 1976, p.9).

Many Cape Breton recreational skaters use racer skates – a skate with a black boot and an extra long blade that allows for greater acceleration. While racer skates are commonly used throughout North America for speed skating, in Cape Breton they are primarily used for pleasure skating. Cy Bowser, a former member of the Sydney Millionaires hockey team and long time participant of the Halifax skating community, indicated that racer skates are not used, nor are they even permitted, in any of their skating clubs (Bowser, 1980).

Rite of Passage

I don't remember the actual process of learning to skate, and yet I don't recall a time when I couldn't skate. I do, however, vividly remember my first visit to the Sydney Forum for morning skating.

At seven years of age and in the second grade, I was driven to the rink by my friend's father. Germaine and I were deposited at the door with our skates, twenty-five cents for admission, ten cents to spend on a treat, and strict orders to be waiting in the same spot to be picked up at 12:15.

Once inside, the sensation was extraordinary – a huge ice surface as smooth as glass, lots of kids (most of whom I didn't know), wonderful music playing on a loudspeaker . . . and it was warm. Having learned to lace up skates with freezing fingers at an outdoor rink, this was a luxury I couldn't have imagined.

Another revelation I was surprised to discover was that there existed a hierarchy at morning skating, and seven year-olds were at the low end of the pecking order. Young skaters with experience were sometimes tolerated by, and in unique cases even accepted into, the elitist circle of pre-teens who enjoyed the status of rink-rats (an accolade denoting a proficient skater who spent a lot of time in the rink). It wasn't that these older kids were unkind to us; in fact, they could not have been more ambivalent toward us if they tried. It was just obvious that their twenty-five cents bought them a more prestigious spot in the rink than ours did. Perhaps it was their inherent confidence or their athletic prowess that set them apart from the younger skaters. But whatever the division, the older skaters were first on the ice at the beginning of each band; they sat in the same spot week after week; they could cut perfect corners (even on the left-bands); and the boys occasionally asked the older girls to skate with them . . . . And then one Saturday we didn't show up for morning skating. We were old enough to move on.

A rite of passage is a ceremony that marks a person's change of status: any ritual or ceremony that marks a transition in the life of an individual. In skating at the Sydney Forum, this rite manifested itself when a skater moved from morning to afternoon skating. Skating from two until four o'clock was an entirely different experience. We now used the bus and not our father for transportation, the skaters were more experienced, and almost everyone skated in couples. Growing up in a predominately Roman Catholic community, where segregation between young boys and girls was rigidly enforced, skating was the one activity where this rule was relaxed. Boys, who were usually bashful, would confidently ask a number of different girls for "a band."

Then, with arms cross-linked and holding hands, we would skate in a style that is typical of this area. At afternoon skating we became more confident skaters and, in some ways, more confident people. We made new friends, we learned about music and movement, we even picked up a few social skills. The whole event seemed somehow more structured, more grown up.

The next level of the hierarchy, the progression from afternoon to evening skating, wasn't at all like the process of moving from morning to afternoon skating. Seven until nine o'clock was reserved for adult skating, so now age and not just experience was a factor. Evening skating was reserved for those who were sixteen or older, and only in special circumstances was a younger skater permitted to attend. It is, however, interesting to note that for most of the senior skaters that I interviewed, the hierarchy seems to have come full circle, because at eighty years of age they have returned to morning skating.

Erving Goffman makes reference to a set of persons engrossed in a common flow of activity and relating to each other through that flow as a "focused gathering" (Geertz, 1973, p. 424). By the time we advanced to evening skating, we had been part of this gathering of skaters for almost ten years. It was little wonder that with this kind of experience and practice, Sydney skaters dared to consider themselves to be among "the best."

The Way We Were (and will always be)

There have been changes and improvements in many accoutrements associated with the sport of recreational skating over the years. Today, nearly every community has an indoor rink with heated dressing rooms, concession stands, and popular music playing on expensive stereo equipment. The hours for skating are flexible enough to accommodate almost any lifestyle. The number of bands has increased from 15 to 30. We can even have our skates custom-made.

But for all those changes, the social context around the activity itself has remained pretty much intact. Whatever one's reason for skating may be, the ritual of donning the blades and spending a few hours blissfully gliding to music played in 1/16th time has been a part of entertainment in Cape Breton for many years. Skating is still a popular winter activity for all age groups, and there has been a resurgence in the number of older skaters who have returned to the sport, as well as an increase in young pleasure skaters.

As I rest between bands at Center 200, which is now "the" skating place in Sydney, I watch some 300 skaters, of all ages, whiz by. I reflect on the past and look forward to the future of a cultural practice that has been part of my life for over 30 years, and I realize that I am proud to be part of a group that some consider "the best in the world."

References

Bowser, C. (Family reunion, 1980). Personal communication.

Eitzen, S.D. & Sage, G.H. (1986). *Sociology of North American Sport*. Dubuque, IA: William C. Brown Publishers.

Geertz, C. (1973). "Deep Play, Notes on the Balinese Cockfight." *The Interpretation of Cultures*. New York: Basic Books.

Howell, N. & Howell, M.L. (1969). *Sports and Games in Canadian Life: 1700 to present*. Toronto: MacMillan of Canada.

Lake, A. (March 2, 1995). Personal communication

MacNeil, I. (April 16, 1976). Sydney Forum. *Cape Breton Post*, Sport Section, p.9. Sydney, Nova Scotia.

Quinpool, J. (1936). *First Things in Acadia*, First Things Publishers, p.123. Halifax, Nova Scotia.

_____ (1984). *St. Theresa's Parish 1934-1984*. Sydney: St. Theresa's Parish

Bungalows and Barbecues

ERNA MacLEOD

Our lives are made up of rituals. Each day we engage in prescribed practices and relationships that seem to us totally ordinary and normal. They are so commonplace we do not even question our associations or interpretations of these rituals; they make up our concept of reality – the world as it exists. Around the world, even within our own communities, these practices can be very different. By examining these aspects of culture, we can gain a better understanding of ourselves and of others.

In North America, we tend to place special emphasis on work-related rituals. We devote most of our waking hours to our jobs and we base our self-perception, to a large extent, on our occupational roles. Our chosen careers motivate us and give purpose to our lives. This is true in Cape Breton, as well; we use our occupations to define our identities, but we have a distinct attitude towards our work. Our main industries have traditionally been coal mining, fishing, and steel production. These are dangerous occupations with little opportunity for upward advancement or variety of experience. Historically, employment has been sporadic – interrupted by seasonal change, strikes, and lay-offs. The nature of our work has resulted in many social and economic problems which, in turn, have promoted a deeply-felt need for structured leisure as an outlet for despair and frustration; but also as a ritualistic expression of ourselves and our society – our beliefs, values, and attitudes.

Among these rituals of leisure, I feel that seasonal rituals have a particular significance. We are an island people, isolated to a certain degree in our own small communities. We live in a harsh climate where winter is long, dreary, and usually cold. Summer is brief, and all the more precious because of its transience. We rely on the promise of the warmth of summer and on our memories of past summers to carry us through the long nights of winter, the months of shovelling snow. Here in Cape Breton, the summer also represents economic stability. For many, employment is seasonal, dependent on the fishery and more recently, tourism. The warmer winds of spring can bring money and security for another year. As the island population swells with visiting tourists and returning family members, we feel a sense of revival and hope.

Our cohesive identity as an island people has been strengthened by our difficult economic situation. We are resigned to, and even proud of, the danger and drudgery of our lifestyles. We have come to view work and leisure as completely opposite. Work is necessary and must be endured so that we can enjoy leisure. We are passionate about entertainment and rejuvenation of the spirit. To many people outside of our culture, we seem rowdy and unrestrained. We are often perceived as heavy drinkers, loud partiers, and feisty brawlers who are somewhat ignorant of life beyond our island's coasts. Rather than disputing these stereotypes, we have embraced them, taking pride in our close-knit relationships to family and friends, bragging about our most scandalous behaviours, and firmly believing that we have it all here – nowhere else on earth are people as friendly, scenery as beautiful, or leisure as laid-back and thoroughly enjoyable. We envision ourselves as hospitable, gregarious, and uninhibited. I feel that two of our seasonal rituals – our bungalows and our barbecues – have become particularly symbolic of our love of summer and entertainment.

It is no coincidence that in its early years the "Summertime Revue" featured songs commemorating the barbecue and bungalow. We have developed our own definition of the word "bungalow," using it to describe our summer cottages. If we are not affluent enough to travel to far-off places and tropical resorts, we are not without breathtaking beauty on Cape Breton Island itself. It is not unusual for some of us to pack up our things and move, for a few weeks (or the entire summer), to our bungalow, although it might be only thirty or even as few as ten minutes from home. The Bras d'Or Lakes, Mira River, or Atlantic Ocean are never far away, and they offer an escape from the monotony of work and responsibility. Our bungalows reinforce our belief that there is no good reason to leave our island. We are surrounded by good company (excluding the flies), water for swimming, and familiar sights and faces. There is no need to fear transgressing some unfamiliar social code; this is our own cultural environment – we know that we can break the rules and be pardoned, because almost anything goes.

The bungalow also presents the perfect environment for another casual summer ritual of leisure, namely the barbecue. In Cape Breton, our summertime barbecues incorporate our beloved seafood – lobsters, mussels, clams, or crab – as well as the usual hot dogs and hamburgers. We savour the rich bounty of the sea around us and are reminded again that life couldn't be much better than this.

Thus, our bungalows allow us to relax in a material sense, as well as an emotional one. There is little pressure here to keep up with the Jones. Although there are many stylishly constructed, well-maintained summer homes in Cape Breton, there are also many rustic, somewhat dilapidated bungalows, built with an eclectic mix of old, new, and borrowed elements. What is interesting about this fact is that even the most humble of bungalows is not ridiculed or scorned. It seems we rate these possessions more for their sentimental value than for their material or resale worth. They represent to us a manifestation of ritual – they provide a link to the past, a sense of place in the present, and continuity in the future. In many cases, the construction of a bungalow is reminiscent of barn raising traditions, with friends and family pitching in to lend their particular talents. This sort of activity fosters a strong sense of community.

Bungalows often make the return of summer more predictable; we know where we will spend our free time, we look forward to seeing certain people each year and to resuming particular activities associated with summer and leisure. Our bungalows grant us freedom from the dictation of society regarding style and good taste. Hand-me-down furniture is perfect here, although it might be too shabby or tacky to use at home. Most of us strive to make our homes meet society's standard of acceptable appearance, but it is not appropriate to be too fussy about furnishing and decorating a bungalow. We want to feel free to leave the dishes in the sink or the bed unmade, or to come inside without removing our shoes. The bungalow presents an opportunity for us to live in closer contact with each other – we share a room or even a bed, and have limited facilities – we leave behind many conveniences like central heating, running water, the television. Not surprisingly, we rediscover conversation, storytelling, and song.

The bungalow endures through all of life's stages. Young children are afforded special privileges and freedoms – bedtime curfews are extended, baths are less frequent, and junk food is permitted, even at mealtimes. Beaches, fields, and forests provide unlimited possibilities for play, and this environment encourages imagination and resourcefulness. Often, children forge friendships with playmates they meet there who do not live in the same neighbourhood or attend the same school. These summertime friends enhance the experience of summer vacations and mark the passage of time. Each year they have changed significantly, yet somehow the feeling of kinship remains.

As children become adolescents, they begin to assert their independence, relying more on peers for companionship and guidance. Often parents leave for the bungalow while teenagers choose to remain at home, enjoying rare freedom from parental authority. Eventually, another milestone towards maturity is reached when teenagers can attend bungalow parties. Those who are fortunate enough to be able to host one of these parties receive particular prestige among their peers, as these are known to be the best of all gatherings – unchaperoned, free from the constraints of "proper" public behaviour. Here, among friends, social barriers are more relaxed; normally inexcusable breaches of conduct will be forgiven and might actually provide for lasting memories and bonds of friendship. The mention of a bungalow party evokes warm feelings of anticipation, freedom, and fun.

Parents develop their own associations with family trips to the bungalow. Many times these feelings become more positive in retrospect when memories of children's squabbles and tantrums, brought on by excitement and lack of sleep, have faded, leaving more positive images of fondness and nostalgia. Away from the responsibilities of work and community, family ties become stronger, memories are made, and the progression of time is recorded through photographs and stories. As children leave home to create families of their own, the bungalow becomes the site of family reunions.

Summer must come to an end, and in much the same way, the dalliances of youth must yield to more practical everyday concerns and adult responsibilities. We do not, however, outgrow the need for fun or release of tension. Perhaps this partly explains why we continue to treasure time spent at our bungalows; it is our brief return to the simpler life of youth. All of these rituals are performed without leaving Cape Breton, reinforcing our deep-rooted ties to home. Although many people are forced to pursue their lives in other places, I think most of us never lose our longing for home; we are profoundly nostalgic and sentimental.

The coming of fall usually means the return to normal routines. Autumn is a beautiful season in Cape Breton, with leaves changing to an array of reds and golds, and breezes becoming cool, crisp, and refreshing. The change of seasons signifies the beginning of the ritual of "battening down the hatches" to prepare for another winter. Children must return to school and adults must resume their obligations at home and work. Those who are only visiting often must leave Cape Breton for another year. It is likely that this limit placed on time spent at the bungalow adds to its appeal. We have been replenished by summer's energy and we are now ready to face another winter – the bungalow has renewed our sense of peace, endurance, and affiliation. By now, children are anticipating their reunion with school friends and adult minds are turning to the upcoming holiday season.

I was walking my dog one rare warm January day, when days at the bungalow were long past, and I caught the scent of my neighbour's barbecue wafting towards me. I was immediately overwhelmed by a longing for the warmth of the summer sun and the company of far away family and friends. I realized that my associations with the aroma of meat cooking on a barbecue are more than just the idea of a quick, easy meal. That aroma makes me think of many things – laughter, conversation, relaxation, enjoyment, sustenance. As I examined my feelings more closely, I realized that several symbols are embodied within the ritual of the barbecue. In a broad sense, the barbecue represents our concept of ourselves as North Americans. It offers traditional all-American food (usually beef) and perpetuates our ideas of family, relationships, and leisure. It represents a "focused gathering"[1] where everyone involved knows the rules of interaction. Our needs for acceptance and enjoyment are met. We escape, briefly, from the "rat race" in which we willingly engage for most of our lives. Barbecuing takes time, forcing us to slow down. Our values of competition and communion with nature are filled to a certain extent. We exchange stories, compare accomplishments, play "catch" or some other sport, and enjoy the sunshine and fresh air. The media legitimize the barbecue as a facet of our culture – there are songs written about the practice; advertisements portray it as symbolic of good times, and there is a vast assortment of commodities associated with it – clothing, utensils, condiments.

Our traditional familial and gender roles are perpetuated through the ritual of the barbecue. Men reinforce their "manliness" on this celebratory occasion; they don the ceremonial garb, take centre stage, and, in most instances, assume the role of cook. The setting is distinctly masculine. Barbecuing is associated most commonly with meat, usually beef. The cook is not hidden away in the kitchen, unobserved and unappreciated. Instead, he basks in the attention and adoration of those he feeds. He also quite often escapes the drudgery of clean-up. There are very few dirty dishes to be washed and those that do occur are usually taken care of by women in appreciation of his efforts. Cold beer, a working man's reward, is often associated with a barbecue. It is reminiscent of past times when men returned victorious from the hunt to enjoy a celebratory meal.

Women, on the other hand, tend to view a barbecue as a release from their usual responsibility of preparing the family meals. While this is true to a degree, they continue to occupy their traditional roles of nurturer and subordinate by overseeing the process – they normally supply utensils and condiments; they also partake in supervising children's play – supplying band-aids and fly-repellent. The barbecue does offer freedom from the kitchen, and women tend to spend this time re-establishing relationships, enjoying conversation and laughter.

Our North American culture teaches us the value of individualism, independence, and privacy; meals are normally eaten behind closed doors with a very select group of people. We tend to retreat from society, relying on electronic devices for connection with the outside world. The barbecue allows us to tear down some of these barriers, if only for a short time. We leave behind the television and the telephone and go out of doors. We are conspicuous – we can call out to neighbours and we tend to expand our social circle. The thought of a barbecue usually brings to mind a larger group than the immediate family. Normally, it includes visiting family members, neighbours, and friends. The setting is informal. The dress is casual. We can ignore some of the more stringent rules of etiquette and allow ourselves to behave more naturally without fear of offending social codes of more-structured dining. We can eat as soon as the food is ready because it is served hot and usually cooked in batches. We can ask for seconds, and we can use our fingers.

In Canada and the United States, there are ideal models of

behaviour regarding health, diet, and fitness that we wish to emulate. We idealize a trim, athletic body and healthy internal organs. We believe that everything we eat has some effect on our body's overall condition and consequently on our social status. Scientific research has been warning us of the relationship between fat, cholesterol, and heart disease for years now. Later studies implicated animal fat with the development of various forms of cancer. More recent claims linked nitrates and cancer. The newest research reveals that harmful carcinogens produced in grilled meat can contribute to colon cancer.[2] The fumes from cooking, when inhaled, can possibly be harmful even to those who don't eat the meat.[3] In spite of all this negative publicity surrounding the barbecue, we refuse to worry about the bombardment of cholesterol on our arteries and stubbornly relish our red meat. We remain in complete denial of the dangers of carcinogens and nitrates as we continue to dish out hot dogs, sausages, and hamburgers. This is our little piece of resistance against the social restrictions we normally willingly accept – the nine-to-five work day, the value of punctuality and refined table manners, the importance of privacy, and the need for a healthy diet.

The barbecue endures through changing times, partly because of its constancy, but also, I feel, because of its adaptability. It has adjusted to our demand for immediacy with the invention of the propane barbecue. It has responded to our efforts toward multiculturalism by offering ethnic dishes, and it satisfies our anxieties about health hazards by incorporating chicken and fish recipes, vegetables, and salads. Yet, our most popular image of the barbecue continues to be that of a meat-based meal, and beef is still the all-time favourite barbecue fare. Finally, the barbecue appeals to the child in all of us. As we grow older, summer is reduced to a few short weeks' vacation and a couple of trips to the beach for most of us. Time is of the essence; we rush through the day's duties and meals are eaten hurriedly to make time for more responsibilities. Only while relaxing in our backyards, enjoying a cold drink and the company of friends can we truly slow down and smell the fresh air, newly mowed grass, and flowers of summer. As children, these were part of our everyday world, and these sights and scents are particularly nostalgic. Perhaps this is the strongest symbolic image conjured up by the familiar aroma of food cooking on a barbecue. That aroma carries the promise of revitalization and replenishment of social and familial relationships. It embodies our perception of good times and good food, of freedom and acceptance, and reminds us of our bungalow days.

Some of our earliest memories are encoded in our recognition of particular smells. Long before we learn to encode memories by verbal association, we can recognize the scent of our favourite people, places and foods. Smells can evoke surprisingly clear pictures of the past. While writing this essay, I have come to realize how intricately these seemingly simple interpretations are connected to our expectations and behaviour. I understand more clearly why the scent of my neighbour's barbecue was able to transport me through time and space to a place where I felt accepted, nurtured, and filled with enjoyment.

The barbecue ritual is certainly not unique to Cape Breton, but we have welcomed it in typical Cape Breton fashion and enriched it with our own symbolism and subliminal meaning. We have combined such cultural artifacts like the barbecue, the bungalow, and the beach with our ideas about relationships, entertainment, and reasons for living that reach beyond the world of work. As technology forges ahead rendering many traditional occupations obsolete, problems such as loss of industry and high rates of unemployment become more prevalent worldwide. Organized leisure might prove to be the source of new avenues for employment; at the very least, it will provide a sense of purpose and a feeling of community in our lives. Here Cape Breton may lead the way, as we have already discovered the value of good, honest fun.

Today, economic difficulties and fears about the future have taken their toll on even the most stubbornly optimistic Cape Bretoners. Conversations are tinged with elements of wistfulness, sadness, and uncertainty, but also with hope. We can no longer ignore the invasion of the outside world due to advancing computer technology and the exodus of many of our young people, but we cling to familiar values using cultural icons and practices to reaffirm our belief that this is truly the best of all worlds, and that we are survivors – able to overcome hardship and oppression.

Winter is upon us again; if it is long and cold and if money seems tight, I hope some day to catch the scent of someone cooking on a barbecue as I pass by. It will sustain me until I am once again in gentler temperatures and more carefree times. The barbecue and the bungalow will continue to symbolize these things for me and for many other Cape Bretoners as long as we keep up their ritual practices. They will bestow upon us a longing for past summers and an anticipation for those to come.

Notes

1. Clifford Geertz, "Deep Play: Notes on the Balinese Cockfight," in *Rethinking Popular Culture*, eds. Chandra Muleerji and Michael Schudson (Berkeley: University of California, 1991), p. 249.

2. Jane Raloff, "Not So Hot Hot Dogs", *Science News*, April 23, 1994, pp. 264-5, 269.

3. Jane Raloff, "Meaty Carcinogens: A Risk to Cook?," *Science News*, Aug. 13, 1994, pp. 103.

'Going Out': A Taxonomy of Cape Breton Drinking Establishments

MICHAEL G. MacDONALD

'Going out' to one of the many drinking establishments on our Island is as integral to Cape Breton life as remarking about the weather. It is an activity that includes seeing and talking to people, listening to music, and drinking. The process of 'going out' is the key to understanding why bars play a role in social life. Bars offer one of many venues outside the home for social inter-action, and 'going out' usually means meeting friends in several different types of circumstances. Cape Breton bars allow one to socialize in ways that run the gamut from dropping by for a quick drink to spending great amounts of time and money. Depending on the particular bar frequented, one can visit with neighbours and friends or one might meet people for the first time. Cape Breton bars provide an important venue for the exchange of con-versation and for renewing or making acquaintances.

There are several basic characteristics of bars: the bar is a place that exists to serve alcohol, a place that is dimly lit, a place in which people engage in various forms of interaction, and a place in which we change our expectations about acceptable be-haviour. Like every different meeting place, the world within the bar is governed by a unique set of rules. This essay examines what people do when they go out to bars in Cape Breton and how their behaviours create the social rules that exist in different

I would like to thank my brother-in-law, Shaun Kennedy, for joining me on many of my excursions into the Cape Breton nightlife. He not only provided friendship, but valuable insights into the nature of bar behaviour in our area.

types of bars. Rather than attempting to answer the question "why do people go to bars?" I asked "what do people do in bars?" I resisted the temptation to refer to particular bars by name, although some are less well-disguised than others. Instead I group bars by types, following the approach of Sherri Cavan (1966), the author of what may be the definitive ethnography of bar behaviour to date.

This Guy Goes Into a Bar: Methodology

The data for this study were obtained by observing behaviour in twenty-three different Cape Breton bars on various occasions between July 1995 and January 1996. Visits ranged in length from less than an hour to more than four hours. As a participant-observer I consciously strived to appear like the typical customer by ordering a beer or soft drink and talking with a friend.

Cavan (1966) did not record data in the midst of other patrons but rather waited until she left the premises. I initially attempted this methodology but within the first month of the study I began to record my field notes right in the bars. This ensured accuracy and enabled me to record direct quotations. I engaged in this unobtrusive note-taking by folding a sheet of graph paper into an eighth of a sheet so that it fit nicely into the palm of my hand. Keeping the paper hidden was easy, and the scrawling of brief notes was done quickly with my own version of shorthand speeding matters further. Throughout the project, I reviewed notes from previous sessions to identify themes emerging from my observations.

What follows is a discussion of the types of bars and the behaviours I observed. I found four general categories of bars in Cape Breton: local bars; Legions and private clubs; night spots; and hybrid bars. These classifications are open for debate and I encourage others to conduct similar research into this interesting aspect of Cape Breton culture.

"Where Everybody Knows Your Name": Local Bars

According to Cavan (1966), the major distinguishing characteristic of local or neighbourhood bars is that they serve patrons who "designate them as 'my' bar . . . a kind of home territory" (p. 205). While many bars have regular patrons, the local bar is one that serves a particular geographic region. The home territory bar is present in many communities and, in some, the local bar may be the only drinking establishment. In larger areas, the local bar might be in close proximity to several other nightspots.

Based on my observations, I would characterize the local bar as catering to an older crowd (usually over thirty, according to at least four informants). Music is almost an afterthought but may be provided in the form of music videos, juke box selections (either an old one with scratchy 45's or a new one with compact discs), or a radio tuned to a local station. Local bars do not rely on a live band to draw people and they rarely feature dancing.

Staff members keep the music on the low end of the volume scale. When a music video competes with a song on the juke box, the resulting cacophony usually results in cries for the bartender to either mute the television or unplug the juke box. Because a patron has invested 25 cents in the juke box, the television generally gets muted. As one bartender told me after unplugging the television to allow people to hear the juke box, "Hey, it's like his quarter, right? Who am I to keep Ricky from enjoying his song?" Bartenders seem to understand the importance of pleasing the regulars, probably because they are usually from the same community.

One feature that sets the neighbourhood bar apart from the club or Legion is that no membership is required. Further, staff is kept at a minimum. Local bars usually have only one bartender who serves drinks, cleans floors, plays pool or darts with the patrons, and takes care of any trouble. When a person drinks too much and gets too loud, the bartender may solve the problem by referring to the person by name and alternating between making a joke of it or being firm. Bartenders never seem to wear any type of uniform, unlike staff in dance clubs.

One homey little bar in downtown Sydney was a favourite with a younger crowd, but it also had a share of older professionals who were known by name to the bartender. This bar was quiet and had a mellow ambience that allowed for conversation, just as many other local bars do. What was interesting was that the crowd differed in age and background, yet the bar shared the characteristics of a local bar in that people knew each other. On entering, I discovered I knew the bartender who went on to tell me the names of others I would (or should) know who had been in earlier: "Oh, you just missed _____." His assumption was that I was interested in the comings and goings of people he thought I would probably know. This attempt on his part was likely a way to make me feel comfortable and at home. He was giving me a framework that could help me situate myself within that bar. It was as if he was saying 'you know these people who come here; you can belong as well.'

"Welcome to the Club": Legions and Private Clubs

In Cape Breton, many communities have branches of the Royal Canadian Legion which serve as centres for interacting, dancing, and drinking. One need not be a member to attend Legion functions, although some events are listed for members and guests only. Legions are different from other clubs in that they are managed by an executive who oversees the day-to-day functions of the hall, and they are part of a nationwide organization of war veterans and their offspring. Otherwise, they are similar to clubs.

Private clubs generally require some form of membership and many are run by executives. How strictly membership is monitored varies from club to club. For instance, one club I visited has open nights as well as nights where only members with keys can enter. Another club requires that members be "buzzed in," although I never met anyone who was not given access. Still other clubs do not seem to screen access at all; customers simply pay the cover charge. Another club requires those entering to sign in, but they do not scrutinize this act very closely. I noticed 'Wile E. Coyote' was among the previous signers the night I attended. When asked why signatures were required, the person at the door thought it was "for the Fire Marshal or something." Perhaps the list functions as a way to make members feel a heightened sense of belonging. I asked the bartender in one club how someone might become a member. The response was, "Well, you come in for a while, we get to know you, find out if you're all right. Then you get a key." He also implied that someone might sponsor a prospective member.

The average age of patrons in clubs varies greatly, although certain age groups are attracted to certain clubs. Clubs have live bands that perform well-liked country, contemporary, or classic tunes, and well-known artists usually play some original material. While country music or oldies are the staples at clubs in Sydney Mines, North Sydney, Sydney, and Glace Bay, Newfoundland, Scottish, and Acadian music are popular in other areas around Cape Breton.

Club partons prefer a "so-so band over good records." When one considers the number of Cape Breton performers who have gone from playing bars to being stars, it is easy to understand why live performances are valued. However, there is no correlation between the quality of the band and the number of people who may show up at the club. A band that is considered "great" might draw a small audience. While expectations for so-called "bar bands" are seldom high, someone like local country artist Bruce Guthro (who receives radio air-play) often draws a good-sized crowd.

"We're Here for a Good Time": Nightspots

Nightspots cater to a younger, college-age crowd and feature loud, live bands and dancing. No membership is required but there is a cover charge of three or more dollars. By attracting lots of young people, nightspot owners make money by selling even a few drinks to a lot of people. People who go out specifically to dance seem to like a crowded bar, so popularity builds a following. One young woman looked around at the fairly large crowd and said, "This is nothing. You should come when it's packed. You can't even move in here." She did not seem to understand my question concerning why anyone would want to be packed in so tightly, so she answered, "It's great, you know? A really great crowd." I felt like an alien . . . an old alien. Some informants referred to a couple of the nightspots as "meat-markets," or places where people "pick each other up." Interestingly, many reputedly popular nightspots were quite "dead" when I went to them.

During this research, I spent less time in impersonal night-spots than in local bars because the latter were more social and nightspots lacked the "personality" of clubs or neighbourhood bars. Nightspots are about the same no matter where you travel throughout the world. They seem to be part of American-influenced popular culture and are clones of nightspots around the globe.

"Eat, Drink and be Merry . . . for a Buck": Hybrid Bars

Some bars seem to defy classification. For instance, there are bars that have live bands at times (like clubs do), but also rely on juke boxes or videos (like local bars do). Sometimes, the bar may serve a slightly older (twenty-five and over) group of people who watch baseball or hockey in the afternoon (a kind of local sports bar), while a disc jockey will play raunchy dance music to a youthful crowd at night (like in a nightspot). The difference between offering patrons an evening of country line-dancing or one of hip-hop party music begins to blur when we realize that the motivation is the same for both: owners want to draw a crowd and make money. I use the term 'hybrid' bars to describe those that are broad in appeal and offer a variety of features to attract customers.

Many drinking establishments have a grill and lure customers by offering cheap, hearty meals like spaghetti or steak. Another popular menu item is barbecued chicken wings, usually ordered by the dozens, in either wimp, mild, medium, hot or suicide sauce. The reasonable price of the meal serves as an enticement for patrons to enter the bar. Once there, the warm, dark atmosphere encourages them to stay on a little longer and drink a little more.

Besides the lure of the grill, lowering the prices on particular drinks on particular days also attracts customers. An example of this is "Shooter Night," during which the bar lowers the price of shooters (layers of different flavoured liqueurs in a shot glass). Other bars offer some form of a "Happy Hour," during which drink prices are discounted for a defined period of time (usually up to 8:00 or 9:00 p.m.). The idea is simple: reduce the price on some or all of the available drinks for a period, then hope the customer stays to buy more at full price. I noticed at least three examples of patrons ordering drinks only to be told that the special had just ended. Without exception, the patrons went on to order the more costly regular-priced drink.

Some hybrid bars also reduce the usual cover charge. For instance, some have a "Ladies Night" where men pay the full cover charge and women get in free. One female informant characterized ladies nights as "medium quality beef at low, low prices. It's pretty disgusting." A male informant suggested that a ladies night special may not draw more women, but "it sure brings out the guys looking for the ladies." Another way to reduce the cover charge is to have a "Loonie Night," which allows entrance for $1.00.

Bars also try to draw a crowd by hosting a contest or event that involves several people entertaining the other patrons. Pool tables, tarabish tournaments, and league darts attract people to clubs and local bars. One bar has a video trivia competition that matches its patrons with those from other North American bars. In another club, members participate in a lottery known as "Snowball." As participants continue to contribute, the jackpot snowballs into a large prize, sometimes up to $700.

Another common way to draw people into bars is to install video lottery terminals (VLT's). I have seen people stay at these machines for up to four hours–they were still there when I left. Seldom did patrons go over and play one or two quarters or loonies. Instead, they put in a full roll of loonies, letting their fortunes rise and fall over a two-hour period, and then put yet another roll into the machine. VLT's served as a spectator sport, often with whole conversations centring on how someone was doing. In one case, a ball team was having a few drinks in a local bar when one team member called out to a VLT player, "Cash that in and buy us a drink for f___ sake." The team did not expect the person to respond, so involved was he with the machine. Sometimes, a man and a woman would be at the machine taking turns or playing together. I noticed a few instances of one patron playing the VLT, while another would stand watching the screen with her arm draped over his shoulder. The VLT was the centre of their evening out.

"What Are These People Doing?": I'll Bet You Wouldn't Do That at Home

In one small neighbourhood bar in Sydney, the only source of entertainment was the sound of a local radio station playing on a small radio that was vintage 1968. Seated about the establishment was a small crowd of sixteen people. Two patrons were playing pool, four people were at the VLT's, and the others were sitting at tables. When the bartender answered the phone, he simply said "hello," rather than indicating the name of the bar. The place had a very relaxed atmosphere.

It was a hot summer afternoon, and like most bars, the interior was dark. I entered to observe patrons as they attempted to cool off and ended up seeing an interesting display. A man rode in to the bar on his bicycle and manoeuvred around the inside the bar.

The man on the bike did not simply move a metre or two but actually pedalled throughout the bar, making several laps. One woman who was apparently new to the establishment said, "I never saw anyone on a bike in a bar before." A man who had come to her table replied, "You never know what you'll see in here." No one, including the staff, attempted to stop the rider. In fact, no one said anything to him at all about the impropriety of riding a bike within the obstacle course of tables, chairs, pool tables, and patrons. Another man playing pool moved out of the way of the bicyclist without comment. The only remark about the incident directed toward the cyclist was, "You could take a heart attack in this weather, I'm telling you." Apparently he didn't think he should ride his bike home in the heat. Finally, the man stopped the bike and sat down. Still, no one mentioned his action, although everyone enjoyed the diversion of his afternoon ride. Cavan (1966) notes that "like unmoderated mutual involvement, a variety of social faux pas may be committed with equanimity in the public drinking place. Patrons may belch, stumble, fall asleep, or fall off bar stools, and such activity is routinely accorded the same status as more socially acceptable activity" (p.72). This clearly holds for Cape Breton as well.

"So One Guy Says to Another Guy. . . ."

What do people talk about in Cape Breton bars? Everything – sex, religion, politics, friends, enemies, games, sports, bars, people, pets, cars, relationships, and any other topic one can think of. I once overheard a discussion of the concept of free will versus determinism by two patrons who had shared approximately four pitchers of beer.

One of the most interesting interactions I observed was a conversation between two men standing at the bar. I left my table and moved close to them, and their conversation continued at a volume that reached me and the bartender. Through the entire conversation, the men paid little attention to my presence, despite the intimate nature of their interaction. They exchanged stories of sexual exploits and bragged about their ability to drive while intoxicated. What was notable about the conversation was not the topics but rather the fact that neither seemed to care who overheard them. They seemed to know that they had an audience which may have influenced the tone of their discussion. Throughout, buying drinks and bathroom breaks served as transition points in their interaction. The following is an excerpt from their dialogue. When I approached them, Man 1 was telling Man 2 about how his father had died recently:

1: Forty ouncer, pint. I drank it with him. We got a buzz.
2: And then it was over? He went?
1: Yeah, a few days later.
2: Were you with him at the end?
1: No. We said our goodbyes. He wouldn't want to see me. We said our goodbyes.
2: He was a great man. I never met the man.
1: He taught me military stuff when I was a kid.
2: Go on.
1: Seriously. Twelve years old and learning how to take people out. Thanks, Dad.

They continued with musings about life and death for a short time, then moved to women as a topic:

1: She bought me beer and pizza and videos, man.
2: Shut up.
1: Yeah, man.

Apparently, the woman in the relationship had a hidden agenda in welcoming the man to her home:

1: Picture it. You laid this one. She calls your fiance and says 'guess who was sleeping in my bed.'

They commented at one point about the time:

2: What time is it?
1: 10:25.
2: Oh Jesus, the wife'll have a search party out for me.
1: A surgical party?

45

After Man 1 made fun of his friend's slurred speech, they ordered another round. The topic that ended the night came about a half hour (and two drinks) later. Apparently, Man 1 had his wallet stolen at a party. His friend was more than sympathetic:

1: I can't wait 'til he tries to cash my cheque.
2: I don't even know who did it and I want to cut his balls off.
1: [To bartender] It had a $1000 cheque in it.

Bartender: How many people at the party? Did you know them?

1: Yeah.
2: I raise my kids the same way I raise my Doberman – if they cross you, kill 'em. Don't worry about jail. I'll bail you out.
1: It's the only way.
2: Yeah. [silence] Come on, let's get our pizza.

In local bars, attempts to initiate conversation may take different forms. One way to start a conversation is to begin speaking to a person near you, but a more interesting way is to make a statement and hope someone – anyone – picks up on it. As Cavan (1966) notes, "declarations. . . are made to the collectivity at large rather than to any specific patron" (p. 53). In one example I observed, a man called out, "And the [Montreal] Canadiens' fourth goal," and then looked around for a comment. Although a Toronto Maple Leaf fan, I managed to keep my comment to myself. No one commented. In another example from November 4, a woman made a declaration about a country music video that featured a Christmas song, "AHHH! Christmas carols!" Another woman called out, "What do you expect? Halloween's over." At this point, the women carried out a brief conversation despite the approximately 3 metres (and two patrons) between them.

"Be It Ever So Humble"

What happens when people drink beyond an acceptable level of intoxication and their behaviour becomes inappropriate? Acceptance of public drunkenness is common in private clubs and neighbourhood bars where the patrons are known. For example, a man was so impaired in a local bar that he staggered and fell into a patron at another table. He was helped up and gently pushed off. No one reprimanded his behaviour. This contrasts sharply with stories by informants where intoxicated people in nightspots are brutally hurled out by uniformed bouncers who maintain a strong presence. I observed two bouncers at one nightspot physically remove a patron who had just laid his head on the table as if to sleep. The action of removing the man was both quick and rough.

A local bar may permit behaviour which is unacceptable in other establishments. I have seen more than one intoxicated patron rest on the table in neighbourhood bars, but they were not thrown out for such behaviour. Cavan (1966) has noted that local bars are more like home-bases than public places, and I have found this to be true in my observations.

Some local bars have old reputations for being "tough," but I never once saw a physical fight in a neighbourhood bar. Informants tell me that they do happen, but such altercations are atypical. During the week, local bars are particularly quiet places where people can have a pop, a beer, or whatever pleases them, while also being able to hear the conversations of those with whom they are speaking. Conversely, the night spots are good places if one wishes to dance, but conversation is a quick casualty in the midst of loud music.

Conclusion

No matter which type of Cape Breton bar you enter, you will encounter people who have come to the bar for a wide range of reasons. Some are looking for love, others are trying to forget problems, some want to dance, and still others are simply at the bar to "go out." This territory is ripe for further research. In this study I noticed a certain surreal quality in bars, no matter what type of bar is involved. The darkness and the music create an environment that is quite different from other public places. As a result, social interaction changes in a bar, and new or different rules seem to govern the patrons. In a mall or a restaurant, people could well resent any intrusion into a private conversation with a friend; in a bar, however, such intrusions are common, and while not always welcome, patrons usually tolerate the intrusions.

I have attempted to describe more than analyze behaviour. However, even a description is an interpretation by the one who is doing the describing, and thus certain events are emphasized over others. During my research, I gathered far more data than I could reproduce in this essay, but I have tried to present those examples that allow the reader to gain an understanding of some aspects of bar life in Cape Breton. I have focused primarily on local bars in various communities because neighbourhood bars, while not big draws for young dancers or great spots for tourists, serve as sanctuaries for members of a community. These bars are not quaint artifacts of this island, nor are they centres of Cape Breton music and entertainment. They do, however, play an important role in the culture and communication of small communities in their capacities as gathering places for local people.

References

Cavan, S. (1966). *Liquor license: An ethnography of bar behavior.* Chicago, IL: Aldine Publishing Company.

Talent Shows in Cape Breton

HUGH MacDONALD

Cape Breton bars that sponsor talent competitions are becoming homes to amateur musicians. Many of these performers are part of a regular crowd who play the talent contest circuit, sitting together and cheering each other on. Cable television stations sometimes tape the contests, and the increased coverage results in more performers and more patrons for the bar. Television exposure also gives the contestants a local notoriety, a semi-professional status, and a downhome kind of fame. However, if a contest does not draw a crowd, it is quickly eliminated from a bar's schedule of activities. Many musicians accurately view talent contests as just a gimmick to bring in the crowds. But as part of the island's musical culture, such contests provide venues and audiences for some of Cape Breton's budding talent.

Amateur talent competition: A live band provides backup music for prospective performers who enter the competition by giving their names to the band or the bartender. The audience rates the performances, and usually the top three acts are awarded cash prizes based on the size of the crowd, the amount paid to the band, and the cover charge. The club records first place winners, who come together one evening for a sort of grand championship. During this championship round, prizes may be higher, but the main attraction is the prestige of winning. Performers may choose to perform any song they wish, but a real constraint is whether the back-up band knows the tune.

Karaoke: Although similar to the amateur talent competition, the backup music for karaoke is played from a tape or compact disc. The lyrics to the song are captioned on a television monitor so the singer can read the words. Quite often, the performer is given a cassette tape of the performance. Occasionally cash prizes are awarded as well. Some contests are judged in the manner of amateur talent competitions, whereas in other, winners are drawn from a hat or by including a "secret song" among the music played.

Jam session: Also called a blues jam, the jam session allows musicians to interact, and it is a lively and spontaneous way to entertain the audience. Amateur or professional musicians will often perform a few impromptu songs with the band, and no prizes are awarded.

"Load of wood" or "load of hay": Semi-professional and professional musicians perform solo or together on stage as a showcase for Cape Breton's up and coming local talent. "Load of wood" was christened in the 1970s by Ronnie MacEachern as a description for the winter entertainment. "Load of hay" was the summer version. These entertainment forms have become regular attractions in Cape Breton, even though no prizes are awarded. Often audiences are treated to performances by well-known professional musicians.

'What Comes Around, Goes Around': Bingo as a Cape Breton Subculture

JEANNINE L. McNEIL

A huge line begins to form as people wait to enter the building. Cars are parked all along the side of the road; it is going to be a crowded night at the bingo hall. As people pay the admission fee and get in line to purchase their cards, the conversations begin: "Did you see what Bertha wore to church last week Ethel? Truly shocking." "I wonder who will hit the big jackpot tonight, Lenny." The topics of conversation consist of everything from funerals to weddings. This activity occurs every night somewhere in Cape Breton.

When I attended my first bingo game, I assumed it was simply a friendly game engaged in by those searching for another form of entertainment in their lives. Was I wrong! I soon learned that bingo players comprise a very distinct subculture here in Cape Breton. I decided to talk to avid players and continue attending games to learn more. Here is what I discovered.

The Game

Bingo is easy to play. Upon entering the bingo hall, you buy a mandatory booklet of bingo cards which costs three to five dollars, depending on the game's sponsor. Additional booklets for regular games and specials may also be purchased if the player so chooses. The game begins at a publicized time, and some organizations have an early bird game. A caller reads out the numbers taken from an electronically-spun basket containing 75 balls (one for each possible number on the bingo card). The balls come up one by one and the caller reads them out. Each number also appears on electronic screens and televisions strategically placed around the hall. Most games are double line bingo; that is, the first player to fill two full lines wins. Other variations include the 't', 'x', and 'l' formations. Games can be played for cash or merchandise, but sponsors are only permitted to pay out a maximum of $15,000 per game, according to the gaming commission rules.[1]

Social Aspects

Bingo is without question a social game, and regular players claim that they are drawn more by the socializing than by the opportunity to win money. For some, bingo is the one place where they can interact with friends. As one woman told me, "Older people go to bingo because there is nothing else for them to do."

Before the game begins, there is a flurry of activity in the hall as local gossip is exchanged or a friendly game of gin rummy is played. Some read or do crossword puzzles. Further, territoriality features heavily in the hall, with regular players occupying the same area each week. In fact, first time players can be reprimanded if they invade a regular's space. Charlotte Boone, the chairperson for the bingo games sponsored by the Minor Hockey Association, related an experience she had at a Mayflower Mall game. A woman unknowingly chose a regular patron's seat and the patron complained to Charlotte, stating that everyone knew it was her seat, and that she wanted the new woman removed. The bingo manager somehow settled the dispute. Clearly, not all players are there to socialize. One person told how he had walked into a hall and noticed a table covered with cards with only one woman sitting there. When he asked if the seats were taken the woman replied, "Not right now." He sat down and soon discovered that all the cards belonged to that one woman. She had spread them out so that she could have the whole table to herself. Some players like a lot of space so that they are not distracted during the game.

Cultural Artifacts

Many cultural artifacts accompany the bingo ritual, some of which are necessities. One necessary artifact is the bingo marker (dabber) used to mark off the numbers on the bingo card. These large, sponge-tipped markers come in a wide range of sizes and colours and regular players are known to have their favourite dabbers and ones that they use for specific games. The players I talked to designated certain markers as "lucky" after they had won a game. For example, if they used their blue dabber for the jackpot and won, then blue became the "jackpot dabber." Other players use different coloured markers just for variety. Avid players may also have good luck charms such as rabbit's feet, troll dolls, baby booties, or lucky pennies.

It is clear that the marketplace has capitalized on bingo's tremendous success, and merchandisers provide a selection of artifacts to outfit the avid player. These include bingo bags that can hold up to six bingo markers, a wallet and a good luck charm. There are also bingo t-shirts, magnets, stickers, necklace charms, and bumper stickers which sport adages like "Happiness is yelling bingo." Others bear a symbol of a bingo card. Such items serve to identify serious bingo players, and at the same time manufacturers make money off their obsession.

Who Plays Bingo

Although bingo does not appear to appeal to any specific race, socio-economic class, or age group, it seems that not everyone plays for the same reasons. Players can be categorized into three types: casual, avid, and addicted.

Casual players enjoy a game once or twice a month, some even less often. They do not consider themselves serious players; they are there because there is nothing else going on at the time. I spoke to a number of my friends at the University College of Cape Breton about the game, and those who had attended claimed it was something to do once in a while "for a laugh."

Avid players are those who refuse to miss a game and may refer to themselves as "bingo bags." Originally this was a pejorative term used for the stereotypical bingo players (old ladies with their hair in curlers), but now players themselves proudly adopt the name. Such players go to bingo regularly (as often as six times a week), arrive at the same time each week, and sit in the same section of the hall. If they are unable to attend, someone else is sent to play for them. I attended a game where a man was playing for his sick mother. He sat among her friends who graciously watched his cards along with their own massive piles. I also heard of a group of women who came from St. Peters to Sydney each week to play a merchandise game in the afternoon and a regular game in the evening. Rarely did they miss their weekly ritual.

Bingo is also home to gambling addicts – players only interested in winning and who are known to spend their entire pay cheques at bingo. A local caller informed me that bingo establishments make more money at the end of the month when social assistance checks are issued than at other times. Some of these players spend a lot of cash thinking that they will be home free once they double their money. Unfortunately, like any other type of gambling, there are no guarantees of winning.

Economic Aspects

Although bingo is a social game, there is no denying the fact that economics are involved as the game promises a monetary reward to a fortunate few. Although a lot of money is paid out at each game, sponsors do not make as much as one might imagine.

Organizations such as the Kinsmen and Minor Hockey Association sponsor bingo as a source of revenue for their organizational needs. In the case of the Minor Hockey Association, bingo earnings defray player registration fees. Parents volunteer their services for three games a year in exchange for such reductions. Volunteers who run the games for the Minor Hockey Association also give their profits to the Association. According to Charlotte Boone, the Association received $140,000 last year before expenses were deducted. These would include the cost of bingo cards, dabbers, table maintenance, and so forth. Sometimes sponsoring groups only break even.

Bingo as a Subculture

Just as Shirl J. Hoffman considers sport as a form of religion, I too see bingo as a ritualistic exercise. The bingo hall is like a place of worship for regular players, a place they attend on a weekly or daily basis. Their preacher is the caller and their prayer books are the bingo cards. They surround themselves with bingo charms and amulets and utter incantations for divine assistance. Winning is like going to heaven: some deserve it, some don't. Missing the game, like missing church, is considered a "sin" and meets with great disapproval from the regular "congregation." And, like any organized religious practice, bingo offers a regular opportunity to socialize with other congregation members, swap stories, and mystically remove oneself from the mundane routine of every day life.

Once you enter the bingo hall, you are in a different world. Although bingo players are very diverse, like parishioners, they have a common bond and share each others' fortunes and misfortunes. For instance, Charlotte Boone plays with a "what comes around goes around" attitude. Whenever she wins, she shares her reward with the person who delivers the money. She feels that if she does not share her winnings, she will "cut off" her source of good luck. By spreading the luck around, she feels that she will be able to hold on to her good fortune. Other regulars have done this as well.

There also seems to be parallels between Janice Radway's analysis of romance readers and my study of bingo players. Radway discusses women who share a bond because they read romance novels. The books become an important part of their lives. Some of the women I spoke to felt the same way about bingo. They consider it an escape mechanism; once they enter the hall they forget their worries. Bingo time is their time – away from the responsibilities of work or home. A time when they can sit back and relax.

It appears that any way you look at it, bingo is indeed a subculture in Cape Breton. Those who attend regularly are there for more than just mere entertainment. For some people, life without bingo would be a joyless existence. An avid player put it best when, during a spell of bad weather, she said, "As long as I can get out to bingo, I'm fine." It is a chance to socialize and see old friends, a chance to be one of the lucky ones to yell "Bingo."

References

Hoffman, Shirl J. "Sport as Religion." *Sport and Religion.* Champaign, IL: Human Kinetics Books, 1992: 1-12.

Radway, Janice. "Interpretive Communities and Variable Literacies: The Functions of Romance Reading." *Rethinking Popular Culture.* (Chandra Mukerji and Michael Schudson, eds.) Berkeley, CA: University of California Press, 1991: 239-277.

Notes

1. Recent provincial law allows Mi'kmaq organizations to exceed this amount.

'You Couldn't Do That in a Hall':
The Social Institution of Tarabish in Cape Breton
JOANNE KENNEDY

Tarabish is a card game that transcends mere leisure activity; in Cape Breton, it is considered an institution. To aficionados, tarabish is considered *the* game. As one player noted, "people take the game very seriously . . . it's a universal game, everywhere you go in the country, Cape Bretoners play tarabish."[1] Claims that tarabish is an institution and *the* game may appear at best exaggerated and at worst quaint, but tarabish is very much integral to the popular culture of Cape Breton. In recent years a World Tarabish Tournament has been organized in Sydney. Popularity aside, tarabish should not be considered yet another folk oddity of Cape Breton. Tarabish is not a card game for the faint of heart. It is a game of skill that requires shrewdness, finesse, and perhaps even a sense of folly.

Realizing that the game of tarabish is held in such high esteem, I began studying it in a slow and cautious manner. By popular repute there are many tarabish devotees in Cape Breton, and many consider themselves "experts." So, if I were going to write about a subject in which seemingly everyone is an expert, I should get my facts straight.

At first I relied on my own knowledge of the game and previous playing experience as I observed tarabish games from September to December 1995. During this time, I tried to discover the manner in which the game is played, then I actively

I wish to thank Stan MacDonald for his assistance on this project.

played the game during December 1995 to better understand its scope. It was during this time that I began to understand why the game endeared so many people. For many players, including myself, the game is not merely the transmission of cards played in a round; it is the development and honing of the skill, the strategy and the cunning that are needed to play this particular card game. Finally during January 1996, I taped interviews with individuals who had a great familiarity with tarabish to ensure that I had a better understanding of the complex rules and the subtleties of the game.

Origins

As with most elements of Cape Breton culture, tarabish is part of an oral tradition. It has been passed down primarily from generation to generation as a lived and social experience rather than as a written document. As such, the origins of the game have become bound with folklore, and tarabish has been associated with several ethnic communities within Cape Breton. It is generally accepted, however, that tarabish derived and received its name from a loose English translation of a card game known as "Klaberjess," a game mentioned in Hoyle's book of games.[2] On Cape Breton, there is evidence that tarabish was played in the coal pits and steel halls, making it something of a working class pastime. Some say that it has Lebanese or Middle Eastern origins. But claims to origins vary from one person to the next, and no definitive roots may ever be determined. Today at the University College of Cape Breton, students in the cafeteria or student pub spend many hours engaged in tarabish games, and they are looked upon as a subculture of sorts among intellectuals. But tarabish is considered the game to avoid if you are a serious student, and in years past, professors warned against the evils of too much tarabish.

From these uncertain beginnings, the name and the game itself have continued to evolve. Tarabish is also known by its simple slang term, "Bish." The actual pronunciation of the name of the game is "Tar-Bish" even though it can be spelled tarbish or tarabish. Also, there are many varieties of the game of tarabish: solitaire, two-handed, six-handed, etc.[3]

Tarabish is a game best understood through verbal instruction rather than in a written form. Nothing can quite prepare an individual for the subtle nuances and strategy of a tarabish card game more than actual observation of a game in progress. It is only when people immerse themselves that they gain an appreciation of why tarabish is considered one institution of popular Cape Breton culture. To fully immerse the reader in the game would go well beyond the confines of this one essay; indeed it would require a book of its own. Therefore, I will attempt to introduce those readers who are unfamiliar with the game to an understanding of its mechanics and cultural aspects rather than an in-depth analysis of various strategies. (See "How to Play Tarabish.") A working knowledge of the game is necessary in order to understand not only the complexity of the game, but also why there are so many avid tarabish card players. Hopefully, those who have not been exposed to the game, intentionally or otherwise, may be inspired to learn to play.

Transcending Leisure – Becoming An Institution

It is said that for every action there is an equal and opposite reaction. This is true of tarabish. Ralph Errington, a local resident, said it best. "I would probably go 45 miles in the opposite direction if I stumbled across a tarabish game."[4] This suggests that not everyone in Cape Breton is taken with tarabish. Errington was not always a local resident. He came from "away." Until he was transferred to Cape Breton, he had never heard of the game. When he arrived at his new job, his fellow co-workers tried to instruct him in tarabish. Although he had played other varieties of card games, he had no contextual framework for the game and deemed it to be "too difficult."

The contextual framework for the game lies not so much in the rules and in the transmission of the cards, but in the fact that the game is part of the social fabric and oral tradition of Cape Breton. This is not to suggest that everyone in Cape Breton is personally familiar with the game. Many people learn to play tarabish in their homes with family or friends who have in turn

been taught by previous generations. Ron di Penta is a living example of this, and he adds that, "I've been playing the game for 54 years . . . since I was six years old and it hasn't changed. I learned it . . . watching my father play it at home. And I've been playing it the same way ever since."[5]

Styles of four-handed tarabish

During my observation period of the game I noticed that there are three basic styles in which four-handed tarabish is played. The "friendly game" is the style in which players play the game in a relaxed and carefree manner. The rules are not as stringent and if a misplay is made it is generally viewed as an error and simply overlooked. This genre is the one in which most people will learn how to play the game as it is most conducive to the learning process. The "serious game" is the type of game in which players rigidly adhere to the rules of the game as well as to the rules of the house. Every card played is paramount to the success or failure of a team as the loss of the round could be a matter of one point. As such, it is a game that requires total concentration. As one player noted, "You've gotta have your mind on it at all times."[6] It is the exacting nature of this game that causes proponents to claim that it is "the" game. To play this type of game, one must be single-minded in one's attention to the game. This attention to detail causes one to develop one's skill in strategy: skill and perhaps even bravado. The third and final genre of four-handed tarabish is the "tournament" style. This is a very serious game indeed, since the ultimate goal is a monetary reward rather than the pure pleasure of playing.

Of the three genres, the "serious" game is one in which the leisure aspect of the game is not readily apparent. There is no room for mistakes as the rules are adhered to in a very stringent manner. It is this exactness, this attention to detail, that is the thrill of the game for the participants.[7] It is also this same exactness that causes people to intensely dislike the game. One opponent of the game was heard to remark, "By golly, if you make a mistake you just never hear the end of it."[8]

'You couldn't do that in a hall'

Because I wanted to reacquaint myself with tarabish, I hosted a game in my home for what I thought would be a friendly tarabish evening. I was wrong. I had neglected to consider the skill level of the other players. Also, I had presumed that all of the players would want to play a more relaxed game, as it was being held in a home and not in a hall where there are generally set house rules that are strictly adhered to. Again, I was wrong. As I made mistake after mistake playing the game, I was told, "You couldn't do that in a hall."

In halls, tournament-style play is stricter and more formal than play in a "friendly" game. By reminding me that I "couldn't do that in a hall," my opponent was telling me that my play was careless. The game was not so friendly after all. Frustrated, I began to question the wisdom of playing this game. Where was the "play?" Where was the leisure element of the game? Weary of being reminded yet again that my performance was lacking, I began to take the game more seriously. As I persisted, it was in the trial and error, the actual playing of the game, that the rules began to coalesce in my mind, and I began to develop my own strategy.

As the game progressed, I was told less frequently that "You couldn't do that in a hall." At approximately the same time, I began to realize that the comment was never intended as a snide remark, it actually was a helpful reminder to pay closer attention to the rules and to the game at hand; it is part of the oral transmission and tradition of the game. As my skill level increased, I noticed that the banter became more relaxed and, as a result, so did I. This is not to say that gentle jibes didn't persist throughout the game. They are as much a part of the game as the actual cards themselves.

Conversation

Generally, the conversation during the game of tarabish is about the game itself or on the merits, or lack thereof, of the actual players involved. This, however does not preclude other topics of conversation.

There are two factors that determine the topics, tone, and volume of conversation during the game: the personalities involved and the genre of the game. These two factors will not affect the tournament style of tarabish because talking (other than calling a bid) during the game is not permitted.[9] This censure ensures that people are not "talking across the table," one partner advising another during the game to advance the team. It was explained to me that one could very easily cheat during a game by devising a code prior to the game to advise one's partner of the cards that one holds. One woman told me of a game in which she began talking to her partner about her dog having puppies. This was a prearranged signal to indicate that she had several good clubs in her hand; the clubs resemble the paw prints of a dog.

Whether or not an individual will talk and, when they do, about what topic depends on the skill level of the individual. Again, one must consider the level of concentration one needs to negotiate this complex game. There is the human factor to consider in this equation as well: the many varied and innumerable personalities in existence. A skilled player may be able to give a discourse on the subject of quantum physics and still maintain focus on the game. Personally, I find it easier to stay focused and develop my own personal strategy if I disregard all other topics of conversation other than the game at hand.

The genre of play will also affect the amount and subject matter of conversation. During a friendly game, there may be little ebb in the flow of the conversation. Since the ultimate goal is not to play a precise game, but rather to enjoy a game that is convivial and perhaps jovial, there is no need to halt or stifle the conversation. However, as previously noted, the "serious" tarabish game commands total concentration. Frequently, a round of tarabish will pass without commentary. Between each round, however, the silence is broken by what might be called "shoulda-been" bish or "after" bish—essentially an analysis of the playing or players of the round that has just passed.

"Shoulda-been" bish

Once each hand (or the whole game) is concluded, participants may engage in an informal discussion of what transpired during play. Some call this debriefing session "shoulda-been" bish, in which what should have happened during the game if everyone had played at a perfect level is discussed. Others refer to the informal session of game-related conversation as "after-bish." Depending on your point of view, the analysis and commentary of the game and the merits of the players involved either heightens or lowers your interest in or the desire to play tarabish. Again, this is where the personality factor fits into the equation; you either like to talk about the game a lot, a little, or not at all.

The analysis and commentary of the game and participants serve three purposes: the transmission of rules, the attempt to assert authority and, finally, levity. As I have noted, it was the gentle reminders, "You couldn't do that in a hall," that provoked me to pay closer attention to the game at hand and to the rules in general. Promoting oneself as an "expert" or, at the very least, more knowledgeable than others is a common practice throughout the game. However, the assertion of authority may be only in jest. Of the two genres in which talking is permitted, the "serious" game is the one in most need of moments of levity so that tensions do not rise to the point where comments are perceived as vicious or vindictive. In one game that I observed, snoring sounds were made by a player when another player was deemed to be taking too long deciding what card to play. In another game, one player, not appreciating the cards dealt, asked another, "Do you have any tar and feathers?"

It was in the actual playing of the game during my research that I began to realize why tarabish is integral to Cape Breton popular culture. The sense of carrying on a Cape Breton tradition, the conviviality of family and friends, and the challenge of besting one's opponents make tarabish a popular pastime. The game continues to flourish as part of our oral tradition, and the verbal transmission of the game from generation to generation ensures that tarabish will continue to exist as part of Cape Breton culture.

Notes

1. V. Boutilier, personal communication, January 7, 1996.

2. R. diPenta, personal communication, January 8, 1996.

3. R. Keough, personal communication, January 8, 1996.

4. R. Errington, personal communication, January 8, 1996.

5. R. diPenta, personal communication, January 8, 1996.

6. T. Boudreau, personal communication, January 8, 1996.

7. R. diPenta, personal communication, January 8, 1996.

8. R. Martin, personal communication, January 8, 1996.

9. A. Campbell, personal communication, January 8, 1996.

How to Play Tarabish

JOANNE KENNEDY

Playing the game of tarabish requires a deck of playing cards and four willing and knowledgeable participants. To some, this will be the only readily comprehensible aspect of what may unfold as a complex and unpredictable game. The premise of the game is actually quite simple: you want your team to reach the goal (through several rounds of play) of 500 points. Since four-handed tarabish appears to be the most common variety played, the rules imparted and the reflections given here are from the perspective of a four-handed tarabish game.

A common deck of 52 cards is promptly divided into the actual playing deck of 36 cards with the remainder disregarded. The discarded cards are those numbered two to five. Of the four suits within the deck of cards – hearts, diamonds, spades, and clubs – one of these will be determined as the suit which is pre-eminent over the other suits during each level or hand of play. This dominant suit is known as "trump." The order of importance and point values within trump are as follows: jack - 20, nine - 14, ace - 11, ten -10, king - 4, queen - 3, eight, seven, six -0. One must remember that the six, seven and eight cards in trump are not entirely valueless; they still are trump cards and can dominate over any non-trump card regardless of its point value. The order and values in a non-trump suit are as follows: ace -11, ten - 10, king - 4, queen - 3, jack - 2, nine, eight, seven, and six - 0.

As in other card games, combinations of three or four cards of one suit in consecutive order ("runs") also hold point values. Three cards of one suit are valued at 20 points while four cards are assigned 50. When players ascertain that they are holding runs, they announce the point value of their runs before the first card is played. When the second turn comes around, players must place their run of cards on the table in full view to be able to collect the point value. If they fail to do so, they forfeit the points.

If there is a scenario of more than one run, the question is asked, "How high is the run?" Only the individual with the highest card of their particular run attains the points. If there is a tie, no points are awarded. If one individual's run of cards is in trump, it prevails. Again, the run of cards must be placed on the table in full view to be able to collect the point value.

If two runs are announced, one player holding a run of 20 and the other a run of 50, the run of 50 prevails. Theoretically, an individual can have two runs of 20 or 50 in one hand (six, seven, eight, and nine in one run, and another run of nine, ten, jack, and queen). Unlike the previous scenarios where one player's run cancels out another's, two runs do not void each other. Again, both runs must be shown to all players in order to gain the point value. Clearly, it is in a player's advantage to show the run and gain the points. From personal experience, I know that one will face the wrath of one's partner if one forgets to reveal a run.

Other methods of amassing points during rounds of play are "bella" and "last trick." Bella, also known as "bells," is the king and queen in trump. An individual holding both these cards must announce bella while putting the last two cards in action. Bella is worth 20 points.

It takes several rounds of play to advance to the ultimate goal of winning the game. The same principle applies with the "trick." Each round (four cards) won within each hand of tarabish is known as a "trick." Each trick won leads to winning the hand which in turn leads to winning the game. The "last trick," as it suggests, is the last trick played in a round and it is worth ten points plus the value of the cards that were taken.

The deal

In a four-hand game of tarabish, one player from each team cuts the cards and the person with the highest point card becomes the dealer. The person seated to the left of the dealer becomes the next dealer. This is not a "hard and fast" rule and it may be unique to Cape Breton. An experienced tarabish player informed me that in Halifax the cards and the determination of the dealer are always to the right.

The dealer shuffles the cards in clear view of the other players until satisfied that each suit of the cards is evenly distributed. Once this is accomplished, the dealer then places the cards on the table to the right. The player seated to the right of the dealer cuts the deck. What was once the bottom is now placed on top of the remaining cards. At this point the cards are dealt to each player. If this procedure is not followed scrupulously, the dealer may be harangued by fellow card players.

Players receive nine cards, three at a time, dealt in a clockwise manner. Once six cards have been dealt, players may pick up and look at the cards. Three additional cards must remain face-down until the trump suit has been announced.

Determining trump

Determining trump in tarabish is perhaps the most important skill that an individual can learn. Not only are the cards in an individual's own hand considered in determining trump, but such factors as an assessment of one's own skill, one's partner's skill, the other team's skill, the "friendliness" of the game, whether money is involved, and what the score is at the present moment are all considered. Essentially, then, this is the moment when the art of strategizing begins; this is a skill that can only be honed and fully understood by repeatedly playing the game. The following must be considered only a rudimentary explanation of determining trump rather than an exposé of popular and current trends in the strategy of playing tarabish.

The player to the left of the dealer has the first chance to determine trump. This player may either choose trump or pass up this opportunity by saying "pass." The chance to call trump continues on from player to player until one of the players calls the trump. Since this is an action that could effectively continue on for a long period of time, a convention was developed that is known as "forcing the dealer." This convention is a house rule – a trademark rule of the establishment (local hall or tournament, etc.) where the game is being hosted – rather than a standard rule of tarabish. Forcing the dealer in effect means that the decision to call trump has been passed by the other three members of the game and the ultimate decision now rests solely with the dealer. The pressure that the dealer may feel was described quite clearly in a conversation at a recent game: "There's no more sinking feeling than being the dealer and hearing everybody say 'pass,' 'pass,' 'pass' . . . . It's like hanging on a rope and someone is kicking you."

Choosing trump is a testament either to the skill of a player or to the quality of the cards that one has been dealt; perhaps it is a combination of both. There are only nine trump cards in a tarabish deck; all others are non-trump. Generally, it is accepted that if you are going to choose trump, you should have a good combination of trump and non-trump cards. A good combination of trump cards might include the jack, nine, and additional cards of the trump suit.[1] Also, several non-trump cards are essential in terms of strategy and point value, and they are commonly the ace and ten of a non-trump suit.[2] If you don't have high point cards in your hand and you have doubts as to your skill as a tarabish player, it may be wise not to choose the trump suit. Again, this is just one method of determining trump, the decision to call trump is a highly individual choice and there are many factors to consider.

Playing the game

Essentially, this is the moment of truth. Once trump has been determined, the cards in the hands of the remaining three players take on a new dimension. What was once viewed as a "good" hand may now have had a complete change in fortune and may now be deemed worthless. The measure of the tolerance for the reversal in fortune of the cards is entirely incumbent on the human nature of the participants involved. Is this a "friendly" game viewed as mere leisure activity? Or is it the type of "cutthroat" game in which egos are involved and every team is for themselves?

The trick

Once trump is called, the game takes off. The person to the left of the dealer makes the first move by placing a card on the table, regardless of who called trump. There is no real "dyed-in-the-wool" rule to determine what card is played first.[3] It is a highly personal decision. Nevertheless, one might consider several factors in determining the lead: Who called trump? What is the score? Do I have a good hand?

In a clockwise manner, the three remaining players follow suit of the card that was led. The choice of card each player lays down depends mainly on the cards that already have been laid down. Players must follow suit if they have a card of the suit led. In the case of a trump card being played, a player not only must follow suit but must play a higher point value card to beat the previous card. For example, if a 10 of trump is played, the next player would have to play the Ace, 9, or Jack of trump (if that person had it). When a suit other than trump is led, players do not have to play a higher card.

Once the four cards are laid down one of these cards will be determined as the dominant card. The dominant card is either a trump card or the highest non-trump card. Playing the card that dominates the other three cards is known as "taking the trick."

The four trick cards are then placed beside the team members responsible for taking the trick. That team will receive the point value of the four cards, if any, at the end of the round. The four players continue to lay their cards down in terms of strategy and according to the rules until all of the cards are played out. Once the points are tallied, another round begins and the play continues until one team reaches the ultimate goal of 500 points.

Tallying points

At the end of each round of play, the tricks are added up. The lowest level of points available during one round of play is 162. This number increases with the inclusion of runs, bella and last trick which theoretically could cause the maximum amount of points per play to be 282. The team that has called trump must receive at least half of the minimum points available during each round plus one point, or at least 82 points. If they fail to do so, they forfeit their points to the opposing team who add these forfeited points to their own score. The failure to receive the minimum points is commonly known as "being baited." The fear of losing a round by as little as one point causes many devotees to take very seriously not only the game but each and every card played throughout.[4]

Misplay

Many a game has been slowed down as players exchange their views on whether or not a misplay has occurred. Misplays are generally the result of inattentiveness to the game or occasionally the "intentional" mistake: that is, cheating. A misplay occurs when a card is played out of the sequence in which it should be played. The penalty for a misplay is loss of the points of the hand in which the error was made. Conversely, if an individual incorrectly calls a misplay, points in the hand are forfeited. Since experienced tarabish players watch every card that is played in terms of their personal strategy, they tend to develop a keen eye and a long memory. Very little escapes the single-mindedness of an experienced tarabish player.

Most often, in four-handed tarabish, there are two situations that would cause a team to have a misplay: first, a mistake, intentional or otherwise, that would cause the offending team to lose a hand; and second, not following suit correctly. In the case of a trump card that has been laid down, the general rule is that whoever has the higher value trump card must play that card. Failure to do so results in a misplay and ultimately the loss of the hand. In the case of the off-suit card being played (a non-trump card situation), all other players must play a card in that suit. For example, if a club is laid down, all other players, if they have a club in their hand, must play a club. You cannot at this time play a trump card if you have a club in your hand; you must play the club. If you do not have a club in your hand, you may then play a trump. Again, failure to do so will cause the offending team to lose the points of the play at that time.

Tarabish is a game best understood by living the experience rather than simply reading rules. (At this point, the reader would probably readily concur.) While the rules and the general mechanics of the game may be taught in written form, subtle nuances of the game are lost in translation. Tarabish games are common enough wherever Cape Bretoners gather. Any interested reader should find a game, sit down, and ask to be dealt in. The rules will become clearer as you play.

References

1. V. Boutilier, personal communication, January 7, 1996.

2. A. Campbell, personal communication, January 8, 1996.

3. A. MacDonald, personal communication, December 2, 1995.

4. A. MacDonald, personal communication, December 2, 1995.

An American Takes Tea

CAROL CORBIN

By rights, or at least by reputation, I should be a coffee drinker. I'm an American, and Americans are known for their love of java. But I don't drink coffee, I drink tea. And if for no other reason than that, I am lucky to be living on Cape Breton Island. In the States, I often travelled with tea bags in my suitcase in order not to inconvenience the people or establishments I visited. A cup of hot water was all I needed to make myself some tea. My disdain for coffee seemed, to many Americans, to be a bit unusual, since coffee is so clearly the drink of choice in the states. Americans severed their connections with most English customs – especially class-bound ones – with the Boston Tea Party and subsequent War of Independence. For most Americans tea became an anachronism associated with upper class little old ladies. Taking tea in the United States was a quaint pastime for recluses and the infirm, often more associated with soothing a sore throat than with sociability.

Canadian friends also have commented to me about the dismal lack of good tea in the U.S. There, when meeting with colleagues, a request for tea is often met with a groan or, more likely, an apologetic shrug. It usually wasn't available. When it was available, tea was prepared in one of several inferior ways. First, one might receive a microwave-heated cup of warmish water and a tea bag. After dunking it in to steep for a while, the bag would have to be unceremoniously removed and left sitting on the saucer rim, or worse on a napkin. Another unfortunate American custom, quite common on airplanes I have found, is to run water through the coffee machine to heat it and then to pour this coffee-flavoured liquid on top of a tea bag in a paper cup.

This is truly unacceptable tea by even marginal standards. The most common serving technique, however, is to pour boiling water from a pan over a tea bag in a mug. Again, one is faced with the question of what to do with the detritus after this mediocre tea has steeped. But few Americans object to the unsightly pile of drippings: wet tea bags look very out of place on a coffee table.

I knew on my first visit to Cape Breton Island that this indeed is a tea-drinker's paradise. From Red Rose's notification that we have "come for the tea," to the Victorian teas held on Sundays in many small towns, and the ubiquitous teapot at every occasion, tea, it seems, is the national drink. An obsession that always had been an inconvenience for me in the U.S. is de rigueur in Canada. Many of my earliest introductions to people were over tea. I could get a good cup of tea at breakfast in a restaurant without causing a stir. And it seemed nearly impossible to enter an acquaintance's house without being offered a cup of tea.

When I arrived in Cape Breton, I didn't own a teapot. I'd been accustomed for so long to pouring boiling water on top of a tea bag, that I didn't even know the etiquette of making and taking tea. After living in Cape Breton for about a year, I became acquainted with a man in the town where I live. One afternoon I was out for a walk for some fresh air after being sick in bed with the flu for a week, when I encountered this new friend who was also out for a walk and who was also recovering from the flu. A typical Cape Bretoner, he invited me into his house for tea. He made a pot and we had a cup. Then he asked if I'd like a little rum in it. And, yes, indeed, I would. Thereafter when we took tea, we took rum as well, eventually giving up the pretence of tea altogether.

Reciprocating, I invited him to my house for tea – no rum, just tea, for rum too was something of an exotic drink to me. Without a teapot, I fell back on my American custom of pouring hot water over the tea bag in the cup. This, needless to say, wouldn't do. What you need, he said, is a "brown betty," another novel accoutrement. Within the week he appeared at my door with a brown betty – a little brown teapot that holds exactly two cups of tea – and I've used it ever since.

At other houses on other visits, tea has been the medium through which I got to know Cape Bretoners. Sitting in spotless kitchens that are steamy warm in the middle of winter, I made friends gathered over the teapot. Sometimes it was accompanied by sweets – cookies, cakes, tea biscuits, or oatcakes. It seems to me that the requirement of tea and assorted snacks is merely a guise to keep a guest longer in the house. The activities of eating and sipping our tea are only preoccupations for the hands. The real purpose of tea is to engage in the ritual of social interaction: to talk, to yarn, to be in the presence of a friend. Ostensibly taking tea is the reason for getting together, as if we might perish from hunger or thirst without the tea break. But the connection among people, sharing space and sharing time, is the real meaning of tea. It is a purely social institution.

As my tea-taking experiences have evolved in Cape Breton, I have learned more about the formalities of the ritual which are second nature to most Cape Bretoners. Each time I offer tea to guests I discover something new about Cape Breton tea habits. My first major social error was serving Earl Grey to a neighbour. Just the smell of it alerted her to a "foreign" type of tea. I poured it out and started over. Then, after making some Red Rose tea, I filled her cup too full, and she had to pour some out in order to add milk. And she needed to add a lot of milk, since I had only 1% on hand. In later ventures into the art of hosting tea parties, I was told that 1% milk simply wouldn't do. In the future I should have canned milk or whole milk on hand.

While we may think of taking tea as an insignificant social ritual, it in fact reflects the culture in which it exists. Tea is a ubiquitous custom in Mi'kmaq homes on Cape Breton. According to my informants, tea is used at just about every social function. There is at least one pot brewed every day in every home; in some homes the kettle is on continuously.[1] One friend calls another and says, "Come over and have tea." Or if a guest arrives without invitation, he or she will say "Make me tea," if the pot isn't already boiling, which means: "I'm staying a while." The entire ritual has been adapted to an informal familiarity among friends and family members. People fend for themselves. Although many Mi'kmaq take tea without milk or sugar, if you want it, you help yourself from the 'fridge, either canned or in a bag. The sugar dish is always available on the table in a condiment tray.

Within the Mi'kmaq community, the taking of tea has acquired a freedom from the constraints of upper class formalities that nearly belies the ritual's origins. What was once a highly stylized English affair of upper class ladies has been converted into spontaneous interactions among truly communal people. It is a ritual of friendship. Tea is a daily custom among Mi'kmaqs living in the United States as well. Although it is probable that most displaced Cape Bretoners observe the tea ritual in a fashion similar to those at home, Mi'kmaqs who are not from Cape Breton use tea as a conversation stimulant wherever they live. No one could tell me why, but one thing is certain: those who have become accustomed to taking tea as a social institution find the coffee klatsch a poor substitute.

Cape Bretoners are known for their friendliness, for their simple, pastoral lifestyles, and for their gift of gab. All of the best qualities of Cape Bretoners come out in the ritual of tea. This social observance has been taken from its genteel, class-based origins and transformed into a structure for interchange and an excuse for enjoying the company of one's friends. The solace that I felt in my first few weeks here was, in part, because of the extraordinary hospitality of Cape Bretoners. And tea was part of that.

References

1. Elizabeth Cremo. (Interview). February 13, 1996. Sydney, N.S.

II. The Arts

Culture for Sale

JUDITH A. ROLLS

McKay (1992) argues convincingly that Angus L. Macdonald's premiership (1933-1954) was instrumental in the tartanization of Nova Scotia's cultural heritage. That is, the province purposely and politically embraced and celebrated Scottish lineage as its common ancestry. From Macdonald's perspective, this "tartanism" presented an attractive tourism package, gave marginal Nova Scotians of Scottish descent a sense of validation, provided an identity that both Catholics and Protestants could relate to, and offered a plain-folk appeal for aloof Halifax lawyers (McKay, 1992, p. 19).

Bette MacDonald from the Cape Breton Summertime Revue.
Gordon Photo

79

With the tartanization of Cape Breton, the Cabot Trail was developed, the provincially owned Keltic Lodge was built, the Gaelic College was opened, and so forth. However, while this Celtic motif may have enticed tourists, McKay (1992) notes that with tartanism, travel writers such as Dorothy Duncan, Neil MacNeil, and others in the 1930s and 1940s shifted focus from Cape Breton's modern mining and steel operations to an invented "ethnic essentialism" (p. 23). This cultivated a conviction that Cape Breton was a haven for simple, stupid, kind, tough, similar-looking Celts. This cliché still clouds present-day perceptions of Cape Bretoners by those living both inside and outside the province. In addition, McKay asserts that Macdonald's strategy neglected to address the "realities of underdevelopment and economic crisis" (p. 40) in Cape Breton and offered no economic or social cures for these ills. Instead, tartanism attempted to reconstruct a Scottish essence strong enough to undermine the left and defuse regionalism (McKay, p. 43) and one that bore little resemblance to the reality of actual Scottish immigrants (Robertson, 1991).

Has Macdonald's scheme, with its hegemonic pejorative essentialism, influenced the commodification of Cape Breton culture today? McKay writes that "Tartanism in Nova Scotia was in many respects an instance of the international phenomenon which MacCannell terms *reconstructed ethnicity*, the transformation of ethnic identities in response to the pressures of tourism, as ethnic forms are used for the entertainment of others" (1991, p. 45). One might argue that the revival and marketing of Cape Breton's Celtic music demonstrates one such reconstructed ethnic form, although Irish musicians too are benefiting from a world-wide wave of revitalization of this music genre. Ashley MacIsaac, Natalie MacMaster, the Rankins, the Barra MacNeils, and Mary Jane Lamond enjoy musical prominence as a result of blending talent and traditional, "Scottish" musical influences. Ashley MacIsaac further personifies the Celtic bard by cavorting about the stage in a kilt and Doc Martins, playing his fiddle with a tatteredly-strung bow. Promoters export a well-crafted Celtic Cape Breton culture resembling the time-honoured fiddle tunes and Gaelic renderings.

For our purposes, McKay's use of the term "tartanism" can be extended to include portrayals of Cape Bretoners that go beyond kilts and fiddling. It may also describe the phenomenon of presenting Cape Bretoners as quaint, backward rubes. This can be seen in films that reflect Cape Breton life. In *Margaret's Museum*, a recent film focusing on Cape Breton coal mining life during the

1940s, the lead male character, Neil Currie, entertains Margaret by playing the bagpipes, a direct reference to Celtic traditions though rarely encountered in ordinary Cape Breton existence. Another example is the two young Cape Breton men leaving for Toronto in *Going Down the Road,* a 1970 work directed by Donald Shebib. They were portrayed in keeping with Dorothy Duncan's earlier derogatory descriptions of Cape Bretoners, and people on the island were appalled at the stereotypical depictions in this film.

Tartanism might also be examined in terms of two exceptionally humorous, "Cape Breton," comedic stage characters – "General John Cabot Trail" and "Mary Morrison." Robertson (1991) points to Dave Harley's "General John Cabot Trail" as an example of a public performance that has passed from an acceptable self-parody to a "personification of the myth of the 'idiot Caper'" (p. 13). On the other hand, Robertson (1991) suggests that "Mary Morrison" (the creation of Bette MacDonald) ". . . frequently moves beyond parody to offer the shock of recognition (of our own families and past, for instance), and the suggestion of actual ongoing life rather than the dead end of cliche" (p. 12).

More poignant to the tartanism argument is the depiction of Cape Bretoners in the Cape Breton Summertime Revue – one of this island's top cultural sellers. Through music, lyric, and caricature, the show endeavours to highlight the everyday existence of life on Cape Breton Island. Maynard Morrison's "Cecil," Heather Rankin's "Shirley," or Bette MacDonald's "The Piper's Lament" all provide an avenue through which our values, hardships, humour, happiness, and spirit are conveyed. The show has been a tremendous financial and cultural success due to production expertise and, of course, its host of talented writers and performers.

The Cape Breton Summertime Revue furnishes a site from which we can examine and judge ourselves with some objectivity, and through the process, many of us have acquired a deeper appreciation for the worthiness of our distinctive lifestyle. It also defines the nature of a Cape Bretoner; it schools us in how to be Cape Bretoners, and people actually communicate from this posture. For instance, in response to often-times humorous daily events, we hear assertions like "Now that should be in the Revue," or "You should be in the Revue, bye." In a sense, it has provided a common language through which we can thread together the fabric of our community. People relate to and love the show.

However, the dilemma that arises is that the type of Cape Bretoner that we are taught to embrace is often a stereotypical caricature that perpetuates the more negative myths and connotations of who and what we are, just as Dorothy Duncan's did when she described miners who required liquor to still their imaginations or who produced slow-witted, small, dull-eyed, children (cited in McKay, 1991, p. 25). Cape Bretoners are often portrayed as loud, foul-mouthed, uneducated, and unrefined individuals. This distortion only adds to the lack of confidence that some Cape Bretoners suffer due to job loss or bleak economic forecasts. When the show tours across Canada, these myths are offered to broader audiences who lack insight into nuances that clarify a scene's intention. That is, what gives meaning to a Cape Bretoner about Cape Breton may not necessarily be passed along to other audiences, and they leave with a limited and literal view of Cape Breton ways. Exaggeration of the Cape Breton vernacular further implants negative connotations as dialect users are generally not perceived as credible or intelligent.

Most Cape Bretoners recognize the dialectical tension that exists in portrayals of ourselves through joke and songs, but we prefer instead to look to the positive influences, and clearly there are many. The Revue has enhanced our island's culture and our lives have been enriched by Rita MacNeil's "Flying on Your Own," Raylene Rankin's "Rise Again," Natalie MacMaster's flying feet and fiddle, Richard Burke's "Placebo Dominion," Maynard Morrison's "Martin," not to mention Bette MacDonald's wonderful "Mary Morrison." They have each touched our hearts.

In all, how and whether Cape Breton has suffered and benefited from Angus L. Macdonald's tartanism is open to discussion. Many Cape Bretoners willingly embrace it, especially tour operators and those of true Scottish descent. One thing is certain however, Macdonald's scheme has resulted in a complicated culture that interweaves tartanism and commercialism with a bold naivety.

References

McKay, I. (1992). Tartanism triumphant: The construction of Scottishness in Nova Scotia, 1933-1954. *Acadiensis*, 21 (2), 5-47.

Robertson, E. (1991). "How's she goin' b'ys?" Cape Breton culture: A critical look. *New Maritimes*, September/October, 6-13.

A Peek Behind The Curtain:
Cape Breton's Summertime Revue

GERALD TAYLOR

It has its fans, followers and fanatics. It has highlighted some of the best talent ever to come from our island. It has been seen by hundreds of thousands of people across the country. Some have attended every show since it began in 1986; many have seen each show several times. There are some Cape Bretoners who mark the beginning of summer with the opening of each new show, usually in late May, go figure! Even those who have never witnessed a performance are aware that the Cape Breton Summertime Revue has been an excellent vehicle and ambassador for that deep-rooted sense of pride and reverence we have

Cast members from the Cape Breton Summertime Revue: Maynard Morrison, Max MacDonald, and Bette MacDonald.
Gordon Photo

when we say, "I'm from Cape Breton."

The origins of the Summertime Revue began with the strong legacy brought by Harry and Liz Boardmore to the theatre activities at Xavier College in the mid-sixties. They emphasized, not only to students but also to the entire community, the excitement and vitality of live theatre. Their innovative style and experimentation led inevitably to a marriage between the stage and those familiar old Cape Breton standbys, music and humour. Most importantly, their influence kindled in artists the impetus and belief that quality entertainment could be "created" right here in "old CB." It took some time, but in 1977 the first production of The Rise and Follies of Cape Breton Island was staged at the Lyceum Theatre in Sydney. This show is still fondly talked about today. A two-year gap followed, and then the 1980 and 1981 Follies were produced back to back; another three-year gap saw the final production of the Follies in 1985. All were memorable shows that blended traditional and local music with original sketches, some comedic, some poignant, to create a unique and ground-breaking phenomenon. It was in fact a revue format.

In 1986 the Cape Breton Summertime Revue was born, and to this day many still refer to it as the Follies. Why the name change? Why the different approach and tactics? The simple answer is "artistic differences." Whenever multi-talented people work together, a variety of opinions exists. Some felt there was not enough original material or audience support in the area to continue the Follies on a yearly basis, others disagreed. They wanted to continue the work and to create a showcase to develop and present local talent, believing that it could be done, and done in a way that enabled artists to make a reasonable living. Summertime Productions Society, a non-profit entity, was established to further that purpose. The founding members and Board of Directors were Leon Dubinsky, Max MacDonald, Stephen MacDonald, Maynard Morrison, and Luke Wintermans. Over the years the Board expanded and many interested and talented people, from all walks of life, sat on the Board to help guide the expansion and success of the Society.

The Society is involved with more than the Revue itself. In 1989 the Mabou Jig was produced, which gave audiences the first opportunity to see the five Rankin Family members as a group. The success of that show was so great that they decided to form their own band and give it a whirl. They seem to have found something there! "It Came From Away," "Ursula and Arlene,"

"Ursula and Arlene Are Back," and 1995's "Cape Breton Gold" are other examples of shows produced by the Society. In keeping with its mandate, the Society also has provided funding to other theatre groups, various chorales, individual entertainers, and artisans to assist in the development, production, and touring of their material. The Revue, though, is far and away the flagship of the Society.

The original plan for the Revue was to stage a compact, entertaining, mobile show that could be moved easily around the island and be adapted to a variety of venues ranging from well-equipped theatres such as the Savoy in Glace Bay and the Rebecca Cohn Theatre in Halifax to the high school in Arichat or the "Rec" Hall at Keltic Lodge in Ingonish. By performing in smaller population areas, usually in conjunction with a local fundraising group, the Revue hoped that some "government" money might be available to help defray costs. Some was, but not a lot. For the first seven years the Society was proud that 90 to 95% of its revenue came from ticket sales. That changed briefly when the expansion into Ontario and the far West began in 1993. One-time-only grants came from a cooperation agreement between provincial and federal governments. They helped to get the Revue to the entire country, but certainly did not underwrite it. The business of touring is "too" very expensive.

So, it all began in 1986. The entire show fit into the back of a rented cube van. A cast of seven performers, the smallest ever for the Revue, and a support crew of three who did sound, lights and production, set out on the first step of a 10-year journey. The most notable departure from the Follies format was that the Revue was electric. It had a complete sound system with hard-wired microphones, a band on stage, and drums! Over the years it expanded into the back of a five-ton truck, involved as many as 11 cast members, required six wireless mikes, staged 70 shows over 12 weeks, engaged professional designers and directors "from away," experimented with air freight, and experienced countless other growing pains.

The first season saw the Revue play to 10,550 audience members in 11 separate venues over a four-week period. Needless to say, that involved a number of the dreaded back-to-back-to-back one nighters. While these were hard on the cast, they had a more debilitating effect on the crew members. That is the nature of the business. In order to succeed the Revue needed to present a tight show; a tight show needs a well-rested cast; a well-rested cast needs to avoid stress and heavy lifting. Their energy is needed on stage.

The setup procedure for the crew is as follows: When the show ends at approximately 10:30 pm, they tear down the light, sound, and stage equipment, pack it up, and load it on the truck – by 12:30 am, if lucky; after a few hours' drive close to the next venue, they catch a little sleep; they arrive at the new venue by 10:00 am, unload the truck and set up sound, lights and stage to prepare for a 5:00 pm sound check, it's not always pretty!; show-time is at 8:00 pm, and it ends at 10:30 pm. Then, deja vu! all over again! One nighters still exist but they are something to be avoided. The worst stretch ever was the first year in Ontario in 1993. The Revue played seven cities in eight days and unfortunately, due to theatre availability, they were not in a straight line. Ah! the roar of the grease paint, the smell of the crowd!

Amazingly, over the 10-year period that cast and crew have been motoring and flying across the island, the province, the Maritimes and the country, not one show has been cancelled due to someone missing the call. It's been close and scary a few times; Doris Mason hydro-planed into a ditch, and Matt Minglewood cut his hand badly, but the only late starts were due to theft and storm. The first year, the Revue was playing at Thompson High in North Sydney for three nights. The second night, a Friday, everyone arrived at 6:30 pm for a sound check only to find that several pieces of sound equipment had been stolen during the night. The system simply would not work. Panicked calls and a wild drive to McKnight's in Sydney solved the problem and the show started at 8:25 pm. The audience was kind, as was the audience in Arichat when a huge storm knocked out the power for several critical hours during the afternoon set up. Another half hour late opening.

The 1991 show was referred to as "The Act of God" tour. Many quirky things happened but the real biggie was the fire that very nearly destroyed the Savoy Theatre in Glace Bay. Only quick response from the fire department and quick thinking by Dave Bailey, the Savoy's Technical Director, saved total disaster. The building was so badly damaged that it was closed for two years. The Revue opened that year at the Savoy on a Thursday for a seven-night run. After Saturday's show everyone sat around the dressing rooms for an hour or so talking, smoking, and having a beer or two. That was the norm. At 5:30 am Sunday morning the "Oh my God! There's a fire!" call went out and it was amazing how many cast and crew members were on the scene by 8:00 am. It was a dismal sight and a few anxious hours were passed worrying that it might have been a cigarette that caused the blaze. Faulty wiring was the culprit, but what to do next? Drums, amps, keyboards, guitars, set pieces and much more were strewn about the parking lot. The downstairs dressing rooms, where all the costumes and props were kept, were under a foot and a half of water; the set itself was waterlogged and reeking of smoke, and the season was only three days old.

The producer that year was Daniel B. MacDonald and in the next 36 hours he earned his pay. His leadership and determination that the show must go on, the fortunate fact that Centre 200 was available that week, and the tremendous, supportive response from the community created a minor miracle. This is what was accomplished. Keep in mind that it was Sunday and all businesses were closed. Two vans were rented; everything salvageable was removed from the Savoy; Centre 200 opened its doors and damage assessment began; merchants provided access to paint, hardware, costumes, anything that was needed; radio ads were aired to inform the public; and people showed up in droves to offer their help. That help was needed! Everything had to be repainted; all electronic equipment had to be taken apart, dried and tested; a stage had to be constructed and lights rehung; what had taken two weeks of preparation had to be recreated in 36 hours. It was an exhausting but exhilarating challenge.

That Sunday night was the only show that the Revue "never gave." Monday, June 3, at 8:00 pm the curtain went up and the season was saved. All Sunday tickets were honoured over the next three nights, creating a headache for the Centre 200 box office staff since the seating plans are completely different. Very few requested refunds, and those who did were mostly folks without transportation from the Bay. The nightmare was over but not forgotten. For the rest of that season, every time the truck door was opened or the set erected in a new venue, someone invariably would ask, "What's that funny burning smell?"

As the Revue grew in popularity and the cast and crew had become a little jaded doing the same circuit each year through the province, thoughts turned to touring farther afield. In 1987 a first feeble attempt was made when the Revue was booked into Confederation Centre in Charlottetown for a one-night performance. It was a financial disaster! The only night available was a Sunday because the annual summer festival was in full swing. Five technicians had to be paid double time; travel, motels, and the loss of two performing nights due to the ferries spelled doom. The show was really an unknown quantity at the time and had yet to prove itself, so the attendance was not spectacular. Mutterings went on until 1992 when Festival by the Sea in Saint John, New Brunswick, expressed interest in the show. That performance received a stunning reception and excellent reviews. When asked back by the Festival the following year, which was unusual since they go for new acts each season, eyes began to brighten and the feeling grew, "Let's go for it!" The following year Moncton was added and the great leap forward to Ontario materialized. The next two years, 1994 and 1995, saw much the same schedule with the mammoth (cost-wise) addition of the far West. Vancouver, here we come!

"Geraldine and Sadie" (Maynard Morrison and Bette MacDonald) can't see the forest for the trees, in a scene from the popular music and comedy production.

The major problem in touring is that no one knows where they are going or where anything is. Trying to book hotel rooms in cities across the country for the height of the summer tourist season, by telephone, can lead to interesting results. Sometimes the rooms, which often differ in style, but hardly ever in price, are within spitting distance of the theatre, other times they are a 25 minute cab drive away from the venue. Some of those cities are big! Most theatres, although varying in size, were adequately equipped, with one notable exception, the Vogue in Vancouver.

In 1987 the Revue first played the Vogue Theatre in Sydney. At the time it was simply a movie theatre. Its storied history of Rotary productions had long passed and there was much to be done to prepare for live performances again. It lacked some amenities, to say the least. It had no running water or washrooms backstage. A port-a-potty was rented and placed at the rear of the building but it saw little use. Most would quickly nip next door to Joe's Warehouse if needed. There were no dressing rooms to speak of, a five-foot stairway led to the stage on each side and there was no cross-over, which meant that actors exiting stage right and next entering stage left had to run around the back of the building. Many a rainy night saw someone on umbrella patrol. In 1995 the Revue contracted a local promoter to set up the Vancouver gig, feeling that someone on the ground there could probably do a better job. The previous year the Revue had played at the elegant Queen Elizabeth complex in the smaller room, Crosby, Stills, and Nash played in the large theatre. They did outdraw The Revue! When it was learned that the new venue was called the Vogue lots of jokes were cracked by the veterans in the crowd, but hey it's Vancouver, it couldn't be the same. Surprise! No cross-over. It did have dressing rooms and wash rooms but was very seedy and located in what was infamously known as a disreputable part of town. Live and learn!

Touring has one major downside: doing it. In 1995 the show was on the road for five-and-a-half weeks in one stretch. This becomes very tedious for the troupe, but more importantly, it is extremely difficult for the families left behind to cope with the rigors of everyday life, children, and loneliness. Yet little moments can make it all seem worthwhile. In 1993 in Brampton, Ontario, two ladies came bursting out of the hall at intermission with tears streaming down their cheeks. They were sisters from Cape Breton who had not been back home for more than 20 years. They wanted to know where the Revue was playing the next night so they could take their children, to show them how wonderful Cape Breton is. What a feeling of pride and satisfaction to move people in this way! What testimony to the true depth of our cultural roots.

The history of the Revue has involved a combination of stability and change. Stability at the core has given the show a continuity in style and application. Theatre managers across the region know the Society will deliver a quality product on time, will present it with the highest professional standards, and, most importantly, will have fun doing it (without creating ripples). This is due in large part to the acumen and persona of Stephen Mac-Donald who has acted as the out-front person for the Revue for nine of its ten years. In the topsy-turvy world of entertainment it helps greatly to have people who are taken at their word. In addition, the founding Board members, the musical director (Leon Dubinsky), two cast members (Maynard Morrison & Berkley Lamey), the two script co-ordinators (Maynard Morrison & Max MacDonald) and I (Gerald Taylor), the production person, have remained with the show from the outset. For nine years, Adrian Gadd was the lighting director, and for the past six years Ian Robertson has handled sound; Joe Bushell and Steve Drake were also involved. Few would argue that the nine years Bette Mac-Donald has been bringing her talent and characters to the stage has any parallel in the entire region. Her fans are legion. This consistency has helped "greatly, dear, greatly" in promoting the show.

The precedent for change started early. The 1986 show was fortunate to have Rita MacNeil and her band leader, Ralph Dillon, available for the production. Rita was just beginning to hit her stride and had the summer off before the release and promotion of her album "Flying on Your Own." Needless to say, she did fly off on her own. In total, 27 different artists have appeared in the Revue. Change happens for numerous reasons; most often it involves personal choice and opportunity, occasionally there is artistic difference. Once it was tragic. Tara Lynne Touesnard, who joined the Revue in 1992 as our fiddler, died in an automobile accident three weeks before rehearsal was to begin for the 1994 show. The spirit of her sister Krista, who played fiddle with Tara in 1993, and the strength of Shawn MacDonald, who filled an enormous gap, got the show through in 1994. Tara Lynne's death is the hardest memory.

The success of the Revue is solely attributable to talent, and Cape Breton has an inordinate abundance of that. That talent covers every aspect needed to foster the performing arts. It includes actors, musicians, song writers, comedy writers, artists, technicians, directors, producers, and can-doers. It is about people working hard at a craft they love, to create a product in which they take pride. When that product, that show, that song, that play, that experience creates, in turn, the laughter or the tears or the applause of an audience, the soul of the island is strengthened. All the hard work, the painstaking chores, the frustration and fatigue are forgotten; replaced by a wide, warm smile inside. That is what the Revue, for ten years, has tried to accomplish: people doing for people. That's Showbiz!!!

Appendix 1 – All Venues

CAPE BRETON	MARITIMES	ONTARIO	THE WEST
Arichat	Antigonish	Brampton	Calgary
Baddeck	Charlottetown	Brantford	Edmonton
Cape North	Fredericton	Brockville	Regina
Glace Bay	Halifax	Cornwall	Vancouver
Ingonish	Moncton	Kingston	Winnipeg
Inverness	Pictou	London	
Louisdale	Saint John	Markham	
Mabou	Truro	Ottawa	
Margaree	Wolfville	St. Catharines	
North Sydney		Thunder Bay	
Port Hawkesbury		Toronto	
Sydney		Windsor	

Appendix 2 – Cast Members by Year

1986	1987 & 1988	1989
Ralph Dillon	Lucky Campbell	Marcel Doucet
Steve Gaetz	Marcel Doucet	Steve Gaetz
Berkley Lamey	Steve Gaetz	John Hollis
Max MacDonald	Berkley Lamey	Berkley Lamey
Rita MacNeil	Bette MacDonald	Fred Lavery
Doris Mason	Max MacDonald	Bette MacDonald
Maynard Morrison	Doris Mason	Max MacDonald
	Maynard Morrison	Doris Mason
	Cookie Rankin	Maynard Morrison
	Heather Rankin	Heather Rankin

1990

Marcel Doucet
John Hollis
Berkley Lamey
Fred Lavery
Bette MacDonald
Marilyn MacDonald
Max MacDonald
Doris Mason
Matt Minglewood
Maynard Morrison
Neil Robertson

1991

Berkley Lamey
Fred Lavery
Bette MacDonald
Max MacDonald
Natalie MacMaster
Doris Mason
Matt Minglewood
Maynard Morrison
Neil Robertson

1992

Richard Burke
Steve Gaetz
Berkley Lamey
Fred Lavery
Bette MacDonald
Max MacDonald
Doris Mason
Maynard Morrison
Tara Lynne Touesnard

1993

Richard Burke
Steve Gaetz
Berkley Lamey
Fred Lavery
Bette MacDonald
Max MacDonald
Doris Mason
Maynard Morrison
Krista Touesnard
Tara Lynne Touesnard

1994

Richard Burke
Steve Gaetz
Berkley Lamey
Fred Lavery
Bette MacDonald
Max MacDonald
Shawn MacDonald
Doris Mason
Maynard Morrison
Krista Touesnard

1995

Richard Burke
Jamie Foulds
Matthew Foulds
Berkley Lamey
Fred Lavery
Bette MacDonald
Wendy MacIsaac
Maynard Morrison
Maura Lea Morykot
Gordie Sampson
Krista Touesnard

'Mary Morrison':
The Quintessential Cape Breton Character

MARIE WESTHAVER

"Mary Morrison" is the creation of local actor Bette MacDonald, who developed the character in 1985 for the stage production "Broad Assumptions." "Mary Morrison's" popularity has grown in Cape Breton and across Canada through appearances in the Summertime Revue. Actor MacDonald believes that the positive response to "Mary Morrison" lies in the fact that most people recognize her as someone they know, understand, and like. Her character is based on very nice Cape Breton people – a composite of attributes of people whom Bette has encountered over the

Bette MacDonald's Mary Morrison from the Cape Breton Summertime Revue.
Gordon Photo

years. "Mary Morrison" holds up a looking glass for us to see ourselves and our relationships as Cape Bretoners.

Bette as "Mary Morrison" walks onto the stage, slowly and deliberately, dressed in a plain house dress, purse dangling from her partially extended arm, and kerchief wrapped tightly around her head – an image Bette constructed from the many kerchiefed women she saw in church growing up. "Mary" looks intently at an imaginary acquaintance, pauses, and says, "Hello. How are you dear?" Then, after a brief lapse, she responds with, "Good dear, good" and the audience erupts into laughter. They're rolling in the aisles over Cape Breton's version of an inside joke.

"Mary Morrison's" signature greeting, "good dear, good," evolved from Bette's recollection of hearing "good, good, good, dear, good" used in telephone conversations when she was growing up. Bette believes that terms of endearment such as "good dear, good" act as communicative markers that differentiate the people of Cape Breton from those living elsewhere. We rarely reflect on our styles of speaking because they lie more in our hearts than in our minds, but terms of endearment like "good dear, good" serve several purposes in Cape Breton conversations. They provide us with markers of self-identification, they close social gaps, and they strengthen friendships. Bette MacDonald believes that we use terms of endearment to affirm our sense of community by linguistically performing our cultural identity. Bette notes:

> That is why you hear 'dear' so often . . . You're
> calling someone 'dear,' you're saying you're one
> of mine, you know, and I'm one of yours. Maybe
> we feel that more here. Maybe that's why we do it
> more. Maybe we need it more.[1]

Repetition of our terms of endearment initiate, maintain, and renew relationships on many levels of interaction – between strangers or between friends, in formal or informal situations.

Even under difficult socio-economic circumstances, "dear" adds a hopeful dimension to Cape Breton talk. Dr. Mary Lynch, Professor Emeritus of the University College of Cape Breton, views our repetitive use of "dear" as a means of compensating to ourselves for our losses. We may say: "Well, they have more material things, that's true, but we have a wealth of our quality of life that we hold on to."[2]

Terms of endearment act to narrow social distances between

people and break down class barriers, thus helping to initiate and strengthen friendships. "Dear" acts as a means of asserting social equality and indicates a desire to interact in a neighbourly way on the same social footing. Rather than say "yes sir or yes madam," which sounds servile and implies a low social status, folks will use "dear" to indicate that they're not putting on airs.[3]

Bette MacDonald's parody of this Cape Breton endearment both legitimates its usage and allows us to examine it more closely. Although its "natural" use in Cape Breton has passed from generation to generation, and it reflects the genuinely good relational characteristics of Cape Bretoners, it also may serve as a form of caricature of the culture. Nevertheless, Cape Bretoners cling tenaciously to this idiom as a means of identification and a way of preserving our down-home personae.

Notes

1. MacDonald, Bette. Interview by Marie Westhaver, December 1995.

2. Lynch, Mary. Interview with Marie Westhaver, December 1995.

3. Terry MacCluskey, Registrar of the Canadian Coast Guard College, Interview with Marie Westhaver, December 1995.

Real to Reel:
Cape Breton on Film

RON KEOUGH

The trestle at Number Eleven in Glace Bay is gone now. But it was in tact when the film crew of *Margaret's Museum* was here in 1994. I recall driving under that trestle, and back in '68 I walked under it to a friend's house after an evening of drinking and partying. It was a stag party, I think, and I had a crush on the groom. But in *Margaret's Museum*, the loving couple who walked under the reconstructed trestle along the quiet highway was Margaret Mac-Neil and Neil Currie who would soon wed. In that frame of film, the trestle was lit by an overhanging orange flashing light and it grabbed my attention. Just as the innocence of their romance eroded, so grew the image in power – the image of a hard coal mining life which held close to its bosom the anger and despair of generations. That amber shining light represented hope. It shone brightly for now, but Neil and Margaret, like generations before them, would soon suffer from the disaster and death that would pierce their future.

I sat across from Helena Bonham Carter with my microphone capturing her thoughts about Margaret, the museum, and mining. Her gratitude for the experience was deep and earthy. And she praised the community from which the story was born. This was real life, not some Hollywood back lot. Helena felt honoured and showed respect for the lives she discovered while she was here. As she met the people and explored the character of the community, Helena wanted to return, not as a Hollywood star, but as Helena, the woman who saw the romance and the tragedy.

Another film that featured Cape Breton life was Daniel Petrie's *The Bay Boy*. Daniel Petrie, a "Bay boy" himself, became a Hollywood director and returned in 1983 to film a semi-autobiographical glimpse of life in the Cape Breton coal mining environment of the thirties. Petrie's own story-telling screenplay laid out the nuances of young love, religious attitudes, economic hard times, and social alienation on a bed of murder and suspense. Sincere to period detail, Petrie relived his boyhood by recreating those streets and play areas where he grew up. This labour of love, painstakingly directed by Petrie, was developed over a number of years. I was sitting in his makeshift office in Glace Bay, soaking in the Hollywood aura, while Petrie was negotiating with Shirley MacLaine for the lead role of the mother. He missed her by a few days, but luckily Liv Ullman was signed to star in his movie.

The scene between Ullman and Kiefer Sutherland (the Bay boy), as they talked about Jean, the daughter who had died so young, is one of the most rivetting scenes shot here in Cape Breton. Ullman tells Donald about a dream as they walk and sit in front of St. Alphonses's Church in Low Point. There is a touch of mist and the colours cloaking the scene on that dreary November day are from a spectrum only found in Cape Breton.

Themes permeating this coming-of-age thriller seem familiar to me. The constant chaos of the economy and how it affects our lives shows up in the father's struggle to keep his soda pop business and his family afloat. Campbell's fierce pride creates tension, yet it provides a beacon for young Donald. The fact that Ullman's character is Swedish fits into the multicultural backgrounds which make up a large part of the Cape Breton mosaic. The woman who lived next door to me in Sydney was from Holland, and so Ullman's character rings true to me – a Cape Breton boy who never got to Hollywood.

Ullman brought box office appeal to *The Bay Boy*. The film did poorly in North America but extremely well in Europe; and Sutherland, just 16 at the time of the movie, got his career off the ground. Cape Breton actors also played pivotal roles: Jane MacKinnon, from Glace Bay, got a Juno nomination for her performance as the girl in love with the Bay boy, and Kathy MacGuire turned in a memorable performance as Sister Roberta.

Stephan Wodoslawski's autobiographical rendering, *Something About Love*, gives us a more contemporary look at life on the island. Wodoslawski takes his turn at the "you can't go home again" story. His character returns to his roots in Cape Breton, while his life back in Los Angeles is in turmoil, his romance is on the rocks, and his career is in limbo. But the life around him in Cape Breton provides little solace or escape from the urban fast lane he left behind. An old flame beckons, boyhood friends are lost in another kind of grind, and the relationship he has with his father becomes the focus of the visit. *Something About Love* deals with a lot of local issues as this father-and-son confrontation unfolds. The legacy of the Tar Ponds is aired. The treatment of aging parents, left behind by children forced to follow their dreams elsewhere, is another strong theme. The inescapable confrontation with small town mind set is given its due as well in this story.

If you have any connections to Cape Breton at all, particularly the "Pier dear," you'll find yourself drawn to the scenery so wonderfully presented by director Tom Berry. Aerial shots of the Pier are breathtaking. The areas in and around Henry, Hankard, and West Streets pull you into the story. The scenes around Holy Ghost Ukrainian Church are unforgettable. And Berry takes us out of this decaying city to give us a chance to experience the beauty of the mountains as they caress the coastline along the Cabot Trail near Ingonish. Berry allows the terrain and the small town backdrop to tell part of the story Stephen Wodoslawski has written.

These three movies offer different viewpoints of themes long connected to Cape Breton, and, as casting agent for *Something About Love,* I got to do Hollywood work without leaving Cape Breton. That's my father in the funeral scene at Holy Ghost Church. My mother waves to me from her 1959 red, finned Cadillac. My three aunts walk down Victoria Road as the sun sets. My friends are dining in one bar room scene. My dinner with Liv Ullman at a local restaurant was a memory maker, and I really don't care if I ever get to Tinseltown. The sparkle is here, and the stories, and the dreams are hidden in the lives.

Music as a Living Tradition

DAVID MAHALIK

At a going-away party held in a garage/barn/shed/workshop type place in Big Pond, heated by a big old barrel-shaped wood stove attended by two generations of family and neighbours and friends, a song was sung about Rita MacNeil. The song was the focal point of the evening in that it told of the relationship of Rita to the community, on a personal level, as well as in the context of her status as a famous singer. People knew the words and sang along; in fact there had been many calls, from both generations, for the song to be performed.

Those in attendance represented many groups of people. The party was organized to say goodbye to the son of the family, who had been home for Christmas from British Columbia after having been gone for a few months to work. There were basically three groups of people there: friends of the children, friends of the family, and neighbours. These groups all overlap to such an extent that it was virtually impossible to distinguish one from another. Food was served, and there was music played by various people until very early the next day. Songs were exchanged as part of what is done at a party in Big Pond. In contrast, I've lived in other parts of Canada where the traditional thing to do at a party, in respect to music, is to invite someone who has a great stereo and selection of music. Different traditions, indeed.

Music in Cape Breton originated in the home where mothers sang their children to sleep, and people of the community gathered to help out with seasonal chores, the completion of which would inevitably lead to a party. These informal parties, or "kitchen rackets," during which there would be much music (this was before the days of the nation's music station) and dancing, would give way to more organized ceilidhs* and dances in community halls. As the communities grew, each one had at least one fiddle and sometimes a piper who became a fixture at local gatherings. The key here is that local gatherings don't mean paying gigs, they mean any time the locals gathered. Playing music has become a tradition in Cape Breton.

For the Scottish settlers of Cape Breton, music was simply a way of life, and the tradition of music the Scottish settlers brought with them has become the cornerstone of music in Cape Breton. Not because all Cape Breton music is derived from traditional Scottish tunes, played on traditional Scottish instruments, or sung in a language that most Scots no longer understand, but because the Scot's love of music has become manifest in the performance. This is the tradition of Cape Breton music. The music is played in such a way that it embodies the spirit of past influences, and because it incorporates these and other influences, it will continue to grow in the future. Past, present and future are used here in reference to place as opposed to time, in telling the story of where we belong.

Cape Breton fiddlers.
Beaton Institute Eachdraidh Archives - University College of Cape Breton

* Ceilidh is a Gaelic word that originally meant a house visit in which people gathered to talk. Later music was added and the term took on the meaning of "house party." Today the use of the word has been expanded further, and ceilidh can mean anything from a small house party to an outdoor concert.

All traditions must start somewhere. In this passage from "The Scottish Touch: Cape Breton," Hugh MacLennan makes note of tradition:

> When the natural water dries up, it is human for people to try to drink at the mirage. Today there's a Gaelic College at Saint Ann's which teaches the old language, the bagpipes, and some of the old crafts. Every summer (since the war) there is a Highland Mod with Highland games, and chiefs are invited from the other side, most of them arriving with Oxford accents and not a word of Gaelic. Now there is a trade in tartans, and you occasionally see, as you never did thirty years ago, Cape Breton boys and girls wearing kilts. An older generation would have known, I think, that the romance about the kilt as a distinctive uniform of the clan was largely a Victorian invention, accepted among the Old Country Scots as a compensation for their near-annihilation in the mid-eighteenth-century wars, after which the kilt was proscribed for years. I record it as a plain fact that the kilt was never worn in Cape Breton before the tourists came.[1]

Kilts and bagpipes may not be directly descended from the highlands of Scotland but they could be descended from the highlands of Cape Breton. Or from the tourist traps along the Cabot Trail.

Do we have to play it up for the tourists? Why does CJCB replace Talk Back with The Music of Atlantic Canada during the summer tourism season? If it wants to support the local music scene, why doesn't it play Cape Breton music one hour every day all year long? Is there a music that can be defined as Cape Breton music? Maybe this is a meaningless question; but nevertheless, let's support our own.

When I first heard the promo for CHER's Wake up to Cape Breton I thought "right on, wake up Cape Breton. Wake up to Cape Breton's music." Two hours every Sunday morning Rick Matheson played whatever he could get his hands on. You were as likely to hear Sunfish as Charlie MacKinnon. This is important as they both represent very important genres in Cape Breton.

When Wally MacAulay completed some demos and was included on a compilation, his tunes were played on the air despite the fact that there was no commercial recording on the market. In MacAulay's case, three of his songs showed up in the Top 20 listings printed in *What's Goin' On.* "Damn Fine Shame" moved steadily up the chart from #17 in June to #6 in September. This chart is based on requests, which makes it an accurate representation of what people who listen to the show on Sunday morning want to hear.

If this island of ours is to have a future, we must look to our strengths, one of which is music. Entertainment/tourism is an environmentally friendly industry that can take Cape Breton into the future if we continue to develop it locally. Music is as renewable a resource as there is, as long as people play and pass it on. With Rita hosting a national TV show, Natalie MacMaster hosting a regional radio show, Ashley MacIsaac, The Barra's, The Rankins, The Sons of Membertou playing all over the world, Sunfish getting rave reviews in Australia, and Bruce Guthro and John Gracie writing in Nashville, our music has an international profile.

But I have already seen the best minds of my generation leave – to teach in the north, to work in the west, and even to make music in Toronto. We really have to stop exporting our natural resources to import products. The music lives here, as much a part of the community as any person or building. It will survive no matter what happens around it because it always has. Through religious opposition, mass migration, and now, a new generation's interpretation, the music has grown stronger.

References

1. Hugh MacLennan, "The Scottish Touch: Cape Breton", *The Other Side of Hugh MacLennan*, Elspeth Cameron, ed., pp. 221-22, Toronto: MacMillan of Canada, 1978.

Cape Breton Fiddle Music as Popular Culture

KEVIN O'SHEA

One Saturday night in the middle of January, I found myself in the small Saint Francis Xavier University dormitory room of my friend Jody. A fellow Louisbourg resident, Jody pulled out his fiddle and began playing some Scottish jigs and reels as I strained to keep up on the tin whistle. Within a matter of minutes, Jody's friend Dan, from the Wolfville area, arrived with his guitar and Will, whom I had met for the first time the previous night, arrived with his bouzouki. Will, who is from Baltimore, Maryland, was well versed in Irish music, but not familiar with traditional Scottish music, and as we soon found he was more than willing to learn. After all the instruments were tuned, the session began. Jody played tunes such as "Sleepy Maggie," "King George the Fourth," and "Brenda Stubbert's" as Dan and Will chorded along and I played the bones. After a couple of hours, the small refrigerator that had been packed with beer was empty, our small audience was smiling, and Jody, Dan, Will, and I were satisfied with our session. Full of energy, we all left the residence building and made our way to one of the local drinking establishments to continue our night.

In a time when many feel that local traditions are being lost, I believe that they are beginning to thrive. Many feel that the steady barrage of popular culture we receive through the media is assimilating us into a generic North American society. The younger generations would rather experience the culture of Hollywood that they see in the movies and television and forget our traditions. However, in recent years the younger generations have started to embrace Cape Breton culture and are now beginning to bring many aspects of it back to life. Two of the four musicians just described are Cape Bretoners, and this type of jam session is a very common occurrence for me and many of my friends. We are not only continuing some of the musical traditions of Cape Breton life, but we also are letting others experience the music that we love so much.

Unarguably, Cape Breton has a distinct culture, and one important aspect of this culture is music – more specifically, traditional fiddle music. Although Cape Bretoners have, for the most part, grown up hearing Scottish fiddle music, it is only recently that people outside the province are experiencing and appreciating this unique component of our culture. Cape Breton fiddling is a descendent of Scottish fiddling that has survived hundreds of years to become a deep-rooted aspect of our culture. According to Dunlay and Reich, "The early settlers left Scotland toward the end of the heyday of Scottish fiddling, the so-called 'Golden Age,' a time in which there was widespread appreciation of the traditional arts in Scotland. While the fiddle music suffered a decline in Scotland after that era, the music flourished in its new home across the ocean" (1986, p. 5). The entire folk music scene suffered this decline after Bonnie Prince Charlie and the Rebellion of 1745. Many restrictions were placed on the population in the Scottish Highlands and those restrictions extended to music. The bagpipes were banned, the fiddle was frowned upon, and the Gaelic folk song tradition was curtailed, as was the language itself (Gillis, 1994, p. 110).

The music and styles of fiddle players in Cape Breton have evolved over the years to become quite distinct from their Scottish roots. Both cultures are musically literate and draw upon a common stock of tunes. Cape Breton fiddling is the expression of the folk musician, whereas a great many of those who play Old World Scottish music are classically trained violinists (Dunlay & Reich, 1986, p. 7).

People in Cape Breton, especially in the rural areas, have for the most part grown up with the music of such fiddle greats as Winston "Scotty" Fitzgerald, Buddy MacMaster, Angus Chisholm, and countless others. Living in the town of Louisbourg all my life, I was exposed to only limited amounts of this music, but friends from places such as Big Pond and Mabou say that traditional fiddle music was so common in their areas that they just took it for granted. It has only been in the past few years, since my brother started playing the fiddle, that I have become exposed to this music genre.

I had no idea the extent to which traditional Scottish fiddling was alive in Cape Breton. I imagined there only being a few dozen good fiddle players scattered across the island, but I was shocked to find that there were actually scores of great fiddle players all over Cape Breton. This form of music is clearly alive in Cape Breton and can be experienced every weekend at church halls, dances, bars, Legion halls and in private homes.

The biggest change in the acknowledgement of this music has come about in the past five or six years as performers such as Natalie MacMaster and Ashley MacIsaac have become well known. Contributing to the success of these two performers is their youth, their energetic stage presence, their ability to entertain audiences, and their talent. They do not just play for traditional fiddle audiences, but they seem also to target audiences who are not familiar with this type of music. Ashley MacIsaac, from Cregnish, Inverness County, has combined traditional Scottish fiddling with musical genres such as rock and has formed his own unique blend of music which inspired A&M Records to sign him to a record deal unprecedented among Cape Breton fiddlers. Even more recently, at the 1996 East Coast Music Awards, Natalie MacMaster from Troy, Inverness County, signed a large recording deal with Warner Music.

At age eighteen, Ashley MacIsaac had already toured across Canada with the Chieftains and performed at Carnegie Hall in New York. At the 1996 Juno Awards, Ashley walked away with two Junos – one for best new artist and one for best grass roots traditional recording. This type of international publicity has brought a great deal of attention to Scottish culture and music in Cape Breton. Many people who live on the island are now taking an interest in this music for the first time, and many people from other parts of the country are finally getting a taste of Cape Breton's unique musical styles. In recent years we have witnessed the growing popularity of concerts and festivals involving traditional Cape Breton fiddle music. These include the Big Pond Festival, the Broad Cove Concert, the Glendale Festival, and the Louisbourg Scottish Festival.

The Louisbourg Scottish Festival was held for the first time in the summer of 1995 in the Town of Louisbourg and was a greater success than organizers ever could have dreamed. The organizers of the festival were completely overwhelmed when the expected crowd of about 2,000 people grew to more than 7,000. It was hard to get an exact count of the audience because thousands of people jumped the security fence in order to catch a glimpse of the newest Cape Breton sensation, Ashley MacIsaac. I attended the concert with my friends and it turned out to be one of the greatest nights we had ever had. I had never been to a concert with such energy and enthusiasm from both the performers and the audience. At one point Ashley MacIsaac, Howie MacDonald, and Brenda Stubbert were all on the stage playing a highly-charged set together as more than a thousand young people, including me, danced hysterically in front of the stage. This scene was no different from that of any major rock or alternative music concert, but it was traditional Scottish fiddle music that the mass of screaming people danced to.

(Left - Right) Shawn MacDonald and Krista Touesnard put a new face on an old tradition of Scottish fiddling in the popular music and comedy production, The Cape Breton Summertime Revue.
Gordon Photo

Walking through the halls of the University College of Cape Breton or sitting in the cafeteria or Pit Lounge, one can frequently hear fiddle music as well as many other forms of traditional music played by CAPR radio. How many other universities across the country can attest to that? As the popularity of this genre of music grows, Cape Breton artists are becoming more commercial, especially the younger ones. The older, more traditional fiddlers do not like the idea of their music being commercialized and prefer playing at local dances or ceilidhs. There has been, to a certain degree, controversy amongst Cape Breton fiddlers with regards to the musical stylings of young performers such as Ashley MacIsaac. Many "purists" are outraged that someone would change the style of traditional fiddle music, and they feel that it should be left as it is; yet other musicians welcome changes and adaptations to Scottish music.

I see both sides of this argument because my friend Jody Harpell and my brother Patrick are both traditional fiddle players. Jody began playing the fiddle around Christmas of 1990. He was instructed by well-known Cape Breton fiddle player Winnie Chafe, who is described by some as a conservative musician with a strong classical background. Since then he has played on his own. Jody feels strongly about preserving the traditional fiddle style, but at the same time he applauds the new and innovative forms of music that have been created with the fiddle. On the other hand, there is my brother Patrick whom I consider to be a purist in the true sense of the term. He began playing Scottish traditional fiddle music in 1993 and was instructed by Cape Breton fiddle player Raymond Ellis. Patrick is a staunch supporter of preserving the traditional fiddle music, and he is not impressed when people attempt to change this musical genre or blend it with other forms of music.

A process that all forms of music undergo, to some extent, is change. Whether classical, jazz, rock n' roll, or traditional, they have all experienced some form of change and progression. Some are fads that exist only for a limited time, while others are more permanent and may completely alter the expression. Resistance to change goes hand in hand with the evolution of any musical genre. There seems always to have been a reluctance to accept new music or changes in music within traditional circles (Cranford, 1992, preface). Some fiddle players see changes to traditional music as refreshing innovation, while others see it as a threat to the very existence of the traditions they are trying to maintain.

Now that Cape Breton fiddle music is coming into its own, we see people visiting Cape Breton to learn more about music, as opposed to Cape Bretoners going elsewhere in the quest for music.

For many years people from all over the world have recognized that there is something in the style of Cape Breton dance music that is not found anywhere else. Cape Bretoners have always looked elsewhere for new repertoire to supplement the old; now the tides have shifted and we see many Irish, Scottish, Canadian, and American musicians turning to Cape Breton for inspiration (Cranford, 1992, preface).

In recent years, our unique form of music has piqued the interest of people from other parts of the world. Even in the video, *Buddy MacMaster: Master of the Cape Breton Fiddle*, we see one of Cape Breton's greatest fiddlers on a recent trip to Scotland where he taught a group of Scottish fiddlers some of the styles and techniques used here in Cape Breton. A great deal of the traditional fiddle playing in Scotland has all but disappeared, causing many to seek their traditional roots in Cape Breton. The beginning of the twentieth century saw a decline in the interest of fiddle music in Scotland, certainly in the number of musicians. Fiddle music continued to survive to an extent in small pockets throughout the country (Hunter, 1988, xv-xvi). Traditional fiddle music has never fully recovered to the state it once was in Scotland, but it is still thriving in Cape Breton where Scottish immigrants played it more than two hundred years ago.

Cape Breton fiddle music is certainly stronger than ever before. It has moved from kitchen parties, local dances, and independent recordings to major record labels, television specials, and world tours. In hard economic times when Cape Bretoners feel left behind, we gain a sense of pride in our unique and much sought after music. As Allister MacGillivray said in his book, *The Cape Breton Fiddler*, "The Cape Breton fiddler is a multifaceted creature, being at once an elderly man with a Sunday suit and tunes that have no names; a young lady, a smile in her eyes and Gaelic in her bow; a little boy clutching candy in one hand, rosin in the other – a motley mosaic as ever you'd hope to find."

References

Cranford, Paul Stewart, ed. *Jerry Holland's Collection of Fiddle Tunes*. Cranford Publications: Little River, 1992.

Dunlay, K. E. & D. L. Riech. *Traditional Celtic Fiddle Music of Cape Breton*. Fiddlecase Books: East Alstead, 1986.

Gillis, Rannie. *Travels in the Celtic World*. Nimbus Publishing Limited: Halifax, 1994.

Hunter, James. *The Fiddle Music of Scotland*. The Hardie Press: Edinburgh, 1988.

MacGillivray, Allister. *The Cape Breton Fiddler*. College of Cape Breton Press: Sydney, 1981.

Stepdancing: Gach taobh dhe'n Uisge ("Both Sides of the Water")

SHELDON MacINNES

As a young person growing up in Big Pond, Cape Breton, I was fascinated by the stepdancing of Harvey MacKinnon from Whycocomagh, Inverness County. I can clearly recall discussing this man's great dancing talent with my mother, and she explained that it was common knowledge that Harvey MacKinnon could dance as many as fifty-one different steps. Harvey is an excellent free-style dancer: his steps are spontaneous, and his enthusiasm for dancing is driven by Cape Breton strathspeys and reels.[1] He has little notion of where his steps or the music will lead him. Another well-known stepdancer and teacher of dance, Betty Matheson, can demonstrate up to one hundred steps including all variations of the jig, strathspey, and reel.

Insight into the art of stepdancing allows one to glimpse some of Cape Breton's history and identity. But the roots of Cape Breton stepdancing are difficult to trace, and this cultural expression seems to be an eclectic mix from several Old World origins. Traditional music, song, and dance, perceived by people as having evolved on Cape Breton Island, are part of a blend of cultures, and this blending has created a stepdance that Cape Breton alone can call its own.

Connections between Cape Breton stepdancing and other Old World styles are not clear. Many Cape Bretoners believe that the Gaelic language and the Scottish violin music of Cape Breton Island have their roots in the outer Hebrides. Naturally, dance enthusiasts also want to be part of this linkage with the "old country," despite the fact that many of the traditional qualities of Cape Breton music, song, and dance are no longer found in Scotland today (MacMaster Video, 1992). Theories about the origins of Cape Breton stepdancing thread in various directions, and the most probable answer is that to a certain extent, all the versions are correct.

During the late 1700s and early 1800s, immigrants from all over the British Isles settled in the eastern half of the Island of Cape Breton. Scottish Highlanders, in particular, settled the western side of the Island between Inverness County and the Grand Narrows region between 1800 and 1820 (Dunn, 1953). These settlers handed down to their children memories of life in Scotland and of the early days of life on Cape Breton Island. *A History of Inverness* (MacDougall, 1972) describes Alan MacMillan who was born in Lochabar, Scotland, in 1820 and who settled in Rear Little Judique in Inverness, Cape Breton. Alan was a celebrated dance-master. After his arrival in the Judique community, he established classes in Judique and in Creignish. Also noted in the publication, was Lauchlin MacDougall who settled in Broad Cove Banks and, like his father and his son, was a noted dancer. As well, the early "group-dance" formations known as the four-handed reels and as the eight-handed reels were a part of the early dance traditions of Cape Breton. Both of these link Scottish dancing with Cape Breton's stepdancing (MacGillivray, 1988).

These early dance masters of rural Cape Breton, in particular of Inverness County, were likely to have been influenced by the dance etiquette of rural Scotland. Henry Graham's (1950) *The Social Life of Scotland in the 18th Century* describes the presence of public facilities to accommodate a country dance or minuet consisting of "nine couples on the floor dancing to the music of the local fiddlers." Graham states that "all society danced and dancing-masters drove as flourishing a business as the barbers." He also notes that the conversation in the hall was in "conservative" Gaelic. Early Cape Breton dance "classes," as described in the literature, appear to have had the same decorum as those described by Graham.

By 1920, Cape Breton had developed various dance styles similar to those in different parts of Europe, and these were also part of the legacy of dance masters from Scotland. Activity at the Gaelic College, founded in 1939, emphasized the more popular forms of dance including Scottish Country Dancing. Clearly, this type of dancing included many characteristics of dance styles found outside the Scottish tradition at that time (Donovan, 1990).

Various scholars have investigated the Celtic traditions found in Cape Breton. Among them, Frank Rhodes (1964), a renowned Celtic scholar, spent considerable time in a number of rural Cape Breton communities chatting with older people. As a result of his visit and subsequent research, he was satisfied that the Cape Breton stepdance had its roots in the Highlands of Scotland. Works by other researchers like George Emerson (1971), J.P. Flett (1964), and Cape Breton's own Allister MacGillivray (1988), support Rhodes' view.

Yet, Scots of the "old country" and advocates of the "old country's" form of music, dance, and Gaelic language typically find many distinctions between "old country" traditions and Cape Breton traditions. These Scottish cultural proponents have determined that the Cape Breton art of stepdancing is not part of the Scottish tradition. One well-known ambassador of Scottish culture and Gaelic singing, Flora MacNeil, engaged the debate on the origins of Cape Breton stepdance in the late 1970s, doubting that the dance had its origins in Scotland. But after many visits to Cape Breton and after many discussions about this art form, Flora determined that, indeed, the stepdance was very much a part of the traditional culture of the Scottish highlands (MacGillivray, 1988). Elders who are referred to in the literature, whose parents immigrated from Scotland to Cape Breton, support Flora's claims that the dance originated in Scotland.

However, the literature about Scottish stepdance does not emphasize the use of "free-style" dancing[2] as an important feature among the early accounts of Cape Breton stepdancing. Today, Cape Breton stepdancing is recognized as a "free-style dance," unlike the Scottish dances where the solo dance is prominent. The Scots describe traditional dances like "Tulloch Gorm" (six steps), "Over the Water to Charlie" (six steps), "Highland Laddie" (six to eight steps), "Flowers of Edinburgh" (six to eight steps), and "Miss Forbes" (five to seven steps). These are identified in the literature as "Hebridean Dances."

A most important feature of the Cape Breton stepdance is the music itself – especially the strathspey, as it is so uniquely played by great Cape Breton fiddlers like Carl MacKenzie and Howie MacDonald. As a matter of fact, the "drive and the lift" of the Cape Breton strathspey may very well be at the heart of Cape Breton stepdancing. Its inclusion in Cape Breton stepdancing makes this dance different than similar stepdances anywhere else. In many Celtic regions, jigs and reels are plentiful, but the strathspey, as one knows it in Cape Breton, is not.

The work by Colin Quigley, researcher of traditional dance, offers some additional insight into another cultural influence of Cape Breton stepdance. Quigley's research culminated in his 1985 publication *Close to the Floor* – named after a traditional dance tune often played by Cape Breton fiddlers. The tune receives the same response as the lively strathspey, "Welcome to Your Feet Again," also a favourite in Cape Breton. Quigley's publication describes the formal structuring of steps commonly used by stepdancers and the notion that the steps are presented in intricate detail and move in rhythm to select music, including jigs and reels. He describes the body posture of the dancer with emphasis on movement from the knees down, while the upper portion of the body is more relaxed so as not to distract from the footwork. The dancer's main objective is to gain equal coordination of both legs and feet, a basic requirement of a "good" Cape Breton stepdancer.

According to Quigley, the art of good stepdancing requires a great deal of individual style as well as an inclusion of some regional variety. Quigley learned that styles may differ in body stance, in arm use, or in characteristic ways of using the feet. He explained that most traditional stepdancers strive to achieve a light and a near-silent dance style-characteristic of four "great" Cape Breton stepdancers such as Harvey Beaton, Mary Janet MacDonald, Reverend Eugene Morris, and Willie Fraser. Quigley goes on to describe how traditional stepdancers aspire to the music played, and he could be describing stepdancing very much as it is done in Cape Breton. But he is not! He is describing traditional stepdance styles from Newfoundland. Quigley's research outlines the similarity between Newfoundland stepdance and Irish stepdance in terms of technique and the terminology applied to both dance and music, making a direct link between the traditional stepdance of Newfoundland and Ireland. Cape Breton Island was not included in Quigley's research, and it is highly likely that Quigley had never heard of Cape Breton stepdance while he was researching in Newfoundland. Nevertheless, the dance similarities are uncanny.

Like Newfoundland, Cape Breton stepdance probably was influenced by an Irish dance tradition. Barbara LeBalanc's 1986 report on "Dance in Inverness County," for the Museum Of Man (Humanities) in Ottawa, supports this theory. She includes conversations with members of the Cape Breton Irish community who purport that the stepdance in Cape Breton is an Irish dance.

Further research by Saint Francis Xavier University scholar A.A. (Tony) MacKenzie (1979) in his publication, *The Irish in Cape Breton*, depicts the presence of early Irish immigrants throughout Cape Breton. MacKenzie introduces the Irish who arrived on the Hybernia (1861) and on the Carrick (1840). They were later joined by others who sailed directly from Ireland and by still others who arrived from Newfoundland enroute to large urban centers, but finally remaining in Cape Breton. MacKenzie identifies the Cape Breton communities settled by the early Irish to include areas near Glace Bay and South Bar; Margaree, especially the North-East Margaree; Louisbourg; Mabou; Port Hood; Irish Cove; Ingonish; and St. Peters. The presence of the Irish in Cape Breton who held fast to their heritage provided opportunity for them to influence many customs and traditions.

Quigley and LeBlanc may not alter one's thinking about the origins of Cape Breton stepdance, but renowned British scholar Hugh Trevor Roper (1983) offers an interesting case for further reflection in his essay, "Invention of Tradition: The Highland Tradition of Scotland." Although his essay is concerned particularly with the place of the tartan among the Scots, it may have some implication for other aspects of the culture like music and dance. As a result of his efforts, Roper has given cause for Highland Scottish cultural enthusiasts to do some serious reflection on the origin of Highland Scottish tradition. Roper suggests that approaching the 16th century, the Highlands of Scotland were culturally deprived, and the literature of the Highland Scot was a crude echo of Irish literature. Roper claims that the bards of the Scottish chieftains came from Ireland and were "the rubbish of Ireland" who were periodically cleared from Ireland and deposited in that convenient wasteland, Scotland. Ireland remained culturally an important nation while Scotland developed, at best, as its poor neighbour. He further claims that Scotland did not develop an independent Scottish tradition. Is it likely that stepdance in Cape Breton is part of an "invented tradition" – an eclectic blend of various traditions and an anti-modernist search for roots? Even with scant evidence, one may be fairly certain that the practice was influenced by many different regional cultures.

Today, as much as any time in the past, Cape Bretoners love the stepdance. The best illustrations of local interest in traditional dance occur today in small rural communities like Iona, Washabuck, Mabou, Glendale, and Glencoe Mills. When one mentions the word "Glencoe" to Lowland Scots, the Lowland

Scots may envision the notorious exchange between the Campbells and the MacDonalds of Glencoe. The Highland Scots think of the ship "the Glencoe" that sailed the waters of Scotland up to 1935 serving commercial transport interests (Cooper, 1977). In Cape Breton, however, people know Glencoe to be a tiny rural community in Inverness County which boasts, among other things, beautiful landscape, pastoral farm settings, a church, a dusty road, and a small parish hall. The hall, to many people, justifies the pride that Glencoe residents feel, as it accommodates one of the most popular dance sites on Cape Breton Island. The "Glencoe dances" have become renowned to people in various parts of the Celtic world.

The star performer at Glencoe is Buddy MacMaster, a well-known violinist from Judique. His music makes one want to dance – to many stepdancers, his music is what dancing is all about. Buddy always gives impeccable performances – but when he performs at Glencoe, it is special. Even the place name conjures up a sense of Celtic mystique!

This seemingly ageless musician wraps his arm around the violin and cradles the instrument for the evening. As he plays, he frequently glances across the dance floor as if looking for some inspiration as he digs deep from his vast repertoire of traditional music to play appropriate jigs and reels. With his heart and his soul, he plays ever so harmoniously as his bow "graces" the violin in an almost effortless fashion. In accord with the dancers, he pours forth a rhythmic sound that keeps the dancers' feet moving all evening and well into the early morning.

Square sets form on a continuous basis: first figures, second figures and, ah, the highlight, the third figures. In the third figure, the foot-work or "free-style steps" among all the participants move in various formations and depict stepdance styles representative of particular Cape Breton communities: the Judique steps, the Mabou steps, and so on. The foot attire is simple: sneakers, high heels, low heels, moccasins, and even work boots. Occasionally, a soloist appears on the floor to dance to Buddy's sudden change to strathspeys like "Miss Lyall" and "Alex MacEachern's Strathspey." The Glencoe "crowd" dances for the pure joy of it.

In addition to many local activities promoting the dance tradition, Cape Breton stepdancers demonstrate their dance styles and their techniques well beyond Cape Breton's shores. Through the medium of television, in particular, and through personal appearances at major festivals and workshops, Cape Breton stepdancers are seen across the continent and in Britain. The rest of the world is becoming aware that dancing is a significant aspect of Cape Breton culture. Dancing is as important to Cape Breton's step-dancers as music is to the Cape Breton fiddler; in many respects, they truly complement each other.

Notes

1. The Cape Breton strathspey is a distinctive musical beat. The slow strathspey usually commands a good listening audience. Otherwise, the strathspey elicits a signal to dancers to dance their "unique" steps. The strathspey steps may vary from dancer to dancer, and may depict various intricacies. Although there are definite strathspey steps, they vary from dancer to dancer. The reel and the jig, like the strathspey, have their own distinctive beat. They also have their own unique steps but, again, the reel steps and the jig steps (used in square sets) may vary from dancer to dancer.

2. "Free style" dance implies a fluid, spontaneous and enthusiastic response to the music. The stepdancer introduces a series of random strathspey and reel steps. Usually, the dancer is not inhibited by repetitive formations, but rather the dancer enters the strathspeys and reels respectively with no preconceived notion of specific steps. In other words, the dancer will draw from a vast repertoire of strathspey steps and reel steps, and the steps are selected depending on the drive and the lift of the music. A classic illustration: when two dancers are performing - each will dance his/her personal choice of steps simultaneously.

References

Brown, Richard. *A History of Cape Breton Island.* Belleville, Ontario: Mika Publishing Co., 1979.

Cooper, Derek. *Skye.* Great Britain: Morrison & Gibb Ltd., 1977.

Dance Nova Scotia, ed. *Just Four on the Floor, A Guide to Teaching Traditional Cape Breton Square Sets for Public Schools,* 1992.

Donovan, Ken. ed. *The Island: New Perspectives on Cape Breton's History.* Sydney, N.S.: UCCB Press, 1990.

Dunn, Charles W. *Highland Settler: A Portrait of the Scottish Gael in Nova Scotia.* Toronto: University of Toronto Press, 1953.

Emerson, George S. *Rantin' Pipe and Tremblin' String: A History of Scottish Dance Music.* Montreal: McGill-Queen's University Press, 1971.

Flett, J.P. and T.M. Flett. *Traditional Dancing in Scotland.* London: Routledge and Kegan Paul, 1964.

Garrison, Virginia. "Traditional and Non-Traditional Teaching and Learning Practices in Folk Music: An Ethnographic Field Study of Cape Breton Fiddling." Ph.D. Thesis, University of Wisconsin, 1985.

Graham, Henry G. *The Social Life of Scotland in the Eighteenth Century.* 4th ed. London: A. & C. Black, 1950.

Hunter, James. *The Fiddle Music of Scotland.* Edinburgh: T.A. Constable Ltd., 1979.

Leblanc, Barbara and L. Sadousky. "Inverness County Dance Project," Museum of Man, Ottawa, 1986.

MacDonald, Keith Norman. *The Skye Collection.* 1987.

MacDougall, John Lorne. *History of Inverness County, Nova Scotia.* Belleville, Ontario: Mika Publication, 1972.

MacGillivray, Allister. *A Cape Breton Ceilidh.* Sydney, Nova Scotia: Sea Cape Music Limited, 1988.

MacInnes, Sheldon, "Folk Society in An Urban Setting," M.A. Thesis (unpublished). Detroit, Michigan: The Merrill Palmer Institute (Wayne State University), 1977.

MacKenzie, A.A. *The Irish in Cape Breton.* Antigonish, N.S.: Formac Publishing Co. Ltd., 1979.

"MacMaster Video," produced by Peter Murphy, Seabright Productions, Antigonish, 1992.

Quigley, Colin. *Close to the Floor: Folk Dance in Newfoundland.* St. John's, Newfoundland: Memorial University, 1985.

Rhodes, Frank. Appendix. "Dancing in Cape Breton Island, Nova Scotia." *Traditional Dancing in Scotland.* By J.P. Flett and T.M. Flett. London: Routledge and Kegan Paul, 1964, pp. 267-285.

Roper, H. Trevor,"Invented Tradition: the Highland Tradition of Scotland," in E. Hobsbawm and T. Ranger, *The Invention of Tradition.* Cambridge, 1983.

Reflections of an Artist

ELLISON ROBERTSON

"The framing of the discourse around identity is . . . important. However, it is equally important, to recognize that the communities to which we think we belong are all imaginary, and thus we live in a world of the 'double' – the community to which we thought we belonged and the everyday, economic, political reality which we have to contest in our everyday lives . . . . Media is one of our imaginary communities, but so is religion, psychiatry, literature, computers, ethnicity."[1]

Oran Luaidh (A Milling Song)
by Ellison Robertson

Staying. Leaving. Sometimes returning. Always hoping to return. These are elementary terms in the lives of Cape Bretoners. We feel passionately about them as we accept them in contradictory ways. Luck plays a role: lucky enough to be able to stay; lucky enough to be able to get out; lucky enough to be able to come back – sometimes, permanently, routinely, never. I've been away, so it seems a natural way to approach any discussion about the island.

Early in July last year, I drove with my wife and daughter from Ontario to Cape Breton. It was two years since I'd been home. There were always good reasons for putting it off – car troubles, jobs that couldn't be left, bad weather, a shortage of money – but finally there we were after a mere twenty hours of driving and an expenditure of less than two hundred dollars on gas and a motel room. That was nothing. Why had it seemed impossible to get here before? Why had it seemed so impossibly distant? If we came home several times a year, perhaps we wouldn't mind staying on in Kingston, a pleasant enough town, where at least there is the prospect of work.

If you're a Cape Bretoner, or from anywhere in the Maritimes for that matter, and have lived elsewhere, you'll know these or even more complicated calculations. Needing to leave, even wanting to, the necessary dream of finding work and opportunity is set against the nagging sense that what you leave behind is worth, if not more, at least as much as what you find. These have been persistent, defining aspects of our cultural experience, and have led many to a sense of displacement whether they've chosen to stay or to leave. Perhaps this is because often the choice is really only one of surviving or not, and rarely on your own terms. Of course this isn't unique to Cape Bretoners, but we are becoming rare in the world in still believing that the isolation and alienation of contemporary life would be relieved if we could just go home.

When not simply ignored, such notions are usually dismissed as romantic, anti-modern, and unrealistic. Here for example is a random quote I chanced upon as I read a recent *Books In Canada.* In 1968 Canadian author Kildare Dobbs wrote that "contemporary man is a nomad, without ancestors, without posterity, and without a country." For effect, Dobbs used the secondary meaning of nomad as designating any wanderer, and ignored its first meaning as that of a race or societal group of no fixed abode. His intention, presumably, was to figuratively emphasize the individual isolation of urban life, its mobility and hence lack of attachment to any particular place. In fact, I would argue that there is increasing evidence that the yearning for ancestral connection, for a role in posterity and a sense of place, far from being eliminated, has been heightened. However, my purpose here isn't to argue with what continues to be a fashionable, and in some ways accurate, view of the fragmentation of contemporary life, but to suggest that such views stand in contrast to much of both the lived experience and the defining mythologies of our Cape Breton communities. Aren't wanderers, even figurative ones, sustained by the tension of their permanent displacement between origins and destinations? And can't the Cape Bretoner's sometimes real and sometimes imagined sense of place and of home be seen as the condition of accepting that the often distopian facts of our origins and the utopian ideal of home co-exist in the singular space of our island? Whether as wanderers or as stay-at-homes, we share a deep sense of our history and a relationship with our varied ancestry that appears simultaneously in the wider contemporary society as both a morbid preoccupation and an enviable source of community solidarity.

If an extended absence necessarily exaggerates my own preoccupation with a Cape Breton of the mind, it has also broadened my sense of how we're seen from a distance. On the bad news side the tourist industry promotional message has been received: Cape Breton is an incredibly beautiful place, the people unbelievably hospitable and funny, and we're all brilliant natural musicians – oh, and we're all hard up as well. The two dimensionality of these received perceptions is fleshed out by the reality of the Rankins (singing in Gaelic on CBC's Morningside as I write), the Barra MacNeils, Rita MacNeil, Ashley MacIsaac, and so on and on. We are somewhat exotic, lovable, and talented poor relations. (Newfoundlanders present a similar image, though one that is more conflicted due to their seal-bashing and cod-eradicating habits, their living mainly on barren, rocky sea coasts, and a penchant for satirizing their betters.) In this we are not scorned but, again, envied. Ontarions, in the occasional absence of a positive or unified sense of themselves, continue to worry about the Canadian identity and to define it mainly by their difference from Americans. In the literary and visual arts, Toronto is the definitive center of the universe, much to the chagrin of those in other Ontario communities whose "T.O." bashing exceeds anything I was used to hearing back home. But when they want to give expression to the existence of a "real" Canadian culture, they frequently (and this is especially true of the CBC from Toronto and Ottawa) turn to the music of the Atlantic provinces, with Cape Breton and Newfoundland predominating.

The good news is that beyond this they barely think of us at all. (There was a bit of fuss when Manpower announced that they were flying unemployed Cape Bretoners to London to look for work – Eastern "wetbacks" taking the bread from the mouths of locals, the real taxpayers who were footing the bill – but that soon blew over, perhaps because Mike Harris distracted everyone.) While the necessary brevity of this essay is suited, I hope, to the preceding flippancy, I offer it to make a serious point. There is a comparatively huge market out here (that is, central Canada) for our cultural productions, one which goes well beyond expatriate Capers, and that market is susceptible to the "reality" of our culture, not only because perceptions of us here are generally positive but because they are so limited. We needn't cater to preconceptions that, for the most part, don't exist – though I have been asked why I don't have "the accent" – and we are more in danger of creating our own stereotypes than of having to combat those of others.

More personally, after two decades of focusing my work on aspects of Cape Breton history and experience, I left home with a baggage of insecurities I didn't know I carried until I set off for this corner of the larger world. I mention this because I know these feelings weren't merely my own, but were a reflection of the real burden of living in small, economically-depressed communities in which a sense of marginality inevitably breeds a defensive posture. Thus, one positive aspect of my time here has been the reception of my work on its internal merit, the knowledge that to focus on a sense of place is not inherently to limit the scope of a work. Indeed, such focus can create a foundation for widely varied understandings and responses.

This points to another of the contradictions of Cape Breton cultural life: it was the one place where I felt I could develop as the sort of artist I hoped I could be, and it is one of the more difficult places to survive as an artist of any sort – to survive period.

When I went home in 1975, what I enjoyed most after the claustrophobia of nine years of art school and the arts scene in Halifax was a sense of active involvement and interest in my work from so many levels of the community to which I most belonged. My painting and writing were influenced not only by my own experience, but by meeting older residents whose memories spanned the social and labour history of the island since the turn of the century or even before. I was introduced to Cape Breton's radical traditions as well by historians such as Don MacGillivray, who returned at about the same time to teach at the University College of Cape Breton.

Calum MacGhilleasbuig 'ic Chalum an Taillear (Malcolm Campbell)
by Ellison Robertson

I began working within a shared community that possessed a strong sense of a common history, values which most contemporary artists have tended either to repudiate or to manufacture in the narrower context of artistic community. This has been a condition of the "elite" arts as they developed in the modernist period through the constantly renewed rejection of, and assault against, established bourgeois values. This also led to a simultaneously increasing distance from and alienation of the "mass" of the population. (This is, of course, an oversimplification, though I hope it is clear enough for the purposes of arguing my point here.) In urban centres, specialized forms of art have been sustained because large enough audiences are to be found or because the state and some individual and corporate patronage of the arts directly supports such work. Variously described forms of pop, mass, or media culture have been seen to serve the needs of most of us. Any other cultural practices that persisted could generally be categorized, and thus dismissed, as folk, ethnic, or multicultural. Broadly, these same conditions and issues have been played out in Cape Breton. The difference is that, if resources are scarcer here, our sense of ourselves has usually been more coherent and our choices clearer, if no easier to enact, than elsewhere.

While my work has not been formally radical or intended to be accessible only to the initiated, I don't believe it has been parochial or merely regional either. I've tried to give expression to a range of experience within my understanding of my community while maintaining an awareness of (and seeking to understand the far wider issues of) artistic production within contemporary Canadian and international culture. Cape Breton is the ground against which I tested such understanding. While the range of individual interest and active patronage I've received on the island could seldom be matched by artists working elsewhere, there were definite limits to what I was able to achieve. Essentially, these limitations, as with most areas of endeavour in Cape Breton, were economic, and the potential to overcome them was narrowed by the lack of existing institutional and social infrastructures.

There are many practical matters that can be, and to some small extent have been, addressed: the island's lack of exhibit spaces, the absence of art education, limited public (municipal, provincial, and federal) support, the cost and sparse availability of art materials, the lack of professional support services, and so on. But there are other matters that can't be affected solely through economic means. Not surprisingly, our community tastes tend to be conservative and so, therefore, does our support for anything with which we're not already familiar and comfortable. The work we produce that is seen as culturally unique is most often in the areas of music and theatre. It is often dependent on either a stance of reaction against the confines of individual experience or on a basis in tradition that is effective elsewhere because its persistence here is so unusual.

Cape Breton has produced theatrical performers and playwrights who have made significant inroads in the wider Canadian context. Some see this as a welcome escape route, but even those who maintain a happier sense of their origins are generally unlikely to be able to return to work at home. Musically, too, we produce performers who quickly outgrow the local market for their talents, and some, such as Ashley MacIsaac or the Rankins, whose relation to traditional music elicits uneasy divisions between fans and detractors alike.

These circumstances aren't unique to Cape Breton, nor are they limited to artists, as the steady loss of our young has long suggested. They are a familiar aspect of the growth of centralized urban culture. However, I think the inevitable departure of such talented cultural producers underlines a potential for crisis in the very conditions which have previously aided their development. The young musician who learns in the presence of or by example from older local performers is becoming the exception rather than the rule. Sounds gloomy, but what can we do? There was never a golden age, never a time when all might be halted, made permanent. There is always good and bad, hope and loss, dominant, emergent and residual forces at play around and within us. But . . . .

But there are histories to recall and memories that confirm them. We had our industries and they're going or gone. The resources of land and sea are compromised and failing. Communities and language which sustained generations through song, story, and wit, are eroding or gone. Still, change is an unavoidable and necessary part of existence. We even welcome it. And yet our sense of our unique cultural personality is partly dependent on our denial of our role in changing social relations. We need to make change, not simply to accept or endure it. To do this I believe we must be more open to developing critical discourse, the means for assessing and creating answers to the difficulties we all face. I've made this argument in the past to mixed response, but that too is in the nature of small communities.[2] Perhaps this book's cultural studies approach will help to address that challenge in the future. I hope so.

On a more positive note, I believe that one of the apparent strengths of the cultural producers of Cape Breton has been the willingness and imaginative ability to create relationships and processes which seek to answer our particular needs. The association of Arts Cape Breton is an example of this potential. Interdisciplinary in makeup and with island-wide representation, it was created in recognition not only of the need for such a body in Cape Breton, but in response to the particularly diverse character of our arts community. Members have also shown a typical island trait of accomplishing much with very limited resources.

The Festival of Plays at the University College of Cape Breton is another longstanding example. Its blend of amateur theatre, professional training, and education has been the foundation of much of the recently flourishing dramatic and musical stage presentations in the industrial area, and it has helped shape talents such as Bryden MacDonald, Audrey Butler, and Daniel MacIvor, who have had significant impact in professional Canadian theatre.

I am also greatly impressed by the Celtic newspaper, *Am Braigh*, one of the finest specialized cultural papers I've seen anywhere, and one which again draws on the enthusiasm and skill of a few people with a commitment to a vision of community continuity. And there are many other examples, of course.

I began this essay with a daunting sense that the issues I might address were far too complex to be treated in the confines of a short essay. Not only were the two months of casual notes I'd made longer than the proposed essay, but they made it clear that I was not considering a single topic, or even a narrow range of experience of the culture of Cape Breton, but reflecting on the scope of my entire experience in the place I call home. Approaching the essay's end, I'm all too aware of what I've had to leave out, and the limits of the little I've written. I've tried to summarize some of the difficulties as I perceive them. Solutions, as always, will only emerge through active experience.

It occurs to me in concluding that it is our own fascination with the contradictory nature of our history in relation to the wider world, with its continual and accelerating influences, that provides much of the tension and interest in what we create. Or even in how we live.

It helps me to remember that we aren't alone in our struggle to centre ourselves within a history of marginalization. A Quebecois woman, for instance, remarked of the *New Maritimes* piece that, specific references aside, she could read the essay as speaking directly to her own experience of cultural marginalization, stereotyping, and community struggle. The issues of personal and community experience are always more widely shared than the dominant representations of capitalist culture, with their insistence on our fragmented and alienated existence as individual consumers. Our alternative is in knowing, as Raymond Williams expressed it in *The Long Revolution*, that:

> Since our way of seeing is literally our way of living, the process of communication is in fact the process of community: the sharing of common

meanings, and thence common activities and purposes; the offering, reception and comparison of new meanings, leading to the tensions and achievements of growth and change.[3]

And finally, I remember a teacher in the Miramichi region, after I'd read to her high school English class, telling me a story about her son who was almost finished his first year at university in Halifax. He'd left home the previous September in great trepidation at going to a city far from family and friends, and one where, he was warned, he'd be looked down on because he came from a small and poor northern New Brunswick town. He was gone a week when he sent his first letter home. "Don't worry about me, Mom," he wrote. "There are Cape Bretoners here and they're just like us!"

References

1. Davies, Ioan. *Cultural Studies and Beyond.* New York: Routledge, 1995.

2. Robertson, Ellison. "How's She Goin' B'ys: Cape Breton Culture, A Critical Look," *New Maritimes.* September/October, 1991: 6-13.

3. Williams, Raymond. *The Long Revolution.* London: Chatto and Windus, 1961.

III. Community
& Family Life

'Once Upon an Island':
The Story of the MacLean Family

JUDITH A. ROLLS

Introduction

When I think of a self-sufficient family living alone on an island in the Bras d'Or Lakes between 1915 and 1943, isolation comes to mind. At least that was my initial impression when I learned that my father-in-law's family, the MacLeans, lived this unique life-style. But as the stories unfolded, I came to realize that with the exception of managing transportation across the lake, their day-to-day routine differed little from their shoreline neighbours. In fact, the MacLeans were considered very much a part of the West Bay community. In those days, West Bay was a thriving centre with a doctor, a lawyer, a good educational system, daily mail service, and Chester Skinner's General Store. There once had been a tannery owned by Hector MacLean, but by the era depicted in this piece, its day had passed.

In this work I attempt to reconstruct a sense of how the MacLeans conducted their life on the island. The data for this research came in the form of stories told to me by four of the eldest living children, now in their seventies, who were raised on the island – Allan Hector (Buddy) MacLean, Lillian MacLean Chapman, Johanna MacLean MacKenzie and Jean MacLean Swiston. Nellie MacLeod MacLennan, the young school teacher who lived with the family for a couple of years, also recalled her experiences. She was 82 at time of the interview.

A Self-Sufficient Lifestyle

MacLean's or Smith's Island, as it is referred to locally, is situated just off the surrounding shores of West Bay, Lime Hill, and Dundee in Inverness County. On navigational charts, however, MacLean's Island and an adjacent one are identified as the Crammond Islands. The Smith family was the original owner and John Hector MacLean bought the island (plus a house and several farm buildings) in 1907 for $1,000. Originally from West Bay and a carriage maker and blacksmith by trade, John Hector was 25 years old and working at the Dominion Iron and Steel Company in Sydney at the time of the purchase. However, it was several years before he took up residence on the island; some said that he was on a mission to find a wife. When he succeeded, he and his bride, Sarah (Sadie) Belle Gillis from Whycocomagh, commenced their island life just after they wed on July 1, 1915.

John Hector and Sadie lived in a fine home. It boasted three fireplaces, four or five bedrooms upstairs, two bedrooms downstairs, an enormous living room, and a large, dark-bluish dining room. The kitchen, which was stained a deep rose tint, was huge and contained the main fireplace. The house also had an extension, or porch, as it was called. It was divided into four small rooms that served as the cobbler room which was used to make shoes and/or repair harnesses, the sewing room where mats were made, the dairy where milk and milk products were stored, and the shop which was used for tools and woodworking. A fifth large room took up half the extension space and served as the entrance way. None of this space was wasted as the young couple went on to raise fourteen children, each of whom was born in Whycocomagh. Sadie travelled to Whycocomagh to have her babies because both her mother and a doctor were there. Lill, one of the older girls, would accompany her to care for any children too young to be left at home.

The MacLeans were virtually self-sufficient. They stocked beef and dairy cows so they had plenty of meat, milk, curds, cheese, and butter. John Hector, Sadie, and the older girls (Margaret, Johanna, and Lill) did most of the milking, and Lill was designated the "star milk maid." Chickens supplied the family with poultry and eggs. But Buddy considered the sheep the most valuable farm animals because they provided meat and furnished wool to knit sweaters, socks, mittens, fishing mittens, and caps.

Further, lamb always fetched a good price in West Bay, even during the bad times. Of course there were the usual barn and house cats, and Buddy related that when his father, John Hector, came in from fishing, the cats would be waiting onshore to feast on the scraps. The family also owned two work horses and a mare, Lady, that was used to draw the sleigh during winters. How the animals were transported to the island depended upon the season; in winter they walked over on the ice and in summer they were carried on a scow that was towed by a boat.

Although the island today is almost completely grown over, when the MacLeans inhabited it, there were about one hundred acres of cleared land used for gardens, hay fields, and pastures. They grew the typical vegetables which could survive the short Cape Breton growing season – potatoes, turnips, carrots, parsnips, lots of red and white cabbage, and so forth. These large gardens required continuous cultivation and the older children contributed greatly to their upkeep. By 1930 or so John Hector had developed a condition which caused such joint pain that he relied on "sticks" for walking and depended on the older children to do much of the heavy work. As Lill recounted:

> I helped Margaret plough with the horses. She held the plough and Bud drove the horse lots of times. Dad wasn't able to do that. But my goodness, I worked so hard – we all did, it was just a part of life. I just did it. We shovelled manure, we picked potatoes, picked stones, planted the gardens, weeded the gardens, transplanted turnips, everything. And when the chores were done there was time to go picking strawberries to sell to Old Donald Beag when he came out to buy cream from Mama. She got a quarter and he would give us ten or fifteen cents for strawberries or blueberries or whatever berries we had and we felt like millionaires.

In addition to meat, vegetables, and dairy products yielded by the farm, the lake offered fish that was eaten fresh, or dried and/or salted to be eaten or sold at a later date. The family had a balanced diet, and Sadie, with Johanna and Margaret's help, prepared plain, wholesome, and tasty meals. For instance, Buddy noted that a particular favourite was potatoes with curds and cream which was both filling and nutritious. Nellie MacLennan talked about the remarkable lamb stew she was served. Sadie also baked bread daily and was noted for producing high, fluffy rolls. Chocolate pudding was often served after the Sunday evening meal and, of course, there were special treats at Christmas including doughnuts, cakes with raisins and dates, chocolate cake, and gooseberry and mincemeat pies.

Although most necessities came from the land, the lake, or the livestock, items such as sugar, tea, molasses, beans, baking goods, soap, and kerosene for the lamps were purchased at either Chester Skinner's General Store in West Bay or at MacLaughlin's in Marble Mountain. And, once a year, usually in the fall, Sadie wrote to the T. Eaton Company to order fleece-lined navy bloomers for the children, long underwear for her husband, bolts of flannelette, and perhaps some silk stockings for herself, if she could afford it.

Cash for these items came from the sale of vegetables, meat, and fish. There was always a market for lamb in West Bay and beef brought 10 to 12 cents a pound, depending on the cut. Fish, which was plentiful and particularly popular during Lent when Roman Catholics abstained from eating meat, fetched about three dollars per hundred pounds. One load weighed at MacKinnon's General Store at West Bay Road came to 800 pounds. John Hector also earned money by making, selling, and maintaining the navigational buoys used to mark the shore.

Clearly, the family lacked neither sustenance nor other essentials. All the girls knit at an early age, either for themselves or for family needs. Lill recalled sitting at the spinning wheel when her father, John Hector, happened by and said, "Now you make a good job of that and make it nice and fine because Mama is going to knit me a pair of long underwear for fishing." And Sadie would indeed knit the whole thing. She also made leggings for the younger children. Often her mother in Whycocomagh would help out because she possessed a knitting machine! Sister-in-law, Kathleen Monro, also pitched in.

But creating clothing from sheep's wool was a long and arduous process. After John Hector sheared the sheep in spring, the wool was cleaned before being shipped to a carding mill in either nearby Balmoral or to one on Prince Edward Island. Cleaning the wool involved picking out hayseed, dirt, spruce needles, or burdocks and then laundering it in a large iron pot of warm water. It was then spread on the grass to dry. White clumps of wool, four to five inches thick, were scattered all over the place. It was quite a sight. When the wool returned from the carding mill, it still had to be spun before the knitting could begin. In all, the family's life-style was similar to other farm dwellers in the area – honest, healthy, and unpretentious.

The School Teacher

Until 1929 Sadie and John Hector, along with their regular farm and household duties, taught the children reading and writing. However, never having had a "real" teacher before, the MacLeans wanted their children to have the benefits that such guidance would insure. They decided to search for a teacher who would live with them during the school year.

Nellie MacLeod, from Sydney, was just 17 years old, right out of grade ten and "green as grass," when she heard about the position. Imagining that it would be exciting, something a little different, Nellie wrote to Mrs. MacLean and informed her that she would be willing to teach for the winter term. Mrs. MacLean gladly accepted.

At that time the Department of Education issued permissive licenses, and holders could teach up to the grade that they had completed. With such a license Nellie earned a salary of $350 per year, paid quarterly. She considered this generous as most teachers received only $300 and were not paid until the term ended. Nellie attributed her extra earnings to isolation pay. After a year with the family, she returned to Sydney Academy for grade eleven and came back for a second term before going on to Normal College in Truro, Nova Scotia. Armed with her permissive license and a sense of humour, she recalled her initial 1929 trip to the island:

> The woman who told me about the job had a car and she took me to the minister's son or nephew to drive me there. I had never been in that part of the country before, I had never left Sydney. It was great. We drove up to Saint Pe-

ter's and on to Grand Anse and then onto a side road down to West Bay. I could see the island, but they were taking me to Morrison's Point which was the nearest point to the island. An old man ferried me across in a row boat. And he was the nicest man and told stories all the way. He told fairy tales, he believed in the fairies and he believed in the ghosts and I'm sitting there thinking to myself how weird he was. But he entertained me and it was a beautiful day – not a ripple on the lake as we made the five mile row.

When we got there the family was getting ready for supper. We had lamb stew and it was the most delicious lamb stew I ever ate in all my life, with fresh vegetables right from the garden and their own lamb and all. I thoroughly enjoyed it and they were so nice and flattered that I would come all the way from Sydney up there to teach. And Mrs. MacLean was a real, real nice woman and just like a mother to me. That's what got me through, she was so good to me.

It's hard to just go into a family and live but we got along well together. And I was telling Buddy when I wrote him a letter one time, that of all the children I ever met, the classes I had in Sydney and other places, the children I taught on the island were the best behaved and they were the easiest to get along with. I thought that because they were out there, isolated, that they would be queer, but they used to go ashore.

Sadie and John Hector had eight children by the time Nellie arrived and five of them went to school, each one in a different grade. Nellie recalled that Margaret and Johanna knew quite a bit and they were all quick learners. She felt she taught them well and was pleased to hear that Buddy retained his interest in history. This may have stemmed too from an early exposure to *National Geographic Magazine*, a personal gift from Gilbert Grosvenor. Gilbert was married to Alexander Graham Bell's daughter and the couple would vacation at the Bell summer home, Beinn Bhreagh, at Baddeck. From there they cruised the Bras d'Or Lakes on their yacht (The Elsie), and each summer in the early

'20s they anchored for a week in the harbour off the island. The Grosvenors got to know the MacLeans, and Buddy and his younger brother Neil were treated to rides on the yacht with Gilbert allowing them to pilot the boat – truly a thrill for the youngsters. The two couples got along well and *National Geographic* was a reminder of their friendship. It also enabled the children to travel the globe without leaving the island and Buddy is still a dedicated *National Geographic* reader.

Although the farm had a small schoolhouse on the premises, the MacLean children took their lessons in the large living room in the family home. The walls were covered with maps, giving it a classroom ambience. They sat on regular chairs and adhered to the typical school schedule, commencing at nine and finishing around three. However, at haymaking time they were dismissed early to join in the work. As in larger schools, the Department of Education supplied text books; but scribblers, pencils, rulers, and the like were the family's responsibility. Regarding curriculum standardization, Nellie recollected, "There was an exam at the end of each quarter. Nothing very scientific, we just went along our way. Out of the little red school houses came some very brilliant people and you wonder sometimes why we have to have all that technology."

Other than doing dishes, Nellie did not participate in the family's daily chores, although she talked fondly about rocking the baby, Dougie, to sleep. As she explained:

> . . . I just loved him, sat there in the rocking chair by the stove, after she got him ready she would pass him over to me and I would rock him and he would love it and go to sleep in my arms. It was something, something I had to love.

Life on the island could be monotonous at times and school work often occupied Nellie's evenings. Without television or radio for diversion, they had to entertain themselves and frequently they were amused by Lill, a natural mimic, and sometimes by Margaret who would also "take people off." Mrs. MacLean too was like a girl with them and often joined in the fun. Margaret shared a room with Nellie and the two became good pals.

On weekends, if the weather was good, Nellie accepted invitations to stay overnight at houses all around the bay which allowed her to attend the dances at Saint George's Channel, Dundee, and

West Bay. Like any young girl, she looked forward to these breaks and met many wonderful people.

After Nellie's second term, Austin MacDonald, another young instructor, taught the MacLean children for a number of years. Nellie went on to teacher's college and Austin obtained a medical degree. The MacLean children finished high school in either Port Hawkesbury or Whycocomagh, and Jean became a nurse. The three older girls (Margaret, Johanna, and Lill) each taught school before they married. Buddy worked at the steel plant in Sydney for 45 years, without once being laid off.

The Lake and the Weather

Like other families in the area, the MacLeans lived a typical, rural Cape Breton lifestyle. What distinguished them from other households was the lake and hence the weather which determined if and how they could get to shore. They developed a sensitivity to weather patterns and made forecasts with great accuracy. I recall an incident at Lime Hill some time back when Rhoda, Buddy's wife and my mother-in-law, asked if it was going to be sunny that day. When Buddy responded that it would rain, she followed-up with, "What time?" We thought this hilarious – quite a joke. But the joke was on us, as Buddy's knowledge of the lake and the prevailing winds allows him to make precise and reliable predictions. To date he keeps us informed of the nature and time of impending weather and we have come to rely on his meteorological prowess.

The first lake anecdote I heard came from Johanna and Buddy. She wanted to attend a dance at the schoolhouse at Dundee and asked Buddy to accompany her. He agreed but when it was time to leave a thick fog covered the lake. This did not deter them. Buddy rowed and Johanna clutched the compass and navigated. In the eerie darkness they made their way to shore, about a 15 to 20 minute row. Reassurance of their bearing came only when the strains of fiddle music began to waft through the air. The music was getting louder and one of them had just finished remarking that they must be getting close when the boat pushed up against the shore. It was so dark and foggy that they literally could not see a thing.

The weather and the lake featured heavily in the MacLeans'

lifestyle – particularly during the winter. The best winters were cold enough for the lake to freeze over so that a "bridge" formed. This allowed them to skate, sleigh, or walk to the mainland. As Lill remembered:

> It was sort of fun. In '29 or in the '30s Dad wanted to go to West Bay but the ice wasn't strong enough for the horse. He'd sit there in the sleigh with a tub of fish, and Buddy, Johanna, and I would pull him, skating. It would be easy, the ice would be just like glass.
>
> Another time you'd come to a drift coming up by Teal's and Dad would encourage us to keep going, this time in our shoes. We almost ran to West Bay. The Teal man a week later said: 'I didn't know what was going on. I thought it was a bunch of crows out there on the ice.' Our skirts going and the coats blowing.

The mild winters made travel difficult, for while the lake might be open, the coves could be filled with ice leaving no place to land a boat. There would also be periods when the ice wouldn't be solid enough to walk on nor broken up enough to row through. The family was truly isolated at such times. If people along the shore did not hear from the MacLeans for a fortnight or so, they had absolutely no recourse. The family was ice-bound once when Johanna was home for Christmas holidays. She had been living in Whycocomagh where she was attending high school and could not get off the island for an additional sixteen to eighteen days. She was rather concerned about missing her schoolwork.

The family was well-prepared for such events and by December they had enough supplies to last the winter. Occasionally they might run a little short of tea, for instance, but not often. Nellie related some of the predicaments she encountered during her winter adventures:

> In the winter time we wondered if the ice was strong enough to walk on. We could skate across or walk across, you know. One of the nicest times I had we all hooked up the sleigh together and drove across to a friend's house, and I

stayed for the weekend there, went to a dance and then went home. And then Monday morning, the fellow in the house had to drive me across. He saw that the ice had gotten kind of rough, you know. And at one place there was ice, and underneath it, it was like a lake and the horse plunged in and I thought we were going to go right to the bottom. But we just made it, he went right fast over that and we just escaped with our lives. Now that happened when I was seventeen.

Another time, I was visiting friends, the Teal family, and all of us from the Marshes, we went out the MacInnis' to what they called the rear. And we had a Victrola, you know, a gramophone, and we played 'Tiptoe Through the Tulips' and all the old songs, and we had a wonderful time. But when we came out about eleven o'clock there was a blizzard, and you could hardly see your hand in front of you. You know, we had to come down this mountain and go across the lake to reach the place where we were going to.

Well, we came down there and when we got to the lake all the boys started to argue. You know, there was open water down further on and if we went in the wrong direction we would go to the open water and drown. And some of the boys said, "No, we should go this way," and some of the others said, "No, we should go that way." And at last the fellow who was driving just let the horse go and the horse's instinct took him home.

But you know I remember Marjorie and I were so petrified that we didn't say a word. From the time we left we didn't say a thing we were so petrified we would end in that open water. They let the horse go and the instinct of the horse, he knew his way home. Things were different in those days, it was a different world. You lived closer to nature, there weren't any of those new inventions. You sensed things, at least the animals did.

On the island, with so much cleared land, the wind whipped off the lake and across the fields, further reducing already frigid temperatures. The cows drank from fresh water ponds which had to be kept ice-free by breaking large openings in them. Then in spring, the ice invaded. Lill recalled:

> In the spring, the ice would hit the island. You were never allowed to go down to the shore and you'd hear it coming and the crash of it jamming together, the ice cakes. Not every day it would come ashore but sometimes it would pile 20-30 feet high and the rocks would come up in the field with it.

But, generally, winter life was enjoyable and they commuted to MacKenzie Point, about two miles away, by horse drawn sleigh in 15 to 20 minutes if the horse was a trotter. The mail was delivered twice weekly to Morrison's Post Office at MacKenzie Point. Other people, too, travelled the ice along the shoreline rather than follow the snow-filled roads. Lill recounted that she hadn't realized how bad the roads could be until they moved to Lime Hill in 1943. There was no such thing as snow removal in those days, not until Duncan MacKenzie, Johanna's future husband, got a truck that could be used for ploughing.

In all, it appears that the family lived a happy, healthy, secure life. With the exception of the usual colds and John Hector's rheumatism, there was little sickness on the island. That is, until February, 1943, when Douglas, the baby that Nellie had so lovingly rocked, then 14 years old, was struck with such a high fever that he was taken to the doctor in West Bay. She instructed Mrs. MacLean to get him to the hospital in Sydney. They made the long drive but he died shortly after arrival of spinal meningitis.

That was the last month that the family inhabited the island. In March 1943 they moved to Lime Hill, directly across the water. While Douglas' death did not precipitate the move, it may have accelerated it. By that time the older children had gone off to work, John Hector was having a more difficult time getting about, and a house had already been purchased. These were changing times and a move to the shore meant greater mobility. Further, that winter was an especially cold one, so the cattle could be transported with relative ease over the ice to the large barn on the new property. It was a big move – all their belongings were sleighed across the frozen lake to their new home. After the family settled in, they continued to grow hay on the island, but over the years, as the younger children grew up, they even stopped that. The children finally sold the island in 1985, and today my husband and I sit on the deck of our Lime Hill cottage, look across at the island's tree-lined acreage, and imagine the life that had been there once.

Conclusion

What is apparent is that the cultural values and sense of community displayed by the MacLeans on that small island between 1915 and 1943 differ little from the "social circulation of meanings, pleasures and values" (Fiske, 1987) that one encounters on Cape Breton Island today in 1996. Living close to nature, experiencing isolation, entertaining ourselves, being unpretentious, and being practical, capable people – these qualities still characterize Cape Breton culture. It was imperative for the MacLeans to be sensitive to nature; they grew their food, fished, and their activities and mobility was dependent upon the weather. Thus they learned to predict the weather with an uncanny accuracy. Cape Bretoners today clearly commune with nature. They go camping, hiking, have country cottages, and cherish the inherent beauty of the island. And just as the MacLeans suffered isolation at times, we too unwittingly display signs of seclusion through our defensiveness or reluctance to embrace ideological positions other than our own. Small town nuances still prevail. Too, like the MacLeans who lived physically close lives, we, Cape Bretoners, possess an intimate knowledge of one another and are well positioned to watch each others' lives unfold. Even young people read the obituaries as the old people weave together entire family histories from just one name.

Before the proliferation of the mass media, rural families like the MacLeans amused themselves. They had good humour and Lill entertained with her flair for parody; dances with local fiddlers at Dundee or West Bay provided an additional welcome diversion. And Cape Bretoners are still entertaining themselves and the rest of the world too. We have a tremendous musical forte and a quick humour.

The MacLeans were essentially self-sufficient. They were practical, skilled, innovative, and capable people. They were jacks-of-all-trades as are many Cape Bretoners. When somebody's hot water heater goes, it's usually not the plumber who is called, but rather a friend or family member. Customs such as these keep the cost of living down, a necessity for most Cape Bretoners.

And last, the MacLeans had simple, honest, unpretentious ways; they had what they needed but not a lot more. Clearly, great material wealth is not evident in Cape Breton and those blessed with affluence mingle easily with the less fortunate. These conventions promote a blending of social classes in Cape Breton that resonates with the value that is placed on family and relationships.

References

Fiske, J. (1987). British cultural studies in television. In R. Allen (Ed.), *Channels of discourse*, (pp. 254-289). Chapel Hill: University of North Carolina.

Cooperativism and Vernacular Architecture in Tompkinsville

RICHARD MacKINNON

Joining together with one's neighbours to aid in construction projects or communal work activities was once an essential part of the fabric of Atlantic Canadian communities. House raisings, barn buildings, and chopping frolics to gather wood for widows or clergy are frequently mentioned in regional histories. Spinning bees, quilting bees, and milling frolics also were essential in passing on work patterns and oral traditions. One neighbourhood of eleven homes in Tompkinsville, Cape Breton Island–a cooperative housing development begun in 1938–is a particularly good example of the way cooperativism among citizens built and maintained communities and neighbourhoods.[1]

The term "vernacular" is interchangeable in much scholarship with terms like "folk," "common," and "native." When used to describe architecture, "vernacular" refers to buildings that are designed and constructed by the owner. Vernacular architecture reflects the unique character, cultural mix, values, materials, climate and topography of a place and a people.[2] It is an expression of a community's personality. Features that make a neighbourhood a distinct region–the public spaces, the types of buildings, the decorative details and the local culture–are all important facets shaping a vernacular building tradition.

Geographers, folklorists, architectural historians, and archaeologists are interested in vernacular buildings because they provide a democratic view of an architectural past and display the interaction of human beings with their built environment. Geographers address the themes of architectural transfer, adaptation and change, and the shape and location of buildings in the wider cultural landscape. Folklorists produce micro-studies of vernacular architecture in specific sub-regions within Atlantic Canada, exploring issues such as architectural transfer and change, the contrast between tradition and modernity, gender and spatial usage, and the patterns of modification. Architects, archaeologists, and architectural historians document various styles and genres of vernacular architecture of the Atlantic Canada region. This study of Tompkinsville vernacular buildings constructs a cultural history through photographs, measured drawings, and interviews with residents.

The "Antigonish Movement" and the Tompkinsville Housing Development

The 1920s were a hard, bitter time of great unrest for workers of Cape Breton Island. The decade saw numerous strikes in the coal industry and sharp class conflict; a culture of resistance amongst coal miners resulted from the workers' struggle with industrial capitalists.[3] One scholar notes that there were at least 58 strikes in the Sydney coal fields between 1920 and 1925.[4]

Many workers were unhappy about their living conditions. Some of Cape Breton's coal mining families were housed in poorly maintained, dilapidated duplexes built by mining companies at the end of the nineteenth century. These houses had rotted sills, badly constructed windows and doors, and lacked cellars.

Mary Arnold, a New York housing reformer who played a significant role in the Tompkinsville housing development, outlines conditions in the 1930s: "It is difficult to tell one house from another. If you are a comparative stranger in Reserve and wish to visit a friend, you take the nearest telegraph pole and count down from it two, three or four houses as the case may be. All the houses are painted a dark green or brown. . . ."[5] These duplexes were over 75 years old with shingles painted dark green or with unpainted clapboards. There were no indoor toilets, and the front and back yards were dusty and dirty. The rent charged by the mining company in 1938 was ten dollars per month.[6]

A 1945 survey of housing conditions, conducted with the assistance of the United Mine Workers of America and the local municipality, verifies the poor conditions faced by miners and their families. The survey of 320 dwellings in Reserve Mines showed that 1,799 people lived in these houses and that 88% had no bathroom or indoor toilet, no sewer system was developed in the community, and 47% of the houses were over 50 years old.[7] Of the 320 houses, 159 or 49% were considered to be over-crowded, and there were at least 30 "shacks," temporary houses found around mine sites at the development stage, which were deemed "uninhabitable."[8] The report concluded that 125 to 150 new housing units were required for the community, that a sewage system should be installed, and that the community should plan to provide for individual ownership, cooperative ownership, and subsidized low-rental, limited-dividend corporation projects.[9]

Moreover, the report petitioned the Premier and Minister of Highways of Nova Scotia, Angus L. MacDonald, about the deplorable conditions of roads in the community. The worst conditions were said to be in the neighbourhood where many of the Tompkinsville pioneers originally lived:

> Bad as these conditions are, the greatest evils [are] . . . on the so-called Company Streets. These serve Belgium Town and Lorway, both very populous areas. These roads are low and soft and wholly lacking in adequate drainage. . . . In the Belgium Town, . . waste from the houses drains directly in the roadway. This adds up to a very nasty, unsanitary condition. . . .[10]

These poor housing conditions helped to steel the resolve of the miners to search for solutions to their housing problems, and thus the "Antigonish Movement" entered Cape Breton.

The "Antigonish Movement"– a social and economic reform movement begun by priests working at Saint Francis Xavier University in Antigonish, Nova Scotia – believed that individuals could raise themselves from economic plight and become better physical, moral, and spiritual beings through adult education and cooperation. They envisioned people joining small study clubs to solve their difficult problems through cooperation and hard work. The movement was successful, and libraries, credit unions, grocery stores, gasoline stations, and housing groups developed in Atlantic Canada following the tenets of this philosophy.

Although there was some opposition to the "Antigonish Movement" in Cape Breton, extension workers had made excursions from time to time into the industrial areas. Soon mass meetings were held at which the value of education and the possibilities of economic and social improvement were set forth, but it was difficult at first to get some miners interested in the study groups. As Mary Arnold says: "You couldn't do anything with some fellows. They never read anything or seemed to care. They don't even know what Father Tompkins or Father Coady are talking about. And as for a study club, just try to get them into one . . . ."[11]

By the mid-thirties, however, a number of Reserve Mines residents had accepted the ideas being presented by Father Jimmy Tompkins. One Tompkinsville resident, Mary Laben, describes Father Tompkins' influence on the community: (Figure 1)

Figure 1 – Mary Laben sitting in her living room or "front room."
Photograph by Richard MacKinnon.

Dr. Tompkins came to Reserve in 1935. And of course the first thing that he did, he gave one look around and saw everybody standing around the corners and going to the taverns and drinking and everything else, and I guess he said, I guess I better start doing something. So he got a library. Organized with the help of the Carnegie foundation, you know.

He'd pinhole every boy or girl that he'd meet in the street to go to the library to read. So Joe

> [Mary Laben's husband] went to the library with Father Jimmy and he'd start reading his books... And at that time we were after organizing the Credit Union. And there was talks of a store. And there was talks of fish plants and one thing or another.[12]

Miners and their families formed study groups and taught themselves to build houses suited to their specific needs. This was the first cooperative housing group in Canada, and much of the architectural landscape of Cape Breton's industrial communities in the 1940s, 1950s, and 1960s was shaped by cooperative housing groups that followed the pattern worked out by the early Tompkinsville residents.

The idea of cooperative housing movements spread throughout Nova Scotia. A survey of cooperative "housing groups," as they are known in Nova Scotia, indicates that between March 11, 1938, when the Tompkinsville experiment began, and July 16, 1952, there were 35 housing groups developed in the province,[13] and from 1953 to 1973, an additional 982 cooperative housing projects were developed.[14] Many Cape Breton communities, including Glace Bay, New Waterford, Inverness, and Sydney, followed the cooperative movement's philosophies to build housing.

The Development of Tompkinsville, Cape Breton Island

Establishing a credit union in the community was the first experience some of the miners had with the cooperative philosophy. A credit union study club was organized in October, 1932, with Joe Laben taking a leadership role. (Figure 2) After much reading, thinking and discussing, the first credit union was started on March 2, 1933, with 43 members and a share capital of $3,700.[15] In 1935, the first community library was established with the assistance of Dr. Jimmy Tompkins. As Tompkins said: "Read. Books are the university of the people. Ideas have hands and feet. Choose your ideas. They will work for you. You must study."[16] In this Reserve Mines' library, the team of cooperators were introduced to many texts on cooperativism, self-worth and the industrial revolution. Mary Laben explains this process:

Figure 2 – Joe Laben.
From Mary Laben's photograph collection.

> In Reserve they had organized 23 study clubs,
> meeting in people's houses. So every Sunday eve-
> ning after Mass there'd be nine or ten or eleven ar-
> rive at my little house in Belgium town. And I'd go
> to another house where there was a bunch of
> women holding a meeting. . . . They had a ques-
> tion box, and everybody was asked to put a ques-
> tion in the box. Something, and if they couldn't
> answer it among themselves they got Dr. Tomp-
> kins to answer it.[17]

By the fall of 1936, a small group was working on the establishment of a cooperative store, and a year later a store for miners
and their families was opened in Reserve Mines. It provided an
alternative to the company stores which had dominated the mining communities until this time.[18] Once the group had established
a credit union, a cooperative store, and a community library, then
the housing project was considered. A housing study club was organized in the spring of 1937 that followed the same format used
with their previous cooperative successes. One of their first tasks
was to make a careful study of the Housing Act of Nova Scotia. At
this stage of the project, two outsiders, Mary Arnold and Mabel

Figure 3 – Housing group members are digging basements by hand. Mary Arnold is in the centre of the photograph with a pick in her hand.
From the photograph collection of Catharine McNeil, Reserve Mines, 1938.

Reid, cooperative organizers from the United States, came to assist them in their proposed endeavour. (Figure 3) Connected to the Saint Francis Xavier Extension Department, these social reformers offered to help the group manage their project because they had previous experience with cooperative housing developments. Reformer, builder, cooperator, and manager of apartments, Mary Arnold assisted in numerous ways in the completion of the Tompkinsville housing project. Mary Laben describes how Mary Arnold came to Tompkinsville:

> They used to have seminars in Antigonish. And Joe went up to the seminar and he gave a talk on what they'd like to do – build some homes for themselves. And this lady from New York happened to be at the seminar. Her name was Mary Arnold. So she went to Dr. Jimmy after the meeting, and she said, 'I'd like to go to Reserve and help those men. I have just finished building a cooperative apartment in New York.' So Dr. Jimmy invited her down.[19]

As soon as Mary Arnold and Mabel Reid arrived, the miners began to plan their homes and bring their wives together with the

women to plan the interior layouts. Mary Arnold stayed in Reserve Mines for more than a year during construction and helped
with planning, organizing, and bookkeeping.[20]

A travel writer, Clara Dennis, stumbled across the Tompkinsville housing group in her tours throughout Cape Breton Island in
1938. She met one of the Tompkinsville pioneers at work on his
home and she quotes him describing how the group was formed:

> 'We're all coal miners – shooters, bottommers,
> loaders and so on', he said. 'We work in the coal
> mines here in Reserve. If anyone had told me a
> year ago that I would build a house! – well, I
> wouldn't have believed him, that's all. When the
> cooperative movement struck Reserve, I joined
> one of the study groups that were formed. We
> studied different things in our group. One of our
> members found a law about housing on the Stat-
> ute Books of Nova Scotia. He sprung it on our
> meeting.
>
> We found we could borrow from the govern-
> ment seventy-five percent of the cost of a house.
> We would only have to pay two and a half percent
> interest and would have twenty-five years to repay
> the loan. We decided to take advantage of the law
> and build homes for ourselves.'[21]

After examining the law for almost two years, the group studied housing, planning, and all aspects of building; in a sense, they
taught themselves the whole process, including how to make
forms and concrete foundations. The members aimed to build
their homes for $500 dollars each; at the time a comparable
house, built by a private contractor, cost approximately $10,000
dollars. On April 1, 1938, the cooperative housing experiment became a physical reality as group members dug the first basements
by hand, eventually digging 11 basements this way. As one miner
interviewed by Dennis stated:

> An expert showed us how to mix the cement for
> the first foundation and we went ahead and did
> the rest. We worked in gangs of three. Three
> would put up the frame, the next three would
> come along and board it in, three would lay the

floors and so on. We went from house to house, till all were finished – co-operation you see, co-operators.[22]

After two years of weekly studies of carpentry, plumbing, electricity and general house construction, the families completed small, cardboard scale models of the houses to be built. As Mary Laben describes, the women played a key role:

> The women . . . all built little cardboard homes like is in that picture. . . . Katie McNabb, she did her whole kitchen around because she had eight. And so she put a window in the middle on both sides. She put whole cupboards [in] because she'd need them, you know. And then room for her table and room for her stove and that went in her kitchen.[23]

Women also aided in the construction of the houses:

> Yes, there's more shingles went on those houses with women then there were with men. They helped put up the gyprock and everything. But we also had women study clubs with somebody that the government sent down from Truro that taught us with a loom to weave, you know. We did quite a bit of that, and we knit, and crocheted. And then when it came the fall they sent down someone that helped us can. We all had a garden, and they sent us down a woman to show us what to do with canning and the canning machine, and what to do with what we had in the garden. . . .[24]

The group decided to use a contractor to build the first house, to allow them to observe the building process and to assess construction time, costs, and materials. As Mary Arnold says in her book:

> [We] let the contract for a budget house to a reliable builder, got the total cost of such a house built under contract conditions, made it similar

> in every way to the houses which the men planned
> to build, and then cost accounted every joist and
> every sill of the budget house as well as every hour
> of work by skilled men. . . . We could obtain accu-
> rate figures against which we could check labor
> and materials in the houses built by the men. . . .[25]

The first house in the neighbourhood was where Mary Arnold lived during her stay in Reserve Mines.

Juggling the difficult shift work schedules, the miners were able to complete the project within one year. On November 27, 1938, the group's dreams were realized when the housing development was completed. The terms of the mortgage were quite simple; one quarter of the total project's value was needed for the down payment. The group used their donated land as collateral for this loan. The government loan was rated at 3.5% per year and their local credit union put up the balance at 1%. The initial term was for 25 years but the group paid off their mortgage within 20 years.

Tompkinsville Houses

The eleven houses in Tompkinsville were laid out in a block of land originally designated for the parish graveyard and situated approximately 300 yards from the centre of Reserve Mines where the church, convent, library, credit union, company houses, and store are located. Tompkinsville Road runs at a diagonal off the highway between Reserve Mines and Sydney, and the land was divided in a grid-iron fashion. Each house was situated on a piece of land on average 100 by 165 feet in size (Figure 4). Nine of the eleven participants placed their houses close to the road, leaving room behind for gardens; only one house on the northwestern side deviated from this arrangement, situating the home in the centre of the lot. Another house on the southeastern side of the neighbourhood was situated in a different manner from the rest, rotated 45 degrees and placed closer to the centre of the lot.

Ten of the eleven builders chose to construct gable roofs; only one used a half-hipped form, known locally as the "Cheticamp Style" because of its popularity in the rural Acadian community of Cheticamp on the western side of the island.[26] Each Tompkinsville house was two stories in height and had a bathroom and six rooms, including a kitchen, dining room, and living room on the ground floor and three bedrooms upstairs (Figures 5 and 6). No two houses were exactly alike in floor plan or decoration, although all chose the three room ground floor plan for their living space. Although the process of construction was communal and the floorplans were similar, individual builders were innovative in their use of cosmetic details and interior arrangements. One of the pioneers summed up the minor variations between plans:

> One has no hall, another has an extra window, another has the bathroom downstairs, and so on. I liked a fireplace more than anything else, so I saved on my floors (they're not all hard-wood) and put the money in the fireplace. One man put his extra money on a ceiling. He saw a fancy ceiling in a church and liked it. So, in one of his rooms he has a fancy diamond ceiling – very pretty – where I have only a plain ceiling.[27]

The owners were proud of their accomplishments and allowed many visitors from Cape Breton Island and beyond to see the fruits of their labor. The interiors of houses were brightly coloured, causing one traveller in 1938 to focus on interior details of the visited house:

> The floor of one room was a royal blue. The walls had light blue paper and the woodwork was white. In another room the floor was pink. White curtains at the windows had dainty frills of pink. 'This is our guest room,' said one house-wife, as she opened the door of a most attractive room. Floor of a delicate yellow, mauve walls and a ceiling of pastel green blended together and gave a most pleasing effect. 'We got the color scheme from a magazine,' the housewife said. 'See the nice big clothes closet,' she continued. 'We never had such a thing as a closet in a room before. The last house we lived in had no bathtub and no hot water – very awkward that was.'[28]

Figure 4 – Tompkinsville houses shortly after completion, 1939.
From Provincial Archives of Nova Scotia Collection, N-7277.

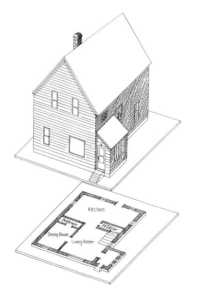

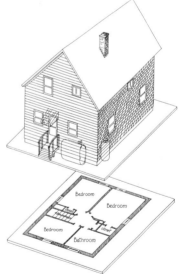

Figure 5 – Floor plan and sketch of ground floor, Joe and Mary Laben's house.

Drawn by Barry Gabriel, University College of Cape Breton.

Figure 6 – Floor plan and sketch of upper floor, Mary and Joe Laben's house.

Drawn by Barry Gabriel, University College of Cape Breton.

While both men and women helped construct the homes, women made most of the cosmetic choices of the house interiors, and they altered their individual spatial layouts, particularly in the kitchen–the place where much activity occurred. Travel writer, Clara Dennis, describes the spacious and well laid-out kitchens:

> There were the most adorable little kitchens in the houses – kitchens that would delight the heart of any housewife. To the miner's wife they were a special joy for with different members of her family working perhaps different shifts in the mine, she might have to prepare as many as seven or eight different meals a day instead of the regulation three. One kitchen had a window built over the sink, and the miner's wife looked out on a beautiful view as she worked. A built-in flour bin and four closets with four closet doors, was an original idea in another kitchen. One kitchen was red and grey, with red and grey linoleum on the floor. Another had black linoleum and the chairs were Spanish red and Royal blue. . . .[29]

On my first visit to Tompkinsville in the 1990s to visit Mary Laben, the last surviving pioneer of this neighbourhood, I was welcomed into her comfortable, sun-filled kitchen at the rear of the house. She said, "I love my kitchen" and she proudly showed me around pointing out its many features and details including a sunny kitchen nook with table and chairs, a large space for cooking, and a wall of cupboards for storage. A decorative overhead valence divides the kitchen into suitable preparing and eating sections.

While the rear kitchen is sunny and inviting, the living room, or "front room" as it is often called in Cape Breton, located at the side of the Laben house, is where the many photographs of daughters, nieces, their friends and acquaintances, and Mary Laben's late husband, Joe, are displayed. The photographs in this "personal museum" show the various rites of passage of family members along with several awards given to Joe Laben for his contribution to cooperativism and housing. A large image of the Last Supper and a picture of Christ keep watch over the living room. It is here where special guests are brought and where Mary Laben now spends much of her time. A small dining room has been transformed into a bedroom because it is difficult for Mary Laben to get up and down the stairway leading to the living room. A bathroom was built off the dining room as well. The up-stairs contains three bedrooms with small closets and another bathroom.

Residents of Tompkinsville chose familiar spatial patterns when constructing their new houses. A variation on the grid-iron plan was used to lay out the neighbourhood, a common town plan used in the many coal mining communities of Cape Breton and other areas of North America.[30] Even though their motiva-tion for building cooperatively was to move away from the company housing, owned and managed by the Dominion Steel and Coal Company, they chose a basic three-room plan with a front room, dining room and rear kitchen that was similar to the company houses built throughout the island as early as the 1830s with the arrival of the British-owned General Mining Association. While some two-room plans were used in Cape Breton's com-pany housing, by 1900 the standard plan in company duplexes built by the mining company was the three-room form; homes of this type still can be found in communities such as Dominion, Glace Bay, New Waterford, New Victoria, Sydney Mines, and In-verness, as well as in Reserve Mines. Even though company houses were considered to be drafty and sub-standard, the build-ers of Tompkinsville stayed with familiar plans and demonstrated a certain cultural conservatism in their selection of floor plans for their new homes.

Tompkinsville residents also followed earlier patterns in their exterior yards. They planned for and planted gardens to help sup-ply their families with fresh produce and root crops. The garden was not a hobby but a necessity for many, especially when the mines were reduced to one or two shifts a week, a common oc-currence throughout the 1930s. Many industrial Cape Bretoners have rural roots; their parents and grandparents came in droves from rural Inverness, Victoria, and Richmond counties of Cape Breton at the turn of the twentieth century when coal mining was booming on the island. Agriculture was not unfamiliar to them. In addition to beans, peas, carrots, squash, turnips, and potatoes, their gardens also contained large strawberry patches, many sup-plying more than 25 baskets each year.[31]

In the last 56 years, most of the original residents have died, and younger citizens have purchased the homes of the Tompkins-ville pioneers. There are no longer any coal mines in Reserve Mines; miners now work in the underground submarine Phalen Colliery in the nearby town of New Waterford. Many of the houses have had aluminum siding applied in the 1960s and 70s in an attempt to cut heating costs during the OPEC oil crisis.

Conclusion

Vernacular architecture exists when people and communities have some element of control over their physical environment. When individuals are able to build homes, barns, or neighbour-hoods following older, conventional patterns in a region, when they are able to adjust and alter their architecture to suit their own needs, or when they are able to express their wishes and desires in making a home or building, we are dealing with architecture at the vernacular level.

The Tompkinsville housing cooperative exhibits many fea-tures of vernacular architecture, including owner control of the entire building process. Despite the poor economic climate, the participants realized that by working together to construct houses they were able to afford decent, comfortable places to live. The residents of Tompkinsville nurtured the idea of cooperative hous-ing through many discussions and study clubs, through readings, conversations, arguments, and debates. They moved from theory to practise as they constructed their own homes. Their tenacious drive has transformed many working class neighbourhoods in At-lantic Canada that have followed their example.

This cooperative building process, in itself an older conven-tional pattern of enterprise, allowed mining families to break away from the confines of the company-owned housing so preva-lent in the community at the time. Barns, outbuildings, and houses were once "raised" in many communities in a communal fashion with entire neighbourhoods of men, women, and children assisting in some way. The Tompkinsville residents adjusted and altered their architectural plans to suit their own needs, modifying each unit to match the particular aesthetics and needs of the fam-ily. The architecture of this neighbourhood is clearly, "product of a place, of a people, by a people."[32]

The Tompkinsville houses would not fare well if evaluated according to architectural criteria developed by governments to assess the significant historical buildings in our communities. These houses are not extremely old, only fifty-eight years. They are not designed by a well-known architect, they do not represent a unique architectural style, and they are not directly associated with a prestigious merchant or industrialist. Moreover, many are sheathed in aluminum siding, a renovation made by working-class people throughout Nova Scotia in the 1960s. Nevertheless, the process of construction and the influence of this housing development at the local, regional, national, and indeed, international levels would suggest that the neighbourhood should be recognized as a significant part of Nova Scotia's built heritage. Vernacular dwellings like those found in Tompkinsville deserve to be represented more extensively in our historic building inventories and in our designated Canadian historic properties, for they offer us a realistic portrayal of the lives of working-class Canadians.

Notes

1. Much of the material for this paper derives from the Beaton Institute Archives, University College of Cape Breton (UCCB), and the Public Archives of Nova Scotia. The most important materials, however, came directly from Mary Laben, the last surviving pioneer of this neighbourhood. She thoughtfully and carefully answered my endless questions about the development of the neighbourhood and allowed me to take measured sketches and photographs of her home. Mary and her husband Joe, who died in 1992, were two of the prime forces behind this housing development. Mary graciously offered her assistance throughout this entire project. I also wish to thank Kate Currie, Beaton Institute, UCCB, research assistants Ainslie White and Kim Stockley, Don Ward, Barry Gabriel, Bill Davey, Del Muise, and the Nova Scotia Department of Culture to whom an earlier draft was submitted for their Heritage Unit. A longer version of the paper is to be published in the fall issue of the *Material History Review*, published by the National Museum of Science and Technology.

2. Kingston William Heath, "Defining the Nature of Vernacular," *Material Culture*, 20 (1988), 5.

3. For a sense of the times see: Dawn Fraser, *Echoes from Labor's Wars* (Sydney: Breton Books, 1992); David Frank, "The Industrial Folksong in Cape Breton," *Canadian Folklore Canadien*, 8 Nos. 1-2 (1986), 21-42; David Frank, "Tradition and Culture in the Cape Breton Mining Community in the Early Twentieth Century," in *Cape Breton at 200*, ed. Ken Donovan (Sydney: University College of Cape Breton Press, 1985, pp. 203-218); Don MacGillivray, "The Industrial Verse of Slim McInnis," *Labour Le Travail*, 28 (1991), 271-83.

4. David Frank, "Class and Region, Resistance and Accommodation" in *The Atlantic*

Provinces in Confederation, ed. Ernest R. Forbes and Del A. Muise (Toronto and Fredericton: University of Toronto and Acadiensis Press, 1993), p. 245.

5. Mary Arnold, *The Story of Tompkinsville*, typescript, n.d., Beaton Institute, UCCB, pp. 10-11. In working on this project I uncovered a first draft of this book in the attic of a cooperative house in New Waterford. A copy of this typescript has been deposited in the Beaton Institute Archives, UCCB. See a later version in the publication: *Mary Arnold. The Story of Tompkinsville* (New York: The Co-operative League, 1940).

6. Edward Skillen Jr., "New Houses and New Men: Nova Scotia Miners Raise Themselves Nearer Security Through Co-operation," *Commonweal*, August 18 (1939), p. 388. PANS.

7. "Housing Survey of Reserve Mines," Beaton Institute, UCCB, 1945 MG 14 184 E. B, pp. 2-3.

8. "Housing Survey of Reserve Mines," p. 4. These kinds of temporary "shacks" were quite common surrounding mine sites in industrial Cape Breton and beyond.

9. "Housing Survey of Reserve Mines," pp. 5-6.

10. "Housing Survey of Reserve Mines," p. 6.

11. Arnold typescript, n.d. , Beaton Institute, UCCB, p. 6.

12. Interview with Mary Laben by Richard MacKinnon, January 7, 1993, Tompkinsville, Nova Scotia.

13. *Coop Housing Nova Scotia*, Public Archives of Nova Scotia, VF, V. 186, 3. p. 37.

14. *Coop Housing Nova Scotia*, Public Archives of Nova Scotia, VF, V. 186, 3. pp. 37-58.

15. "History of Arnold Credit Union," People's Library, Beaton Institute, UCCB, MG 14, 184, B.

16. Arnold, typescript, Beaton Institute, UCCB, p. 8. The present-day Cape Breton Regional Library developed from this first Reserve Mines library; today there are thirteen branches and two bookmobiles to service the counties of Cape Breton and Victoria.

17. Interview, Laben.

18. In Cape Breton Island, company stores were referred to as "Pluck-Me's" because the stores were viewed by miners and their families as part of an exploitative system. The bill at the "Pluck Me" store was taken directly off the paycheck before the miner was able to collect the pay. During the bitter strikes in the 1920s, some "Pluck Me" stores were burned because of their symbolic associations. See: David Frank, "Tradition and Culture in the Cape Breton Mining Community in the Early Twentieth Century," pp. 203-218.

19. Interview, Laben.

20. See Mary Arnold's book, *The Story of Tompkinsville*. New York: The Cooperative League, 1940) for her version of how this neighbourhood came into being. Mary Arnold was involved in cooperative development in New York City where she was manager of a group called Consumer Cooperative Services. The liner notes in her book, *Father Jimmy of Nova Scotia* (Chicago: Cooperative League of the USA, n.d.), state that she produced a film, "The Turn of The

Tide," about lobster fishers along the coast of Maine and a book, *In the Land of the Grasshopper Song* (New York: Vantage Press, 1957.)

21. Clara Dennis, *Cape Breton Over* (Toronto: Ryerson Press, 1940), p. 108.

22. Dennis, p. 109.

23. Interview, Laben.

24. Interview, Laben.

25. Arnold, typescript, p.23.

26. For a discussion of this roof type see JoAnn Latremouille, *Pride of Home: The Working Class Housing Tradition in Nova Scotia 1749 -1949* (Hantsport, Nova Scotia: Lancelot Press, 1986), p. 37. Latremouille points out that the high winds in the Cheticamp area led to the choice of this roof form: "The builders around Cheticamp oriented their houses to face the hipped gables into the prevailing southeast winter wind . . . ." Even though the wind conditions were different in the industrial communities on the eastern end of the island, people from Cheticamp brought this roof style with them when they went to work in the mines.

27. Dennis, pp. 109-110.

28. Dennis, p. 110.

29. Dennis, p. 111.

30. For an article examining the vernacular nature of grid iron plans see: Howard Wight Marshall, "A Good Grid-Iron: The Vernacular Design of a Western Cow Town," in *Perspectives in Vernacular Architecture*, II. ed. Camille Wells (Columbia: University of Missouri Press, 1986), pp. 81-88. For a description of the layout of a Cape Breton coal mining town in 1928 see: Debra McNabb, "A Company Town, Glace Bay, Nova Scotia," in *Historical Atlas of Canada: Addressing the Twentieth Century,* ed. Donald Kerr and Deryck Holdsworth (Toronto: University of Toronto Press, 1990), Plate 37.

31. Interview, Laben.

32. Kingston William Heath, "Defining the Nature of Vernacular," *Material Culture,* 20 (1988), 5.

Kaqietaq 'All Gone':
Honouring the Dying and Deceased in Eskasoni

DAVID L. SCHMIDT

Death is simultaneously the most profound and most banal of all human phenomena. Human societies ease the tension this paradox engenders through shared rituals of closure, including deathbed visits, wakes, and commemorative meals. In the following essay I share my observations of Mi'kmaq conventions for honouring the dying and deceased in these settings. During the nearly three years I lived in the Mi'kmaq community of Eskasoni, I was able to participate in a number of wakes, funerals, and post-funeral dinners when my personal relationship with the families of the deceased allowed. My thanks are extended to those families and to my friends Helen Sylliboy, Murdena Marshall, and Joe B. Marshall for their insights on this meaningful facet of Mi'kmaq life.[1]

Kespisawe'k 'The final shore'

"To die a Mi'kmaq is to die a Catholic." So one elder native man told me in 1992 in response to my queries about his views on life's greatest mystery. Certainly the prominence of Catholicism among Cape Breton's Mi'kmaq people is well documented. The first Mi'kmaq conversion is attributed to Grand Chief Membertou who, in 1610, was baptized by missionaries at Port Royale (modern-day Annapolis Royal, Nova Scotia) in a ceremony of alliance between his people and the French court. Even after making peace with the Protestant British in the 1760s, Roman Catholicism persisted among the Mi'kmaq as a bond that could not be broken by colonial and provincial administrators and became an integral part of their tribal identity. Since that time the Mi'kmaq Nation, whose members lived on and off reserve throughout Nova Scotia, New Brunswick, Prince Edward Island, Newfoundland, and eastern Quebec, has been known as the "eldest daughter of the [Holy Roman] Church among the Indians of North America (Lenhart 1932). Today divergence from Catholicism is rare: in Eskasoni, for example, there are small coteries of Baha'i enthusiasts and native traditionalists who promote decidedly anti-Catholic spiritual philosophies. The total number of self-identified non-Catholics is no more than five per cent of the population, however (Schmidt and Marshall 1995).

In almost all cases the elder man's statement "to die a Mi'kmaq is to die a Catholic" is apropos: Mi'kmaq families have long comforted the dying and buried the dead according to the church's teachings. These conventions are not purely acculturative but are rooted in indigenous concepts of an "appropriate death" (Weisman 1980). To die an appropriate death is to be surrounded by visiting relatives and friends for, as one Mi'kmaq friend told me, "no one comes into the world alone and no one should leave it that way" (J.B. Marshall, personal communication). Over a century ago a Catholic missionary to the Mi'kmaq described their deathbed visits this way:

> If any one is sick, every one visits him continually; they will travel twenty to forty miles to visit him. Everyone will bring something; they prepare medicine for him; go to the white people to get something better than they can give him themselves; they speak to him of heaven, of Jesus, of the Great Spirit, of our Mother Mary, of St. Anne, etc. They say prayers for him; if his sickness increases, every one considers it an honour to go for the priest, and even if the priest's house be very far off. In a word, each strives to alleviate his position, and prepare him for eternity (Anonymous 1868).

An appropriate death therefore is one blessed by visiting siblings, cousins, godchildren, neighbours, and schoolmates from long past, many exhausted from driving overnight from Big Cove or Halifax or Boston and all toting gifts of food. At the bedside of one very ill, elderly acquaintance, I watched as a riot of newly arrived cousins and casserole dishes turned his dreary hospital room into a Cape Breton kitchen party, Mi'kmaq style. Raucous humour is quickly replaced by Christian solemnity when the dying person or others begin to pray, for prayers "ease the way for both the dying and those to be left behind and are taken very seriously" (H. Sylliboy, personal communication). These prayers include Catholic texts (e.g., the Confiteor, Act of Contrition) as well as the non-Christian prayer *Apiksiktuaqn* in which the dying person expresses his regrets to the elements of the natural world he may have wasted or exploited. In *Apiksiktuaqn* "the creatures of the air, of the water, under the water, and all of creation are asked to forgive the person for any disrespect he showed them during his time on earth" (M. Marshall, personal communication).

Most importantly, to die an appropriate death is to have those who have known and loved the dying person "bid him farewell with peace in their hearts as his boat heads for *kespisawe'k*" or 'the final shore' (H. Sylliboy, personal communication). The presence of loved ones enables the dying man or woman to resolve past conflicts and estrangements, thus granting survivors "peace in their hearts." This act of resolution, called *Apiksiktatimk* or 'forgiveness', is the definitive act of an appropriate Mi'kmaq death. When the dying person senses the end is imminent she meets individually with each of her adult friends and family members, saying "*Apiksiktuin*" ('I forgive you') and asks for forgiveness in return. Each one confesses to the dying person the wrongs she's committed or the grudges he's harboured; the dying person, if conscious, will do the same. In that moment all sins are pardoned and, as one elder woman told me, "now the person is ready to die." Humorous stories told in Eskasoni illustrate how *Apiksiktatimk* conventions can go awry, however. In one such story a prominent woman dying of an undiagnosed illness beckoned her family and friends to her bedside. When her oldest daughter (who has a reputation as a flashy clotheshorse) began to speak, instead of asking her mother to forgive her past transgressions, she inquired whether she could have the dying woman's wardrobe. The woman was so incensed by the request that she rose from the bed, vowing not to die in order to spite her daughter's vanity. She remains quite healthy as of the publication date of this volume.

When family members sense their loved one is drawing her last breath, no one is allowed to cry or to call out her name for any loud noise will distract the person's spirit as it searches for the "good spirit path" to the next world. The spirit will then be compelled to return to its corporeal host and the dying person will linger between pain and the release of death. Thus only when visitors are completely silent can the dying loved one pass on; at that point he or she is said to be *kaqietaq* 'all gone'. Family members stay with the body until it grows cold since any remaining physical warmth is believed to signify the abiding presence of the person's soul (M. Marshall, personal communication).

The subjects of death and dying are sometimes accompanied by ghost stories and references to a realm of numinous power inhabited by both benevolent and malevolent forces. Mi'kmaq oral tradition holds that the souls of the recently deceased are transformed into stars and embedded in the *Wjijaqamijawti*, 'the soul road' or Milky Way. From this heavenly vista deceased elders are said to safeguard those they've left behind, and the dying have been known to promise post-mortem protection to their relatives. A teenage girl's description of her maternal grandmother's passing is illustrative in this regard:

> You know the room where Stevie, Ida, Johnny, and me sleep in? That used to be my grandma's room. She had a bad cancer, in her stomach, I think, and she used to complain that her mouth was always feeling bitter, sour-tasting. I'd make her some warm milk and carry it in to her. She didn't say nothing much to me, but I knew she liked me to sit next to her while she had her milk . . . one day I brought in the milk as usual 'cause I heard her calling, that is, making them little noises in her throat. I brought in the milk and Grandma put her hand on my arm and kind of pulled me near her. I said, "What is it?" She whispered to me that she would come back after she died and give me special help . . . I told my mother what she said and she got afraid. She told me to stay away from Grandma after that. She died the next day. My mother and my aunts washed the body and dressed it. After the funeral, my mother didn't want to put me in that room. I wasn't afraid. I was only twelve at the time but I told her that Grandma

had promised to help me, not to frighten me
(Guillemin 1975).

Restless souls are believed to return to their homes as *eli'sasitewk*
or 'patchwork' ghosts, amorphous spectres held together by the
hand-sewn shrouds in which they were buried. Surviving family
members can release these wayward spirits by administering a
blow to the jaw known as *klujjieweyapika'tun* or 'swinging in the
sign of the cross': the mortal forms a fist and, with outstretched
arm, makes the sign of the cross and strikes the *eli'sasitewk*
smartly. The deceased is then able to find eternal rest (H. Sylliboy, personal communication).

Nipapultimk 'All night praying'

After the deceased person's body is embalmed in Sydney and returned to Eskasoni, it is waked in an open casket in the largest
room of the family home for three days and two nights. A white
sheet symbolizing a pure shroud is tacked to the wall above the
casket, and the white and red flag of the Mi'kmaq Nation is
posted as a protective sentinel over the corpse. In former days,
the casket was constructed from barrel staves or rough fir boards
by men who were proscribed from speaking or eating while they
worked (Wallis and Wallis 1955). A factory-manufactured casket
is employed today but, in keeping with indigenous beliefs, it must
be kept well away from walls so the deceased's spirit may flow
freely about the body. For reasons not known to my Eskasoni
friends, Mi'kmaq tradition associates flowing movement with
peaceful passage into the spirit world, whereas chaotic, random
movement is thought to inhibit the soul's release. Thus, in order
to aid the deceased person's transition to the spiritual plane,
friends and family members move around the casket with careful
deliberation.

Because the deceased is considered to be vulnerable to negative spectral forces until interred in sanctified ground, wakes are
twenty-four hour affairs. During these *Nipapultimk* or 'all night
praying' sessions (as wakes are sometimes called in the Mi'kmaq
language), the body is attended by family members, friends, and
visiting relatives. Bolstered by bottomless cups of Red Rose tea,
mourners read from prayer books and place small personal items

inside the casket, including jewelry, photographs, feathers, sprays of sweetgrass, and personal notes written to the deceased. The kitchen hums with cooks, hungry children, and the rich aromas of broiled eel and lemon meringue pie. The men in attendance often gather in the kitchen, while the women are usually found huddled in bedrooms comforting grieving family members. The sometime taciturn social face of Mi'kmaq individuals is suspended at wakes, and visitors feel compelled to comfort with deep expressions of emotion all family members, even those they do not know (H. Sylliboy, personal communication).

On the final morning of the wake a *nujialasutmat* or 'prayer leader'[2] reads the Mi'kmaq Catholic text "Leaving the House" two hours prior to the funeral; indeed, the wake is not considered complete until "Leaving the House" is recited before the assembled mourners. The text's importance to the Mi'kmaq appears to lie in its eloquent expression of the unpredictability and inevitability of death for, as the final line reads, "today it is this person's turn, tomorrow it may be me" (M. Marshall, personal communication). The body is then taken to the church for the funeral and burial. Except for the Mi'kmaq-language hymns sung at the beginning and end of the funeral itself, these church ceremonies are Catholic in content and style.

Salite Charity

Immediately following the church and cemetery services, mourners drive to Eskasoni's community hall to attend a commemorative feast and auction called *salite* (from the French *charite'* or 'charity'). To the Mi'kmaq people a *salite* signifies the final earthly gesture of the deceased, for it is the deceased who is the true host of the feast and who honors the living by breaking bread with them one last time. When attending a *salite* one is immediately struck by the dignified yet convivial mood of the mourners. Each moves from table to table, offering condolences to the grieving relatives and sharing with them a humorous story about their loved one. Great bundles of gifts lie stacked on tables around the room's periphery; these have been brought by the mourners for the auction to follow. Plates of moose meat, eel, boiled turnips, and corned beef are dished out pell-mell from the hall's tiny kitchen. After everyone has eaten, the gifts (including handmade clothes, birch bark baskets, electric appliances, tea towels and other kitchenwares) are auctioned to the highest bidders. All proceeds go to the deceased person's family in order to defray the funeral costs, and wealthier Mi'kmaq families often donate this money to the Eskasoni parish or to a foreign Catholic missionary society.

One fascinating aspect of today's *salite* conventions is that the items mourners bring to auction are often those they bid on with the greatest passion. Indeed, the same item may be donated and repurchased, sometimes at prices many of us would deem outlandish, at every *salite* the person attends. "This is the one part non-natives can't understand," my friend Murdena told me with a smile, "How can someone buy a coffee cup at Walmart for $1.44, take it to a *salite*, and then buy it back for $100? Then they donate it again the next time someone dies, only to buy it back again for another $100?" Such generous behaviour may be traced to the origins of the *salite* in post-funeral gift-exchange ceremonies documented in the nineteenth century (Anonymous 1868). At these ceremonies mourners presented small items to one another as an emblem of mutual respect and ethnic-religious solidarity. By honouring those who remained behind after a loved one's death, it was believed, one honoured the deceased herself. It can be suggested, then, that paying relatively large sums for humble items at a *salite* in modern-day Eskasoni recreates and perpetuates these public expressions of respect and solidarity.

Conclusion

Researchers have been blind to the rich source of cultural information on native spirituality in apparently acculturative Christian traditions, including those associated with Mi'kmaq Catholicism (McElwain 1990). Although this examination of Mi'kmaq deathbed visits, wakes, and *salites* is all too brief, I believe it illustrates the intense and abiding value the Mi'kmaq people of Eskasoni and elsewhere place on honouring the souls of their dying and deceased loved ones. Truly, no Mi'kmaq person "comes into the world alone" and nearly all members of the native community strive to ensure no one leaves it that way. A substantial portion of this contemporary Mi'kmaq "death work" appears to reflect non-Catholic cosmology and ceremonial practice; determining the

exact degree and loci of native-Christian accommodation requires – and deserves – further research.

Notes

1. The beliefs concerning death and dying quoted in this article are not necessarily
held by all Mi'kmaq people, and further research is required to demonstrate the
breadth of their distribution. Any errors of interpretation are my own.

2. The role of prayer leader originated in the 18th century when, anticipating the
victory of British and New England forces over France's colonial army and navy
at Fortress Louisbourg, French missionaries trained natives to serve as lay
catechists to their communities (Schmidt and Marshall, 1995).

References

Anonymous. 1868. The Catholic Church of the Wilderness. In *The Irish Ecclesiastical
Record*, Vol. 18, April 1868.

Guillemin, Jeanne. 1975. *Urban renegades: The cultural strategy of American Indians.* New
York: Columbia University Press.

Lenhart, Rev. John. 1932. *History of the Micmac ideographic manual.* Sydney, Nova
Scotia: Cameron Print.

McElwain, Thomas. 1990. "The rainbow will carry me": The language of Seneca
Iroquois Christianity as reflected in hymns. In C. Vecsey, ed., *Religion in native
North America.* Moscow, Idaho: University of Idaho Press.

Schmidt, David L. and Murdena Marshall. 1995. *Mi'kmaq hieroglyphic prayers.* Halifax:
Nimbus Publishing.

Wallis, Wilson D. and Ruth Sawtell Wallis. 1955. *The Micmac Indians of eastern Canada.*
Minneapolis: University of Minnesota Press.

Weisman, Avery D. 1980. Appropriate and appropriated death. In E. Shneidman,
ed., *Death: Current perspectives.* Palo Alto, California: Mayfield Publishing.

The Irish of Rocky Bay

MOIRA ROSS

The north shore of Isle Madame was settled by Acadians, French, Basques, Channel Islanders, English, Scottish, and Irish. The 1752 census – compiled by Sieur de la Rogue of Louisbourg – shows Basque and French permanent settlers in the area of Rocky Bay as well as itinerant Basques employed in the summer fishery. During the 19th century the principal town on Isle Madame, Arichat, commissioned the building of an imposing cathedral, and the island's harbours supported a vast and prosperous merchant shipping industry which launched schooners laden with dry cod fish.

The first Irish settlement on Isle Madame probably took hold when Laurence Kavanaugh and his associates from Louisbourg moved to St. Peters around 1777. Kavanaugh's father, also Laurence, was prosperous in business at Louisbourg after the defeat of the French by the British in 1758. The extent of his wealth is apparent in the 1772 census of Louisbourg: he had 42 employees, 60 cattle, 10 horses, 30 sheep, and 50 pigs – this represented more than half of the wealth of the entire Louisbourg community. He also operated a farm, owned fishing and retail businesses, and owned three of the twenty-two houses and eight of the seventeen storehouses remaining in Louisbourg. After the death of Laurence Kavanaugh the family moved to St Peter's where fourteen year old Laurence Junior ran the family's business interests in Isle Madame, Main-à-Dieu, St. Peter's, and New Brunswick.[1]

An early reference to Irish settlement at Rocky Bay was made by Father Joseph-Mathurin Bourg, an Acadian priest, who may have visited Isle Madame in 1786. He noted in a letter: "In Cape Breton, about 60 leagues to the east of Halifax, there are at Annaréchaque [Arichat] . . . at least 140 families, all French-Acadi-ans, and many Irish people."[2]

The Catholic Church played an important part in retaining the identity of the Irish community in Rocky Bay. Before the founding of St. Hyacinth's Parish in 1845, the area was served by missionary outpost priests based in Arichat. The first of these was an Irish doctor, William Phelan, who was pastor from 1786 to 1792. He spoke Irish Gaelic and English, but little French. Rever-end Denis Geary, born in Waterford City, Ireland, in 1794, became the first resident pastor of D'Escousse serving from December 1845 to March 1849. Geary conducted a census of the parish in 1846 to record the dues paid by each family. Payment could be made either in cash or cod.

Rocky Bay Irish inhabitants often walked the nine kilometres to D'Escousse for church services at St. Hyacinth's. Some with relatives in D'Escousse attended Saturday evening confession then stayed overnight to attend Mass on Sunday morning. Many of the Irish congregation chose to sit at the west side of the bal-cony close to the statue of St. Patrick. When the church caught fire on July 20, 1954, some Irish members of the parish rushed into the burning building to rescue the statue of St. Patrick.

Mary Norellen James, born in Pondville near Rocky Bay, was the fourth generation to grow up on the family farm.[3] Her great-great grandfather was one of seven brothers who came to Canada from County Cork, Ireland. As a young girl, Mary often visited the farm of neighbours Paddy and Kitty-Ann Doyle who also had come from Ireland to Rocky Bay. She remembers visiting her neighbour's house where the unmarried brother and sister Doyle spoke Irish Gaelic to each other. She recalls these visits:

> You couldn't believe how they lived – the hens and the chickens lived right in the house with them. And the lambs and the sheep, on cold nights they'd take them in. Just a dirt floor. A thatched roof. I don't know what it was built with. It looked like rushes to me, it was all interwoven – looked like rushes from the swamp. The floor was just plain old earth . . . and there was a big fire-place and it had two doors on either side, . . and there were stools in there you'd sit [on] to get warm – benches like. . . . You couldn't see for smoke. Paddy and Kitty-Ann they'd tell us all

these stories from over in Ireland – ghost stories and witches and what have you. We spent most of our time there as kids, no light, no nothing, just the light from the fireplace.

The house was huge, really big. Just parted in two; one side was a huge kitchen, sitting-room, everything went on there. And it looked like it [had] two bedrooms, but we never got in those rooms. They used to milk the cows in those rooms, and they had big tables in there and they'd put basins [in] and leave them set over night and take the cream off in the morning. And then the hens would go in the morning, and get on the edge of the basin and drink the milk – right in the bedroom! And old Kitty-Ann used to make bannock as we call it today. I don't know what they called it. It was some kind of a bread, you cook it in a pot, hang it up in the fireplace. It would be so hard I don't know how they ate it. I remember my brother Leonard, she gave him a piece and he threw it at the hen and broke the hen's leg!

Paddy and Kitty-Ann's house built in the last half of the 19th century is a type of vernacular architecture common in Ireland, but not often used in Canada by Irish settlers who favoured log construction. The Doyles may have used the wattle and daub construction because they were familiar with this method of building in Ireland, and it was less labour intensive than log construction. The house was situated on the beach because the land closest to the water would have been cleared of trees for boat building, fish flakes, housing, and firewood. The fireplace Mary described is also the style found in homes in Ireland and in Irish houses in Newfoundland.[4]

Mary James continues her description of her neighbours in Rocky Bay:

The old woman [Kitty-Ann] herself was bent practically in two, and she walked with a stick. And I remember when she died, I was young. It was Will Kelly that was going to make her coffin to put her in. And if you pressed on her head her leg would come up and if you pressed on her leg her head would come up. And he couldn't get her straight, so he said he had to put her in a barrel! They got her straightened out after a while, whatever they did with her. The priest had to come here and they had to put boards down for the priest. Everybody else went and done what they had to. I remember seeing her lying on the boards before the coffin came. Her hair was [turned] white with the smoke, and [it was] the prettiest blonde you want to see.

And Patrick (Paddy) he was waked up at our house. They brought him up to our house. You put them [the corpses] in the sitting room that no one ever went into hardly. If it was in winter it was as cold as a 'fridge. They'd keep forever in there. The corpse would be along the side. A candle burning. That would go on then – after they buried them they had a real ho-down. And everybody came in there and they brought food and they had the big party – but that was after the funeral.

Wake games, story telling, jokes, singing, and even wrestling were common at wakes throughout Ireland. Evans states that wake games ". . . were generally reserved for the deaths of old people who had survived the ordinary span of life, or young children who could not be looked upon as irreparable loss."[5] These funeral customs, which may date from pagan times, are probably the source of the somewhat irreverent Irish Wake that has been popularised in stories and folksongs.

Mary recalls that St. Patrick's Day was a day of communal work and celebration:

They'd start in the morning, [and] that's the day they made the most of thirty lobster traps [out in the shed], because they had all kinds of help. They used to come from everywhere. The Poiriers from down in Poirierville, they never missed – they came up home. They'd have drinks and they'd sing the songs – sing Irish songs. They'd get mama singing, she had all the old Irish songs. Mama was a beautiful singer. And they'd cook a big feed.

> There was a method to their madness – have a
> big party and get all your lobster traps made.

The visit by the French Poiriers from nearby Poirierville on St. Patrick's Day demonstrates a cultural transfer between the French and Irish communities in the region. Mary also refers to the Irish participation on mi-careme, a mid-lent festival, celebrated by the Acadians – similar to the Christmas mumming tradition of Ireland and Newfoundland. The tradition in Rocky Bay of communal work to make lobster traps on St. Patrick's Day has been recorded in Ireland and Eastern Canada. Manion states that "Saints' days were also observed in Ireland as a time to commence certain farm tasks."[6] St. Patrick's Day was the time for sowing gardens in Ireland, and it appears that this folk custom was adapted to the Canadian seasons. The party afterwards illustrates a fusion of the North American form of St. Patrick's Day celebration with that of Ireland.

Although Isle Madame was a hub of religion, commerce, and education in the mid-18th century in Cape Breton, the economic stability and the population of the area have declined since the 19th century. Confederation, steamships, railways, the 1920 collapse of the fishing industry, and the depression years of the 1930s transformed a mercantile centre into a rural and declining district. World War II brought further depopulation to the area, and the recent closures of the local school and post office have continued to undermine the community of Rocky Bay.

The future appears a little brighter: Maritime studies programmes in the school and a general cultural reawakening have increased an awareness of family and local history. Retirees are returning to strengthen the community, while the combination of a sagging economy in the rest of Canada and improved social programmes have induced families to remain at home. Rocky Bay has its own recreation hall, which hosts a lively St. Patrick's Day celebration and provides a venue for other community activities. The people of Rocky Bay still have a strong Irish accent, and Irish supernatural beliefs persist in Rocky Bay long after they had been forgotten in other areas.

Many Irish communities in Cape Breton gradually assimilated with other cultures. Although Irish people intermarried with Acadians and others, the isolated location of Rocky Bay and the common religion and origin allowed the community to retain

much of its Irish character. In his book *The Irish of Cape Breton*, A.
A. MacKenzie gives this description of the people of Rocky Bay:

> They acquired the name, rightly or wrongly, of be-
> ing a pugnacious irritable lot. Perhaps this could
> be attributed to efforts to maintain their 'Irishness'
> when surrounded by Frenchmen.[7]

Even today the Irish of Rocky Bay pugnaciously maintain
their distinct Irish identity.

Notes

1. Wagg, Phyllis MacInnes, *Lawrence Kavanaugh I: An Eighteenth Century Cape Breton Entrepreneur*. Nova Scotia Historical Review. Halifax, NS: Vol 10, Number 2, 1990; Johnston A.A., *A history of the Diocese of Antigonish*; MacBeath, George. "Lawrence Kavanaugh." Dictionary of Canadian Biography. Toronto: 1966.

2. Evan, Estyn. *Irish Folk Ways*. London: Routledge, 1957.

3. Living Archives Student Project. Isle Madame District High School, Arichat, N.S., 1994. See also Ross, Moira and Silver Donald Cameron, *An Island Parish:The 150th Anniversary of St. Hyacinth's*. St. Hyacinth's Parish, D'Escousse, N.S. 1995.

4. Evans.

5. Evans.

6. Mannion, John. *Irish Settlements in Eastern Canada*. Toronto: U of Toronto Press, 1974.

7. MacKenzie, A. A. *The Irish in Cape Breton*. Antigonish, NS: Formac Publishing Co. Ltd., 1979.

Conversations and Cultural Maintenance in Louisbourg

CAROL CORBIN

Many media scholars worry about the breakdown of community that seems to occur with the unchecked proliferation of mass media. The global village that Marshall McLuhan predicted is really no village at all. It is more like a network of people without geographical or historical grounding. They float, so to speak, in cyberspace.

Is E Dia Fein As Buachaill Dhomh
The Lord is my Shephard
by Ellison Robertson

Humans have experienced changes over the past 150 years that altered their very notions of reality. Industrialization (the shift from local production of hand-made goods to factory production of mass-produced goods), urbanization (the shift from country to city dwelling), and the spread of mass media have combined to work against the formation and maintenance of communities. The television, as just one example of the mass media that have entered our homes, has the power to break down the distinctions between communities, between the "here and there, live and mediated, and personal and public."[1] Where once people living in close proximity would focus their community attention on local events, now we are drawn away by the lure of the spectacle beyond our doors. As our living rooms become receiving centres for simultaneous international news events and entertainment spectacles, our cultures seem to lose connection with their places of origin.

In 1991 I came to live in a small community in Canada on the island of Cape Breton. Louisbourg has a population of 1,200 year-round residents many of whom made their living by fishing or working in fish processing plants. Those numbers grow somewhat during the four-month summer season when some 150,000 tourists pass through town.

When I moved to Louisbourg, I was intrigued by the town's cohesiveness and closeness that, in part, made many of the stereotypes about small towns apparent: everyone knows what everyone else is doing; one's fragile reputation could be marred in the grip of the relentless rumour mill; the town's pace seems slower, less driven, than the cities I had come from; the church features largely in people's lives; and the reputation about the horrors of "small town politics" is apparent in Louisbourg's local political struggles that are often gruelling and very personal.

After living here for several years I began to investigate the relationship between the mass media and the local culture. How could a small Canadian community like Louisbourg hold itself together and retain its identity while being bombarded by media messages – primarily American media messages – produced by different cultures in distant places? In Louisbourg there seemed to be little erosion of the sense of place that many media scholars have feared, although I qualify that statement with a recognition that Louisbourg does not live as it did in the 18th or 19th centuries. Certainly it has changed and is no longer as isolated and culturally distinct as it once was. And certainly many of the social changes lamented by media scholars have affected most communities around the globe. Yet, somehow these small towns have survived as cohesive communities without the schizophrenic cultural identity problems that theorists have looked for. What is it that keeps a small community strong, despite the proliferation of the symbols of mass culture?

Marjorie Ferguson, a media scholar who writes about Canadian culture, suggests that Canada retains its ability to remain culturally distinct in the face of ubiquitous popular culture and the power of American media because media act on the surface rather than the depth of a culture. Although media's role is integral to cultural formation and its symbolic representation, media do not diminish the importance of history and place as primary sources of culture.[2] The power of media and consumer culture works on the surface of a culture. And while these messages have the ability to transform deeper cultural values and traditions, they may not have the all-pervasive power to displace or uproot long-standing deep cultural traditions such as those created by religion, race, ethnicity, family,[3] and, I would add, place.

Canada has maintained its own sense of identity in the face of the proliferation of the forces of global culture that are easily transmitted across an open border in what is considered an extension of American market territory. But it has done so, I suggest, not through nationalism or "melting pot" politics as might be discerned in American examples, but through a strong sense of place tied closely to history and family roots. Residents of Canadian communities, like Louisbourg, identify first with their particular place – Louisbourg, or Cape Breton – and then, they consider themselves Canadian.

To extend Ferguson's study of Canadian culture, I have considered the relationship between the "surface texts" of mass-mediated, consumer-cultural symbols, and the "deep texts," those connected in time to place, heritage, family, and religious traditions. The distinctions between the surface texts and the deep texts are played out and negotiated within the cultural webs of the community. I suggest that there are three ways a community like Louisbourg maintains its own sense of identity. The first is through a high level of interpersonal interaction – a strong oral tradition. The second is by defining itself as what it is not – against other communities that it considers different, inferior, or simply "not us" – thus establishing symbolic boundaries that separate and distinguish the community from all others. The third is the continual recounting of its community history – mythologizing on a day-to-day basis to tie current events with the history of its past. The community retells stories about its history and re-establishes its context every day in personal interactions. It is plausible that through these three techniques, a community like Louisbourg screens out or selects only those surface messages that allow it to retain its sense of identity. The deep texts are not only stories and myths, but they are the very process of connection. The high level of orality within the culture diffuses and subdues mass cultural symbols.

To verify these culture-building and culture-maintaining concepts, I conducted a written survey among the adult residents of Louisbourg (114 residents, or 9.5% of the population) to find out how much time they spend in conversation with each other, where they meet for conversations, and what the topics of conversation are. A researcher randomly approached residents in houses throughout the town and administered the survey during May and June 1994. The results were not surprising and probably could have been predicted by most people living in the community. Yet they corroborate the contention that small Canadian communities like Louisbourg maintain a tightly knit culture in spite of the power of mass media. And, in fact, it appears that the content of mass media simply adds a minor text to the repertoire of topics talked about in the everyday interactions of the residents. The study also supports the theory that communities remain cohesive in these three ways: through a high level of oral interaction, through symbolic construction of boundaries, and through everyday mythologizing.

Orality

One dimension of my theory of cultural cohesiveness focuses on the high level of conversational interaction, or orality, that exists within the town. Conversations among residents are important pastimes, and many hours are spent in interpersonal conversation with friends, neighbours, and families every week. Hence the bonds formed among the people of this small Canadian community, I suggest, are based primarily on orality within the community.

Orality is, according to Walter Ong, "harmonizing," "situational," and it tends to be the factor that brings humans into "close-knit" groups. These oral qualities counteract the heterogeneity that is possible in a literate or post-literate society.[4] Jack Goody and Ian Watt note that orality counteracts the homogenizing tendencies of mass-mediated culture because:

> each individual exposed to such pressures is also a member of one or more primary groups whose oral converse is probably much more realistic and conservative in its ideological tendency; the mass media are not the only, and they are probably not even the main, social influences on the contemporary cultural tradition as a whole.[5]

Orality, I suggest, is tied closely to a geographically-based community, whereas literacy and connections through electronic media know few geographic restraints. Although other pseudo-communities can emerge through media (networks of linked Internet users, penpals linked through ink, webs of like-minded scholars in intellectual communities sharing space in publications), communities of neighbours who co-exist in a certain geographical space maintain and strengthen their communities through perpetual oral interactions, even as they join other communities in mediated networks. The voice is the link. This may also contribute to another feature of many Louisbourg residents that I have observed: a strong, highly developed, storytelling ability. The very soul of the community depends upon residents' abilities to transmit their culture orally through stories and continuous interaction.

This study revealed that residents spend an average of seven hours per week reading and 16 hours per week watching television; while a national survey indicated that Nova Scotians spend just over 24 hours per week watching TV.[6] Louisbourg residents also reported that they spend an average of 21.6 hours talking with family members, and they spent an additional 15.4 hours talking with neighbours for a total average of 37 hours per week in conversation; that comes to 13 hours more time per week spent in conversation than spent in front of the television set based on the national survey statistics. And residents spend nearly 21 hours more in conversation than watching TV in the Louisbourg survey.

The topics of conversation most often stated were weather (64%), children and family (62%), and local events (53%).[7] Births and deaths ("as they occurred") were sometimes topics of conversation in about 72% of the surveys. Television shows were also sometimes discussed (70%), thus suggesting that events on TV enter the cultural dialogue as easily as events within the town. However, the topics least often discussed were international events (28%) and old stories (20%). It is most likely that information about international events is gleaned from mass media. Therefore, although the topics derived from mass mediated sources are sometimes talked about, they hold no significance over local issues. Indeed, the survey indicates that topics from beyond the geographical region are subordinate to the deep texts (such as family and local events) associated with place.

The most pressing local issue at the time of the survey was the closure of the fishery and the high rate of unemployment in the town. Fifty-five percent of respondents stated that the employment situation (or lack of it) in Louisbourg was a topic of conversation, and 26% said that the fishery was a topic. Together these two specific local topics surpassed even the weather as a topic of conversation in Louisbourg, thus confirming the highly contextual nature of the culture of this small community. Not surprisingly, local situations are much more pressing than the vast array of topics brought to every home through television and radio.

Another survey question asked about the venues in which residents had conversations with their neighbours. Conversations are held on the street (93%) or at a friend's house (93%), on the phone (88%), and at the respondents' homes (85%). But a large number of respondents also conducted conversations in public places including the post office (80%), the churches (70%), the four convenience stores in town (67% on average), the gas station (57%), and the town hall (57%). Following these sites, respondents noted work and the three local pubs as places of conversation. Most residents also indicated that they are familiar with the owners or employees in many of the shops and stores – knowing them by name and, in turn, known to them by name. Less than 1% stated that they knew no one working in Louisbourg stores, and 79% knew by name the people in more than three shops in town. Less social interaction occurs at the school (my respondents, again, were all adults), at bingo games, tarabish games, or the local Coast Guard station in comparison to the amount of interaction at the other sites.[8]

Before the 1980s, the main gathering place for local conversations was the Lewis Store. Located on Main Street in the centre of town, the store had been a ships' chandlery, a grocery store, and a furniture store through the years. It had big picture windows facing the street that allowed passersby to see who was inside having a yarn and, in turn, allowing the yarners to see what was going on in the street. After the main road to Sydney was improved and most town residents had automobiles, the store was closed. It could no longer compete with the discount prices in Sydney, and the earlier truck system[9] of paying fishers had long since been eliminated. The loss of that conversational venue was felt by many people, and although interactions shifted to other venues, these too continued to decline in number. The post office no longer has Saturday delivery, the restaurants close in the winter after the tourist season, and generally people have fewer places to gather.

Nevertheless, what these findings suggest is that residents find places to hold conversation even as the number of venues for conversations dwindle. Although there are some people who never frequent some of the local establishments, the majority of Louisbourg residents enter into conversation with their neighbours for several hours every day. In their discussions they concentrate on local issues – the fisheries and the employment situation, the weather, families, and children.

Negative Identification

In addition to the great amount of interpersonal interaction, I also observe that Canadians as a whole, and small town Canadians in particular, maintain their sense of uniqueness by identifying themselves as what they are not. For example, Canadians in general are quick to remind you that they are not Americans. When my uncle, an American, came to visit me in Louisbourg, I introduced him to my Canadian friends as "an American." My uncle corrected me by saying that in fact we were all "Americans" because we all inhabit the Americas. But my Canadian friends showed lacklustre response to his inclusiveness. By most accounts, to call oneself an American is to indicate that you are from the United States, and few Canadians that I know would have any interest in calling themselves Americans. In fact, Canadians visiting Europe make explicit that they are Canadian by wearing maple leaf pins or placing Canadian decals on their luggage. Most Europeans cannot distinguish a Canadian from an American by accent or attire, but once it is known that the guests are Canadians they are treated royally, according to my students who have traveled abroad. Whereas Americans are often associated with the "ugly American" wearing plaid shorts and a cowboy hat, and giving locals the benefit of unsought American advice.

Even as Canada defines itself in negation to the U.S., so do all communities define themselves by marking boundaries of some sort. Cohen believes that as geographical distinctions between places are eroded through mass transportation and mass communication, their symbolic distinctions are, in fact, strengthened.[10] "Communities erect boundaries that are the mask presented by the community to the outside world; it is the community's public face."[11] If one is from Louisbourg, for example, one is clearly not from Main-à-dieu, although Main-à-dieu is only five or six miles away. In Louisbourg, residents separate themselves from even the closest neighbouring communities with tongue-in-cheek statements like "She can't have much taste if she's marrying a Main-à-dieuer." Or, when a street fight broke out late one summer night, Louisbourg residents placed the blame for it squarely on men from a nearby town, even though just as many Louisbourg residents were involved. Some of these contrasts emerge from old rivalries, from having played softball or hockey against a team from Lorraine or Main-à-dieu. Negative identification is less an attempt to make the other community seem inferior than it is to make Louisbourg seem distinct, and, somehow, superior. Yet, I would imagine that Main-à-dieuers feel exactly the same way about Louisbourgers.

Distinctions are just as great between Louisbourg and Sydney. For many years Louisbourg was isolated from Sydney because of poor roads. With the exception of young people who frequent the nightclubs and malls, many Louisbourg residents still spend as little time as possible in the city. Although major shopping is done in the Sydney malls and discount stores, most people express a certain displeasure about making the trip. Some people who are able to drive don't even acquire a license, because they are content to spend all their time in Louisbourg. Rumour has it that in certain bars in Sydney, merely to mention that one is from Louisbourg could start a fight. Yet, I suspect that the animosity is mock enmity feigned primarily to mark territory and define the two communities as separate and distinct.

Another defining mechanism is the "us" and "them" of hiring practices. Louisbourg residents sometimes attribute poor economic conditions in the community to their disgruntlement about hiring of outsiders for local jobs – both in permanent positions and in stop-gap grant hirings. One hiring decision created such wrath among locals that special town meetings were called to discuss it.[12] Residents jealously guard jobs for local students during the summer because every additional income helps feed the family and pay the bills. Even when jobs are posted for residents within the telephone exchange (which includes several small nearby towns) dissatisfaction is often expressed if those hired are not from Louisbourg proper. Catalone or Main-à-dieu residents are seen as intruders hording in on the scarce resources of jobs created within the confines of Louisbourg.

Not only are jobs privileged, but opinions are too. I have been told several times that because I am not from Louisbourg, I have no right to express opinions about the town or its workings. Once a discussion of this sort begins, locals play one-up to determine whose family has lived in Louisbourg the longest, and thus who has the greatest right to speak about town issues. Living in Louisbourg for several generations seems a prerequisite to having voice in local affairs.

These examples illustrate the way in which this community stakes its boundaries to distinguish itself from all other communities, privileging those who have spent the most time in this particular geographical space. While these predilections smack of xenophobia and bigotry, they are manifestations of a deep feeling of connectedness to and custodianship of this place. In the local mind, the "true" residents of Louisbourg, whose parents and grandparents have struggled and died here, are bound in time to this one place and are thus more closely associated with the deep cultural symbol systems that differentiate this town from every other town.

Everyday Myths

"Have not all races had their first unity from a mythology that marries them to rock and hills?," asked Yeats.[13] Yeats suggests that our myths tie us to place, and it is the sea to which Louisbourg is married. Today few people in Louisbourg make their living from the sea, yet it remains one of the central motifs in daily mythologies. In conversations and hours of storytelling, Louisbourg residents bind themselves to the past, not only by recounting old seafaring tales, but by incorporating current stories and events into a long chain of narratives. Thus, present day fables are legitimated through their association with past events, or the traditions of the community.[14]

Louisbourg's sea-faring history is well represented far beyond Louisbourg's shores. The present-day town shares its harbour with an 18th-century French fortress that was located near the easternmost part of Cape Breton in order to have direct access to the lucrative fishery on the Grand Banks. That fishing history is told as part of Canada's national heritage both in textbooks and at the site of the reconstruction of the Fortress of Louisbourg. And although John Cabot's famous words about fish so plentiful that they fairly jumped into baskets lowered from boats still can be heard today, what was once boasted about in terms of plenty is now lamented for its demise.

The Atlantic ground fishery was closed in 1991 by the Department of Fisheries and Oceans after years of over-fishing by Canadian and international fleets. That closure has had profound impact on Louisbourg. How and why it happened is argued over and over again by local Louisbourg fishers and their families. Unemployment in Louisbourg now stands at about 50%.[15] In an open survey question about the future of Louisbourg, many residents expressed feelings of despair as they face uncertainty in the fishery and few opportunities for employment. Words like "bleak," "declining," "sad," and "not good" far outnumber optimistic statements. Thus, the community hangs together in its discouragement, bound by shared symbols of hopelessness.

But the current fisheries crisis is part of a larger mythology that has been handed down through the generations in this maritime community. Fishing has never been a sure thing. One fisher, who remembers fishing on the Grand Banks in the days of sail, stated that there have always been cycles in the fishery. Some years the fish are scarce, according to Louisbourg resident George Barter, but they always come back eventually. In addition, the uncertainty of employment in the fisheries has existed since Europeans first plied the waters of the North Atlantic, and governments have historically subsidized fishing communities in order to ensure the protein sources necessary to feed the nation when the fish returned.[16] So the stories that this fishing community tell today have been repeated many times. They seem new to each generation, but elements of them are repetitions from stories the elders of the community have been telling for years.

Although few people in the Louisbourg survey reported that they recount old stories, many old stories become incorporated into new ones and are thought of as current events. Even as remnants from other mediated surface texts, such as news stories and fisheries bulletins, enter the community's conversations, they are amalgamated into the ongoing story of the fishery and of the town. Thus the fishery crisis that is a pressing current event has its roots in fisheries' crises from days gone by. Even as current myths are created and related, old ones are repeated.

Closely connected to the fishery as a topic of discussion is the employment situation in Louisbourg. This is a theme that I call the "rationalization of hard times." This theme appears both in local conversations as well as in locally-written songs.[17] The stories surrounding this theme place the blame for hard times on several different culprits: the government, foreign fishing fleets, seals, industry, scientists, and environmentalists. In general, the justifications suggest that no one in power listened to what the fishing communities had to say about the fate of the fisheries, a feeling supported by recent studies.[18] The fishers felt that government didn't listen to the people who knew the sea the best; foreign fleets were overfishing Canadian waters in political deals made in exchange for other concessions; protected by bleeding heart environmentalists like Bridget Bardot, unculled seal herds were gobbling huge amounts of cod and other ground fish; industry's only objective is to make a profit as quickly as possible, an ideology that ensures continued overfishing, yet their tight connection with the government allows them privileged access to regulating decisions; and environmentalists and scientists knew little about actual conditions on the sea, were often unable to even identify one fish from another, and thus (along with industry) they were the least qualified people to regulate the fishery. These themes and variations of them are replayed frequently as fishers debate their situation. While current culprits are identified, they are added to the traditional stories of hard times in the Maritimes.

One local story recently incorporated into the fishing myths was about Tom Fudge, a long-time inshore fisher holding a practically worthless cod fishing license. Tom owed money on his boat, and, unable to make the payments because he couldn't fish, the boat was repossessed by the bank.[19] But the story became more complicated when Tom revealed that the officer at the bank who confiscated the boat had made a personal offer to purchase the boat only weeks before the seizure. One thing led to another and soon a theme of collusion by those in power – the Nova Scotia Fisheries Loan Board, fishery officers, politicians, and so forth – was constructed that characterizes both the fisheries crisis and other myths in Louisbourg. That theme I call the "conspiracy" theme. Conspiracy filters into stories on a wide variety of topics, from the fisheries closure to local politics, from the hiring practices of major employers such as Parks Canada or fish plants, to aboriginal rights, federal bilingual requirements, and immigration laws. Local residents find a conspiracy to keep them down in each of them.

Again, conspiracy themes separate Louisbourg from others of the outside world, thus distinguishing Louisbourg in its abjection. And they add to a theme of outside control that has been a staple of local mythology since the French placed a massive fortress on the shores nearly 300 years ago. One would be hard pressed to find a time when Louisbourg did not feel taken advantage of by someone from the outside. But this theme may be a common one in resource-based communities which depend on the outside world for their markets.

Together these local stories act as binding agents. They are tales tossed out in bars and at the post office. And, for the most part, audience members participate in the narrative, adding details or new theories to each retelling. Although there is a certain amount of commiseration in the stories, they act like glue that holds the local populace to its history in time and each other in place.

Conclusion

Listening to stories in Louisbourg can be a full-time occupation; it is usually going on somewhere – in public places, in kitchens, at the wharves, or on the back steps – at almost every hour of the day. The content of these conversations is comprised primarily of local issues, although from time to time topics from the mass media emerge within the narratives and broaden the discussions beyond Louisbourg's geographical space. Residents of this small community spend many hours interacting orally, thus binding themselves in historical time to each other through the continuous recounting of local themes.

Louisbourg residents also distinguish the town from all others by expressing what they are not, although expressing why they are not like "the others" would prove difficult; and distinguishing themselves in positive terms would be even harder. In addition, the community affiliates itself with a long tradition of symbolic construction by bringing old stories into the ever-changing contexts of the day.

The breakdown of community brought about by more and easier access to mass cultural symbols is, I contend, a change primarily in the surface cultural literacy of small Canadian communities. Surface cultural values, however, eventually influence and alter the deeper values.[20] Concerns must be raised about the amount of U.S. or Canadian content in mass-mediated symbol systems, but we must also address, as Marjorie Ferguson notes, the deep cultural narratives that are tied to geographic place, home, family, traditions, ethnicity, and religion. Of concern to me in this discussion are the public venues where conversations occur. When a post office or school closes, when a store shuts its doors because it cannot compete with nearby discount malls, important community-building places are lost. These changes seem to me to be more significant for the maintenance of deep cultural traditions in Canadian communities than does a nightly menu of American sitcoms. Conversations, I believe, are the heart and soul of the community.

Notes

1. Meyrowitz, Joshua. *No Sense of Place.* New York: Oxford, 1985: 308.

2. Ferguson, Marjorie. "Invisible Divides: Communication and Identity in Canada and the U.S." *Journal of Communication 43.* Spring 1993: 43.

3. Ferguson, 45.

4. Ong, Walter. *Orality and Literacy.* London: Metheun, 1982: 73-74.

5. Goody, Jack, and Ian Watt. "The Consequences of Literacy." *Communication in History.* (Heyer and Crowley, Eds.) White Plains, NY: Longman, 1995: 50.

6. MacKenzie, Rennie. "Nova Scotian grannies enjoy Oprah and soaps." *Cape Breton Post.* August 24, 1995: 20.

7. Totals do not add up to 100% because most respondents checked more than one topic area.

8. It must be noted that those who attend bingo and tarabish games or frequent the Coast Guard station engage in conversation in those venues. As a whole, however, most of the townspeople interact in other circumstances.

9. The truck system was based on the company store model. The ship chandler who owned the main provisional store also owned the fishing boats. Fishers would receive payment in provisions, rather than cash, for their work. Thus the ship chandler constructed a closed system of producers and consumers that often left fishers in debt to the chandler and without any options for purchasing elsewhere.

10. Cohen, 72.

11. Cohen, 74.

12. MacInnis, Steve. "Unfair hiring alleged on wharf project." *Cape Breton Post.* January 19, 1994: 15. See also MacGillivray, Dan. "Hiring board established to aid Louisbourg commission." *Cape Breton Post.* January 24, 1994: 3; and Vallis, Cecil. "Blatant favoritism being shown in Louisbourg project hirings." (Letter to Editor). *Cape Breton Post.* January 18, 1995: 5.

13. Cited in Goody and Watt, p. 52.

14. Cohen, 99.

15. Louisbourg Survey, 1994.

16. Candow, James A. "History of the Newfoundland Fishery." In *How Deep is the Ocean?* (James Candow and Carol Corbin, eds.) Sydney, N.S.: University College of Cape Breton Press, (forthcoming).

17. Lahey, Ernie. (Videotaped by Billy Barter), Louisbourg, N.S., 1994.

18. Wright, Miriam. "Fishing in Modern Times: Stewart Bates and the Modernization of the Canadian Atlantic Fishery." In *How Deep is the Ocean?* James Candow and Carol Corbin, Eds. Sydney, N.S.: University College of Cape Breton Press (forthcoming): 21.

19. Greer, Darrell. "Fisherman says not informed of repossession." *Cape Breton Post.* August 18, 1995: 7.

20. Ferguson, 43.

A Sense of Family

BARBARA RENDALL

When my husband and I were faced with transplanting ourselves from a small prairie town to Cape Breton Island, we felt confident that it would be an easy move. From everything we had heard about Cape Breton, there would be all sorts of reassuring similarities: lots of countryside, a slower pace, friendly, hospitable people, a human-sized way of life – in short, even though Sydney was a small city, we would be able to continue to enjoy all the benefits of small town living.

The surprise has been that, paradoxically, we have found Cape Breton even more closely knit than a small town. Moving to Cape Breton is like finding yourself in the middle of one big family gathering – you're welcomed with open arms, enthusiastically entertained, but as an outsider you're at a bit of a loss at first trying to penetrate the language, the customs, the long-shared history, and all the other things that bring Cape Bretoners even closer together than small town neighbours.

The special Cape Breton sense of family seems to owe its existence, fortunately or unfortunately, to relative geographic isolation and economic sluggishness. There are few newcomers here compared with other parts of Canada, and this results in a homogeneousness within the population that is striking in North America in this day and age. It is one of the first things a visitor to the area notices. Half of the population is named MacDonald or MacNeil, or so it seems at first, and a particular Celtic handsomeness – broad-faced, bright-eyed, and thick-thatched – runs through a large segment of the population, as anyone strolling through a mall can testify. And there is also the family accent and the family codes to further solidify the sense of identity, the main code being that anyone not belonging to the family is defined simply as someone from "Away." Where they are from is not important; what most distinguishes them is that they are not of the family.

In a small town there is always a significant segment of the population that feels suffocated and longs to get away. But in Cape Breton, just as in a family, people seem loathe to leave, and if they are forced to, they feel exiled. In both cases, there is an emotional bond that is painful to break and also the sense that everything truly important is right here at home. Cape Bretoners living elsewhere seem to feel a little like orphans. As a friend said of two homesick Cape Bretoners living in Ottawa, "All they can talk about is that island."

After living surrounded by this sense of identity and solidarity for our first months here, it came as a surprise and a puzzling contradiction to discover that passionate rivalries exist between different parts of Cape Breton. Turf wars among different parts of the Sydney area, for example – one side always seeming to feel that the other is getting more because of connections, favouritism, or politics – are much more passionate that any rivalry we had seen among small prairie towns. Even more surprising was the existence of an urban/rural polarization in a place where only one not-very-citified city exists, and where "rural" is not a stretch of dilapidated, dustblown farms, but as close to heaven as one can come on the east coast of North America. But callers on radio phone-in shows harp on about "industrial Cape Breton getting everything" and "You might as well draw a line where Kelly's Mountain is – everything goes to the Sydney area and the rural area gets nothing." This hardly seems in keeping with the larger Cape Breton sense of family unity – until you realize that these complaints are just textbook cases of sibling rivalry on a bigger scale. Members of the same family are always on the lookout for favouritism, and squabbles and intense competition always exist, as any parent knows. But just as typically, let an outside element – Halifax or "the Mainland," for example – attack the family as a whole and watch the siblings close ranks.

We have also discovered that Cape Breton's intricate networks of relationships, communication, and understanding go far beyond that of the small town, to the point where the comically coincidental and the almost mystical converge. Blood and history go so deep, without much disturbance from the outside world, that there is frequently (not just sometimes) a connection between two seemingly unrelated events in your life here. For instance, as in the case of a friend of ours, a person in Ontario with whom you speak on the phone every week in relation to your business turns out, inevitably, to be the sister of a good friend of yours in Sydney. Or, the wrong number you dial by mistake gives you a person who can nevertheless help you with your problem. This goes beyond that joke about the small town: "You know you live in a small town when you dial a wrong number and talk for fifteen minutes anyway." My husband was trying to track down a missing Priority Post letter. A Priority Post official in Ottawa gave him a number for Sydney, but it turned out to be a wrong number, not the Sydney Post Office. However, the woman at the wrong number just happened to know a postal worker who could help us, right in our own neighbourhood post office, and she promptly gave us her name and number.

But our favorite "Weird Cape Breton Coincidence" story is about the dog from Baleine. One beautiful fall afternoon we decided to take a hike along the coast between Main-à-Dieu and Louisbourg. We parked our car at the beach near the village of Baleine and started out along the headlands. Just as we set out we were joined by a friendly yellow lab who seemed eager for a walk as well. He ambled along with us in a sociable way for several hours, kept us company when we stopped and ate our picnic lunch, and accompanied us all the way back to the village at the end of the day. He even seemed interested in hopping into our car but we shooed him away. We were sorry to see him go, though, because he reminded us of our old dog in Saskatchewan. As we drove out of the village, the dog halfheartedly followed the car down the road, but when we reached a house trailer he slowed down and then trotted up the drive. We were glad to see him safely home, and on the way back we talked about what a nice dog he was and idly wondered whom he belonged to and what his name was.

The next day my husband had to attend a conference at the Delta Hotel in Sydney, and while he was talking with some people at the reception the topic turned to hikes in the Cape Breton countryside. My husband told them about the beautiful afternoon we'd had the day before at Baleine, and one of the men said he'd grown up there. My husband asked if he still knew people there and he said, "Sure, they're all my relatives." "Do you know the people in the trailer?" my husband asked. "They're my cousins." And he also knew all about the dog. And so it was that my husband was able to breeze in the door that evening and amaze me no end by saying, "Remember the dog we met down on the coast yesterday? His name is Trudeau."

For all these reasons we have found Cape Breton to be even more closely knit than the town of 1,500 we left in Saskatchewan. What draws Cape Bretoners together is that they have a deep sense of who they are, and they know and can rely on each other as well – like family. Cape Breton may be economically disadvantaged at the present time, but it is rich in this sense of identity. I think that this may prove to be, in the long run, one of its most valuable resources.

IV. Culture and Identity

The Use of Nicknames in Cape Breton

WILLIAM DAVEY & RICHARD MacKINNON

Nicknames are a pervasive feature of English and probably of language in general.[2] In England, political leaders have always been given nicknames, at times complimentary like Alfred the Great, and at times derisive like those given to some of the Viking rulers who led invading armies into England, Ivar the Boneless, Eric Bloodaxe, and Harold Bluetooth. Even monarchs who have long been dead have new names attached to their memory: combining history and modern technology, a London woman recently described Henry VIII as the Wife Dispatcher. The British press continues to delight in using nicknames for political leaders. When Prime Minister Thatcher first came to power, she was called the Grocer's Daughter (because she succeeded Edward Heath who had business interests in the food industry); one of her current names is the Iron Lady. This list might go on to include two other groups that are notorious for generating nicknames – professional athletes and teachers – but this paper considers nicknames of ordinary people in Cape Breton from three perspectives: the naming practices, classification of the nicknames, and the social importance of these names.

Before considering these names, however, two qualifications and a definition are needed. While some of the names are unique to the area (such as Biscuit Foot McKinnon), other names like the Red MacDonalds and Joe Priest are as easily found in Cape Breton as they are in any place where red-headed MacDonalds live or where a priest has a caretaker named Joe. Secondly, because of the oral nature of nicknames, one cannot claim that nicknames are more numerous in Cape Breton than in other areas or cultures. At the same time, however, evidence indicates that the practice of nicknaming is a lively and important oral tradition in Cape Breton that reflects the cultural values and local history of the various communities.

In order to better understand the term nickname, it might be useful to consider the origin of the word and its etymology. As Jan Jönsjö notes in his study of Middle English nicknames, "Etymologically OE *ekenama* (OE *ecan* + OE *nama*) is synonymous with ME *surname* (OF *sur* + OE *nama*) and both terms mean 'additional name', i.e. a name added to the name (the Christian name) that a person was already known by" (1979: 11). Historically, then, the *surname* was an additional name but through the centuries it has lost the sense of being something added to the person's name. It is now an oddity for a person to use only one name, an aspect that some entertainers like Cher have exploited. In a similar way, many nicknames in Cape Breton are perceived as the person's actual name rather than an additional name. As one male informant explained, his wife once tried to call him at work but failed to reach him until she used his nickname rather than his given name. David Crystal gives a working definition of the term:

> The word *nickname* is first recorded in the 15th century: 'an eke name' (Old English *eke*, 'also') was an extra or additional name used to express such attitudes as familiarity, affection, and ridicule. Nicknames are usually applied to people, but places and things can have them too. (Crystal 1995: 152)

This broad definition accounts for additional nicknames like Allan Big Hughie, but substitution is also used for some nicknames such as the Cow Hooks for the surname of a family in Glace Bay. Nicknames are also applied to places and things, but these will not be considered in this paper (cf. Davey 1990).

There are several conventions or naming practices followed in the formation of Cape Breton nicknames. An obvious but nonetheless important feature is that nicknames survive in an oral tradition. Occasionally nicknames appear in print, but more usually they are kept alive by word of mouth in the local community. There are at least two consequences of this oral circulation. First, these nicknames are subject to the strengths and weaknesses of the human memory. As occupations change and generations die, names are lost, and it becomes impossible to answer statistical questions about the prevalence of nicknames one hundred years ago or to define the exact origin or meaning of certain names. An associated characteristic of oral circulation is that several versions of even a current nickname may exist. For instance, a family from Glace Bay are known there as the Big Pay MacDonalds but are remembered as the Pay Cheque MacDonalds by an informant from Sydney. A further consequence of their oral nature is that the survival of certain nicknames depends on phonetic qualities, but more detailed consideration of this factor is found in the following classification.

A second naming practice is that many are traditional and familial. Although some nicknames are, of course, short lived, other nicknames last a lifetime or may be passed to the second, and occasionally to a third generation. As several informants commented, these names have a habit of "sticking" to the person being named. One woman was born during a storm and has been called Stormy ever since. In Ingonish, Allan, the son of Big Hughie, was called Allan Big Hughie; both father and son were known and respected for their strength. Such compound names are common all over Cape Breton Island: John Joe Red Angus, Allan Paulie, Willie Duncan and his brother Jimmy Duncan. A family of MacDonalds are known as the Piper MacDonalds because a grandfather was known for playing the bag pipes.

As well as being traditional and familial, nicknames are mainly patrilineal (Dunn 1953 and Frank 1988). For example, three generations ago the community of Black Point called Angus MacKinnon, Big Angus; his son Derrick later became Derrick Big Angus; in the third generation Derrick's two sons are known as Philip Big Angus and Johnny Big Angus, taking the grandfather's name rather than their father's. Similarly, when a woman marries, she is often known by a compound name consisting of her own Christian name and her husband's Christian name or his nickname, thereby creating an oxymoron such as Aggie Tom to identify the Agnes who married Tom. Jessie Big John is the wife of Big John and their daughter is called Katie Big John. In the same way, Maggie the Sailor does not sail but is the daughter of Alex the Sailor. About 32% of the women's names in this study follow this pattern. While the nicknames are usually patrilineal, occasionally the woman's name is attached to her son's Christian name. The son of Lizzy MacKinnon is called Simon Lizzy, and Tommy Peggy MacDonald refers to Thomas, the son of Peggy

MacDonald. Alec the Plug is the son of a short woman called Peggy Plug, and Angus the Widow has a mother who is known as the Widow. Only about 1.5% of the names in this study follow this pattern. In general, the first name of the compound identifies the individual, and the second reveals the family relationship – similar to the way that last names are, or used to be, passed from one generation to the next.

Because of the traditional nature of these names, the nickname often outlives or fails to describe the social reality that generated it. In Dominion a family is widely known as the Bore Hole MacDonalds because two generations ago, the grandfather bored holes in the coal mines. The name persists although none of the present generation bores holes. Similarly, because Joe Doucette has a lame leg, he is called Joey Peg, and his family – all of whom have healthy legs – have inherited the nickname Peg: for instance, his wife is Mary Peg. As Alexander Laidlaw, a native of Port Hood, points out, the names can be misleading: Young Donald is always called Young, even if he dies at 95, "Or maybe Little Sandy goes through life with a name which does not very well describe his giant stature at six foot two" (Creighton 1962: 72).

Although most people receive one nickname that remains with them for life and that may survive into succeeding generations, a small group have multiple nicknames. Morgan, O'Neill and Harré (1979: 42) found multiple names among school children in England, and Apte (1985: 54) states that occupational nicknames often differ from those known in the community. For example, a big man from Sydney Mines is known to his friends as Moose because of his size but for a short while was called Jesus because he had a beard and long hair, and he is also known by his family nickname, the Dukes.

With these naming practices in mind, it is now possible to classify nicknames according to the factor or factors that generated them. In their study of school-age children in England, Morgan, O'Neill and Harré conclude:

> A fundamental distinction in all naming systems is between internal methods of formation where a name is generated by some feature of language, such as alliteration or rhyming, and external methods of formation where matters of history, appearance, family relationships, local culture, and so on are involved in the genesis of the name. (1979: 37)

This fundamental distinction between names generated by internal methods, or some phonetic feature, and by those generated by external method, or social factors, provides a useful starting point for analysis. Within these two general classes of nicknames, Morgan *et al.* (1979: 35-45) discuss several features that are also found in the nicknames common in Cape Breton.

Since nicknames exist primarily in an oral tradition, one would expect to find that phonetic elements foster the survival of many of these names. The most frequent phonetic feature of Cape Breton nicknames is the suffix tense or slack i. Instead of Big Dan or Tom Cod, the two names are Big Danny and Tommy Cod (the smallest kind of cod). This suffix is found on many Christian names. Examples abound: Johnny Mink, Mickey Hay Cove, Tommy Peggy, Big Hughie, Big Johnny, and Charlie Beaver. Similarly, the substituted names frequently end with this suffix: Birdy, Scratchy, Sharky, Sporty Peter and Mossy Face. Approximately 31% of the names collected in this research have this suffix. Although Morgan *et al.* (1979: 41) found suffixes like *-bo*, *-kin*, and *-bug* popular among school-age children, this study found only one such suffix for a man called Johnnikin, who apparently received the name as a child because as an adult he is known for his toughness.

Alliteration is another common feature of these names. Examples are the Court Crier (who habitually visited the court), Bully Brown, Beer Bottle (who was short), and Billy the Brat. Other nicknames combine alliteration with some physical characteristic such as Freckly Flora, Red Randy, Spotty Steward (who had a growth or spot on his eye), and Monkey Malcom (who reminded people of a monkey). Other names combine phonetic derivatives and alliteration. For instance, Ronald the Rooster at first suggests some physical affinity to the bird family, but, in fact, the name is a phonetic derivative from Garbarus, the man's place of origin. According to one informant, Gabarus is referred to as the Roost and people from that area as roosters.

Other nicknames are generated from contractions of, or substitutions for, longer names. Accordingly, names like MacDonald and Buchanan become the clipped forms Mack and Buck. In the Italian community in industrial Cape Breton, a man called Calisthanius is called Cal, and Cassamiro is reduced to Miro. In the previous generation many long European names were replaced by substituted nicknames: a Mr. Calavisortis was called Nick the Greek, and a man named Szerwonka was called Bubble Gum, partially because he chewed bubble gum in the coal pit instead of tobacco, but partially because the name may have been hard to pronounce by the speakers of English.

Phonetic derivatives are responsible for some nicknames as well. One man is known as E-Boy because as he heaved and pulled in his nets, he would say "Heave Boy." Because a man named Dougall habitually stutters his name as "Dou-Dou-Dougall," he is known as Dougall Dougall. Other nicknames resulting from phonetic derivatives are generated by mispronunciations of words. Mossy Angus received his name because he habitually mispronounces "Mercy me" as "Mossy, Mossy me." Jim the Jampion pronounces *champion* with the initial sound of *jump*, and his pronunciation is recalled in his name. Other nicknames originate from childhood mispronunciations. For instance, one man widely known as Bucko or Buck, received this name because as a child he mispronounced the name of his father's fishing boat, the *Buckaroo*. Similarly, a family from the north east are known as the Bootchers because the father mispronounced the word *butcher* as a child. The nickname was reinforced because the child looked like a butcher who visited the community. As an adult he is called Bootcher and his wife is Mary Bootcher. Other phonetic derivatives depend on rhyme and on partial rhyme. For instance, Carl Snarl and Jake the Snake rhyme, but these belong to boys aged seven and twelve in contrast to the other names in this study which belong to adults. Far more usual for adults is partial rhyme: Cute Hughie, Pan Dandy, Sam the Wake Man (who used to go from one wake to another), Hucky Tuck Finn (who smoked a pipe like Huck Finn), and Hobby Gobby (who was associated with hobgoblins because he worked as a watchman on Halloween night).

A small but interesting group of names is formed as a result of semantic association. As Morgan *et al.* (1979: 41) point out, a name like Gardener is altered to Weed by the association between gardens and weeds. During the 1930s, the president of the Orange Lodge was called – not surprisingly – Orange Dan, but, by association, the treasurer became known as Yellow Jack (McCawley 1936: 4). The nickname of a brother or of one's friends is often the source for semantic association. The brother of John the Bear became Allan the Buffalo as one big animal apparently suggested another. The brother of Joey One Time became Tony Half Time because of a semantic slip made by a friend's mother. Again semantic association seems to be responsible for the nickname of a man called Birdie in Glace Bay: he lived beside a man with the surname of Sparrow. Similarly, a group of boys who grew up together in Sydney Mines all have names associated with the animal kingdom: Duck, Goat, Toad, and Moose. Within this group, some names combine both phonetic and semantic changes. A man from Sydney Mines reflects this pattern. Originally called Moose because of his size, his name was shortened to Moo, which by semantic association became Moo Cow. Following the same principle, Ray MacDonald was given the name Doug (for reasons unknown to the informant); then Doug became Rug as a phonetic derivative, and finally the name became the alliterating Ray Rug.

Finally, when the nicknames are considered in a family grouping, the result is often more lyrical, and the phonetic similarity is more evident than when the names are considered individually. In a sense, when considered together, some of these names have the quality of oral formulaic. For example, there is little to suggest phonetic similarity in the nickname Joey Peg, but there is when his family are described as Joey Peg, Mary Peg, Eddy Peg, Teddy Peg and Granny Peg. Using formal names, one might say that Marcella MacLellan is married to Archie MacKinnon. Locally, it would be stated more lyrically as Micey is married to Archie Gookin. The phonetic similarity is also seen in the nicknames of children in a Glace Bay family: Googie and Boogie, a sister named Booboo, and a cousin called Butchy. In part, at least, phonetic similarity and near rhyme seem to generate these names.

Although one might expect phonetic or internal features to play a more prominent role in these nicknames, especially given their oral transmission, a partial explanation is suggested by Morgan, O'Neill and Harré's study (1979: 40-41) of students in junior and senior high school. Citing a study by Peevers and Secord (1974) and their own research, they conclude that as students grow older, they depend more on physical or social aspects to provide nicknames rather than the free wordplay that is characteristic of younger children. This tendency to rely more on sense than on sound is also true of nicknames in Cape Breton, as roughly 70% of the nicknames collected in this study depend on external or social features. They are generated by various factors: physical characteristics, habitual actions and expressions, events of local importance, character traits, occupations, and references to places. Closely related to these are the descriptive nicknames or aptonyms that are given because of humour and popular culture. At times more than one cause may generate one nickname, and consequently some nicknames could be placed in more than one class. For example, the nickname Livers originated because of an event and habitual behavior: this man was once caught stealing cod livers, but the name was reinforced because he was an habitual thief.

Within this broad class of nicknames, the largest group is that referring to physical qualities of a person. Since physical size and strength are valued in rural and industrial Cape Breton, adjectives like *big, little,* and *long* appear frequently in nicknames. In addition to these common names for size, Hunk and Ox indicate large people in contrast to those called Stump, Bump, Splinter and Pancake. Adjectives referring to size also distinguish two or more people with similar names. A generation ago, Big and Little identified the two Carlos who worked at the same coal mine in Dominion. Where a surname such as MacDonald is common, nicknames like the Red MacDonalds distinguish that family from the Blue MacDonalds and from the Ditty MacDonalds. In a small town, three men in their thirties have the name Kenny (two of whom have the same last name); they are known as Kenny Turk (because of his dark complexion), Kenny Mugs (because of his ears), and Kenny Auger (because of his neck). A fourth Kenny who lives just outside of the town is Lame Kenny from the Creek. The two Lisas in the area are Black Lisa and White Lisa because one is brunette and the other is blonde. Thus, physical appearance is an important means of generating nicknames, but even slight differences may be used in nicknames to distinguish people with identical or like names.

Others receive their nicknames because of habitual actions. A miner from Dominion who habitually carried sugar cookies in his lunch is called Sugar Cookie Smith. Dan the Dancer was known for his habit of dancing for money during the Depression. And a man who repeatedly sat on a pickle barrel in the Company Store was dubbed Pickle Arse MacLean, and his family are known as the Pickle Arse MacLeans. Spider and Sammy the Flea are nicknames of two men known to move quickly on the ice flows, and Dynamite Dan earned his name by breaking dynamite boxes with his bare hands as a sign of his strength. Occasionally, the nicknames given in childhood because of habitual actions last longer than the habit itself. A man from New Aberdeen is still called Scratchy even though he has outgrown his childhood scratching. A young boy who used to hide in a wood box is still called Billy Wood Box now that he is an adult, and Charlie Beaver bears his name because as a child he liked to chew sticks. Little Hell, a man with teenage children, received his name when misbehaving as a child.

In addition to repeated actions, habitual expressions can also be a source for nicknames. Oft-repeated expressions and expletives, and even the manner in which one speaks may be commemorated in a nickname. A couple who owned a store in Sydney habitually responded to comments with "Is it?' They became Mr. Is It and Mrs. Is It. In like manner, two other men are known as Johnny What Is It and Joe Me Fix. A pair of identical twins, Malcom and Norman, received their name because of their mother's habitual greeting to the boys when they were small. Apparently the mother found it difficult to distinguish one from the other, and so she would greet the unidentifiable boy with "Malcom, Is that you Norman?" As the boys grew older, the expression stuck to them, and they are now both called Malcom Is That You Norman as adults. Others receive their names from characteristic expletives. One man who habitually said "Jingers, Cripes of war" was christened Jingers; through family association, his son became Little Jingers. By the same process others are called Gee Hosifer Dan, By Cracky Tom, and The Bloody Awk (for a Cockney living in Sydney who used this term to criticize others). One's manner of speech might also generate a nickname. When John Eliot laughed, he sounded as though he were crying; he is accordingly called John Eliot the Crier. A man with a high pitched voice was christened John the Piper, presumably because his voice sounded like bag pipes. Swearing Dan and Swearing Peter use profane language, and man from the southern part of the island who used to strike his breast while speaking is called Through My Fault.

Other nicknames are formed because of some event that is historically important or unusual. For example, when a group of strikers raided the Company Store in 1925, a man named McKinnon was injured when a box of biscuits fell from a top shelf and crushed his foot (Mellor 1983: 306). Thereafter, he was called Biscuit Foot McKinnon. Another well-known nickname also comes from the practices of the Company Store. Before miners received their pay, the Company Store deducted money from the workers' wages to cover the bills owed to the store. When Johnny MacDonald collected the small pay left after the deductions (two cents according to one informant), he sarcastically boasted about his big pay. He is known as Big Pay Johnny and his family as the Big Pay MacDonalds. Other nicknames are created from unusual events rather than those of interest to local historians. One man is called Turkey because he once stole a turkey from his mother-in-law. An Italian man from the industrial area received his nickname Tony Vin from his habit of selling his homemade wine on Sunday afternoons, but his lasting fame was assured by an incident well known locally. Having been served a new batch of wine made from unknown berries, his customers were stricken with diarrhea. With only one toilet on the premises, the afflicted drinkers retreated to the trees and bushes in the yard to seek relief. The informant explained that this story is often retold and just as often embellished in the retelling.

Character traits or quirks of personality also foster nicknames. One man is called the Silver Fox partly because of his white hair and partly because of his characteristic of reporting infractions of fellow workers to his brother, who worked for the administration of a local company. Billy the Brat, an engineer, received his name because of his characteristic arrogance, and a Leo (Italian for lion) received this nickname because of his noisy, aggressive behavior. A man called Two Dans received his name because of his "two faced" character.

In industrial Cape Breton, nicknames associated with occupations are also common, especially those connected with the coal mines and the steel plant (Frank 1988). One family is known as Twelve-to-Eight because the husband regularly worked this shift. Two MacDonald families in Glace Bay are identified as the Bore Holes and the Bevellor MacDonalds because of the respective occupations in an earlier generation. The family known as the Gobs probably received this name because of a father or grandfather who worked in the gob, the place in the mine where the coal has been removed. Jack Hammer refers to the Joe MacKenzie who used a jack hammer, and John Klinker MacMillan pulled the klinkers (pieces of fused coal) from the furnace used to generate steam power. Two of the Joe MacNeils from Dominion are called Joe Priest (a caretaker for a local church) and Radio Joe (a steel worker who repaired radios). Jimmy the Barber is better known in Glace Bay by his nickname (according to one informant) than by his official name, Jim MacDonald.

Geographic nicknames indicate either a place of origin or a place visited by the bearer of the name. Danny Plaster designates the Dan who comes from northern Cape Breton where gypsum was mined for plaster. Smokey Joe refers to the man who lives at the base of Cape Smokey. The Light House Brothers, Donald Bridge End, Hughie Alders, and the Goose in the Bog are nicknames which depict where these people live. Yankie Dan, one of the few general nicknames, is used in Port Hastings, industrial Cape Breton, and in the Ingonish area for men who came from or visited the United States (except that in Port Hastings the son is known as Danny Yankee Dan). Some people received their names as a result of a prolonged or important visit to a place. Montana Dan worked in Montana as a shepherd for several years before returning to Cape Breton, the Klondike MacKinnons lived in the Klondike during the gold rush, and Ottawa Angus visited the capital only once but repeatedly referred to the trip in conversations.

Other nicknames are generated because of various kinds of humour. Occasionally, the humour depends on irony. Hairy Johnny describes a balding man, Tiny Power describes a man who is six feet tall, and two town drunks were called the Senator and Dr. Angus. Three Sydney men better known for their drinking than for their boxing ability used to fight in the preliminary matches behind the Harness Shop. Because of their comic attempts at pugilism, they were ironically called Knock Out Kelly, the Belgium Panther, and Slippery Tom. Other humorous nicknames seize upon a physical or personality trait to ridicule. Cassie Skillet is a thin woman, and the Blob is a man with the opposite characteristic. Bump, Leo Pancake and the Pancake family are all short. In the days before artificial limbs were as sophisticated as they are today, those who had lost a limb might be called Wooden Allan or Stiff Angus. Yet even in the face of these grim injuries, humour was used against the dangers faced every day by miners and soldiers. As D. MacDonald (1980: 14) notes, "A Cape Breton miner with one arm shorter than another was dubbed Alex the Clock." Another Alex who lost a leg in World War I had to swing his wooden leg as he walked. Because of his need for a wide path, he was called Broadway Alec. Other humorous names emphasize disreputable characters: Sharky (described as a "wheeler dealer"), Eco Bis (*bis* is Italian for snake), Slick Jim, Turkey George, and Livers. A sly bootlegger from the Coxheath Mountains avoided being caught and earned his name, the Fox. A man from Port Hastings who talks excessively is called the August Gale. Other names depend on vulgar language for their humour: Piss Pot Mary, Flat Assed (the smallest of a short family),

Pickle Arse, and probably many more that informants were too well-mannered to mention. Other humorous nicknames depend on incongruous sounds for humour such as Alec the Boo, Bozo, and the group of children called Boogie, Googie, and Booboo. A few humorous nicknames are connected with stories that probably have some truth but have become apocryphal in the retelling. One such story explains the nickname given to a derelict from a small town on the west side of the island. One night the man was lying drunk on the road when an old lady ran over him. Surprised by the bump, the woman supposedly backed up to discover the problem and ran over the man a second time. According to the story, the man survived the accident, continued to drink, and was christened with the whimsical nickname Speed Bump.

One small group of nicknames have their genesis in what might be called popular culture as these names are borrowed from a well-known person, a character on a television program, or a famous event. Names like Ghandi, Tokyo Rose, Squiggy (after Squigman on *Laverne and Shirley*), Smurf (for a short cleaner who wears a blue uniform), and Sputnik (a girl born in the year when the spacecraft was launched) all attest to this cultural influence. Other names recall notorious characters: Jack the Ripper and Captain Kidd (for a man who sailed on a ship that smuggled rum during Prohibition in the United States). One of the local characters who habitually moves his head from side to side is called Wimbledon.

Clearly, then, these two broad categories – internal and external methods for forming nicknames – provide a diverse array of nicknames. In part, the social function of these names within the community is implicit in this classification. The most obvious of these social functions is identification. The frequent occurrence of certain surnames among the Highland Scot immigrants and the custom of naming a child after a relative are two factors that encourage the use of additional and substituted names to distinguish one person or family from another with a similar name (Creighton 1972: 71).[3] Even within a single family, there may be a need to use nicknames to identify two children because occasionally members in the same immediate family have the same Christian name. Reporting on the nicknames used in Port Hood area during the 1960s, Alexander Laidlaw states:

> Many of the Cape Bretoners have large families,
> very often eight or ten children, and sometimes
> the same name was used twice, perhaps for lack
> of imagination, or respect to some relative. Thus
> we have such names as Big Sandy and Little
> Sandy, Old Donald and Young Donald, or
> Brown Jack and Black Jack after the colour of
> their eyes. (in Creighton 1962: 72)

Three informants reported a similar tradition in their areas, one of whom mentioned high infant mortality as a reason for giving the same name to two children in one family. Because of this similarity in first names and surnames, clearer identification is needed at home, in the community, and in the work place. Thus, Black Allan is distinguished from his younger brother Red Allan, and the two Dan MacDonalds from East Bay are easily identified as Business Dan and Sydney Dan. As one informant from Glace Bay noted, nicknames were essential in the coal mines as workers were paid according to the daily tonnage that they produced. Those recording this information each day had to have a more specific name to identify each worker accurately.

Another important function of nicknames is social control. Many of the derisive nicknames stigmatize the bearers of the names for some behavior of which the community disapproves. Derogatory names such as Livers, Slick Jim, Jimmy Skunk, Sharky, Bully Brown, and the Silver Fox clearly criticize those engaged in either criminal or antisocial behavior. While useful in identifying the antisocial or deviant members of the community, these pejorative names also have a negative side. Those with a physical defect or a conspicuous physical feature have a more difficult life if they have to bear a name like Lumpy (because of the bumps on his head), the Hook and the Nostril (because of their noses), or Popeye (because of a bulging eye). At the same time, however, it is difficult to generalize about what names are derisive as people react differently to their nicknames. In the previous generation Allan Big Hughie did not mind being called Ox, but another family called the Oxes resented the name. While *boozer* is usually seen as insulting, it is not for one family because the name was given as a joke when the person was a child. As mentioned above, the nickname Spider is valued by one man as it refers to his speed on the ice, but the same name is derisive to another person as it refers to his appearance when wearing glasses. As with most names, the context in which the nickname is used determines its meaning and the reaction to it.

One final importance of these names is to preserve the local values, culture, and history of a community. As indicated above, strength is admired and consequently reflected in the many epithets like Big, Tall, Long, Hunk and Ox. Names such as Tommy Cod and Paul Fish, and others like the Gobs and the Bore Holes attest to two of Cape Breton's major industries, fishing and coal mining. Big Pay MacDonald, Biscuit Foot McKinnon, and Pickle Arse MacLean all record the importance of the Company Store in industrial Cape Breton and to some extent the animosity between managers and workers. Tony Vin and the Fox – for those who know the origin of the names – recall the custom of selling alcohol illegally. Nicknames like Ghandi and Sputnik indicate an interest in people and events of international importance.

In conclusion, the naming practices, the diverse classification, and the social functions of these names indicate that the use of nicknames is a lively and important tradition in Cape Breton. Although adjectives like *big, little, long, black,* and *red* recur frequently in the nicknames gathered, these four adjectives account for only 11.3% of the nicknames in this study. With a few exceptions, most of the nicknames do not recur and show remarkable creativity and imagination. Instead of using a nickname like Speedy to describe a man known for his speed in hauling logs out of the woods, he was given the imaginative and memorable name of Split the Wind Billy. While a thin person might be called Skinny, there are also interesting variations like Hair Pin Angus (McCawley 1936), Splinter, and the Spaven (a disease contracted by horses that makes the bones become pronounced). This imaginative use of language is also inspired by humour as illustrated by the examples given above and by many other names such as Ten to Six to christen one man who had the habit of tilting his head to one side. Martin Two Times was the witty name given to a man whose legal name was Martin Martin. The examples given in this paper illustrate a sensitive ear and an intelligent interest in words.

While this study provides some insight into the use of Cape Breton nicknames, there is more research to be done. Although trying to cover representative areas, this study does not analyze any one area exhaustively, nor does it cover every location in Cape Breton. Of the fourteen informants used as sources for this study, most come from industrial Cape Breton, with one or two informants from the north east, the west, and the south of the island.[4] The most important written sources report on only two areas: Port Hood (Creighton 1962) and the industrial area (McCawley 1936, and Frank 1988). More thorough research is needed on the nicknames in each of the island's regions, on occupational nicknames, and on certain groups such as the Mi'kmaq, Acadians, and Gaelic speakers.

Notes

1. The *MLA Bibliography* (1981-1995) contains articles discussing nicknames in over thirty languages including Russian, Portugese, Greek, German, French, Gaelic, Spanish, Dutch, Czech, Serbo-Croatian, Scottish Gaelic, Italian, Peruvian, Hindi, Mandarin, and Old Norse. The practice of nicknaming spans continents and the ages.

2. Of the nicknames in this study with known surnames, 75% are Scottish in origin, with MacDonald and MacKinnon being most frequent. In conversation, Prof. A. M. Kinloch mentioned that the practice of giving the same name to members of a large family also occurs in some areas of Scotland. Studies (e.g., Smith 1968) indicate a parallel situation among the Amish where both first and second names recur frequently, and nicknames are needed to identify individuals and families.

3. We are grateful to the following people who generously volunteered their time to be informants for this study: Terry Campbell, Mary Margaret Chiasson, Peyton Chisholm, Kate Currie, Redmond Curtis, George Hussey (who provided nicknames from Meat Cove to Cape Smokey), Dan Alex Macleod, Brenda MacKinnon, Mr. and Mrs. L. MacSween, Robert Morgan, Percy Peters, Lino Polegato, Lois Ross, and Mr. and Mrs. Arthur Severance.

References

"Acadiennes de Chéticamp, St. Joseph Du Moine et Magré." *Genealogie Des Familles.* Unpublished paper available at the Beaton Institute, University College of Cape Breton (UCCB), 1977.

Allen, Irving Lewis. *The Language of Ethnic Conflict: Social Organization and Lexical Cultures.* New York: Columbia UP, 1983.

Apte, Mahadev. *Humor and Laughter: An Anthropological Approach.* Ithaca: Cornell UP, 1985.

Beaton, Elizabeth. "Nicknames." Unpublished paper available at the Beaton Institute, UCCB, 1974.

Creighton, Helen. "Cape Breton Nicknames." *Folklore in Action.* Ed. Horace Beck. Philadelphia: American Folklore Society, 1962. 71-76.

Crystal, David. *The Cambridge Encyclopedia of the English Language.* Cambridge: Cambridge UP, 1995.

Cumming, Peter, Heather MacLeod, and Linda Strachan. *The Story of Framboise.* Framboise: St. Andrew's Presbyterian Church, 1984.

Davey, William. "Informal Names for the Places in Cape Breton: Nicknames, Local Usage, and a Brief Comparison with Personal Nicknames." *Onomastica Canadiana* 72 (1990):69-81.

Dunn, Charles W. *Highland Settlers: A Portrait of the Scottish Gael in Nova Scotia.* Toronoto: University of Toronto P, 1953.

Frank, David. "A Note on Cape Breton Nicknames." *Journal of the Atlantic Provinces Linguistic Association* 10 (1988): 54-63.

Jönsjö, Jan. *Studies on Middle English Nicknames.* Eds. C. Scharr and Jan Svartvik. Lund: Gleerup, 1979.

MacDonald, David. "Nova Scotia's Wacky Nicknames." *Reader's Digest* (October 1980): 13-14.

MacKenzie, Catherine. "Creating a New Scotland in Canada." *Travel* 47 (June 1926): 16-19, 42, 44.

MacPhee, Russell. "Sydney Mines, Cape Breton Nicknames." Unpublished Poem available at the Beaton Institute, UCCB, n.d.

McCawley, Stuart. "Cape Breton Tales." *Sydney Post-Record.* 13 Oct. 1936, 4 and 7.

McCrum, Robert, William Cran, and Robert MacNeil. *The Story of English.* New York: Viking, 1986.

Mellor, John. *The Company Store: James Bryson McLachlan and the Cape Breton Coal Miners 1900-1925.* Toronto: Doubleday. Rpt. Halifax: Goodread Biographies, 1983.

Monteiro, George. "*Alcunhas* among the Portuguese in Southern New England." *Western Folklore* 20 (1961): 103-07.

Morgan, Jane, Christopher O'Neill, and Rom Harré. *Nicknames: The Origins and Social Consequences.* London: Routledge and Kegan Paul, 1979.

Noble, Vernon. *Nicknames Past and Present.* Foreword by Eric Partridge. London: Hamilton, 1976.

Peevers, B. H. and P. F. Secord. "The Development and Attribution of Person Concepts." *Understanding Other Persons.* Ed. T. Mischel. Oxford: Blackwell, 1974. 117-42.

Rees, Nigel and Vernon Noble. *A Who's Who of Nicknames.* London: Allen and Unwin, 1985.

Seary, E. R. With Sheila M. P. Lynch. *Family Names of the Island of Newfoundland.* St. John's: Robinson-Blackmore Printing and Publishing, 1977.

Smith, Elmer L. "Amish Names" *Names* 16 (1968): 105-10.

Urdang, Laurence. *Twentieth Century American Nicknames.* Compiled by Walter Kidney and George Kohn. Foreword by Leslie Alan Dunkling. New York: Wilson Company, 1979.

The World Which Is At Us

SILVER DONALD CAMERON

Once upon a time – not very long ago – there lived in Inverness County a man named Dan Rory MacDonald. "Dan R," as he was known, was a fiddler by calling, and probably the greatest Scottish composer who ever lived in Canada, author of more than 3,000 tunes.

Dan R had no home at all. He wandered Cape Breton Island with his fiddle – an unkempt pot-bellied genius, a musical gypsy with his spectacles taped together, staying with friends and family for a week, two weeks, a month. He paid his keep by chopping wood, helping with farm chores, and entertaining his hosts with his fiddle. Sometimes he would compose a tune for them, writing it down on the back of a fuel bill or an envelope. His hosts felt honoured: they were supporting a great artist, and they knew it.

From time to time, Dan R would stay with his sister, Katie Ann Cameron, in the village of Mabou. Katie Ann was also a fiddler, and she did have a house, though the house was not important to her; her housekeeping was universally acknowledged to be . . . um, imperfect. Katie Ann could not have cared less. Possessions were not a priority for her, or for Dan R. They reserved their passion for higher things.

"Look," says Maureen MacKenzie, a Gaelic teacher who lives on Mabou Harbour, "Those people would sell their boots for music."

So now you know something about the making of John Allan Cameron, who is Katie Ann's son. And you know some important things about Gaelic culture, its values, its world view. But despite the reverence which people still feel for Dan R – and for literally hundreds of lesser Celtic musicians – Cape Breton's Gaelic culture is gravely endangered.

"If you look back at the records, roughly every 20 years there's a lot of talk about a Gaelic revival," says Frances MacEachen. "And after every 'Gaelic revival' there are fewer people speaking Gaelic than there were before."

Frances MacEachen is a tall, handsome woman in her twenties, sitting in an office cluttered with books, papers, and cassette tapes. The office is the former living room of a house trailer on the main street of Mabou, Nova Scotia, pop. 594, as Celtic a village as any in Canada. The sign on the post office says Tigh Litrichean: House of Letters. The Mull Restaurant serves bannock, oatcakes and marag, a spicy white Scottish sausage. Opposite MacEachen's office is a small brown house, the home of the Rankin Family. Next door, more or less, is the home of the late Donald Angus Beaton, a great fiddler whose sons Joey and Kinnon now carry on a family musical tradition stretching back 200 years to Lochaber, Scotland.

Mabou is not far from Creignish and Judique and Port Hood, which have recently spawned a whole generation of brilliant and famous young musicians, notably Ashley MacIsaac and Natalie MacMaster. Cape Breton boasts a Highland Village and North America's only Gaelic College. In summer, tens of thousands flock to Broad Cove, Big Pond, Iona, and Glendale to hear literally hundreds of fiddlers and step-dancers perform at Scottish concerts.

And Frances MacEachen herself is the editor and publisher of *Am Braighe,* a year-old tabloid newspaper of Celtic language and culture partially written in Gaelic. Its 2,000 subscribers span the continent and indeed the world.

All of which suggests that Celtic culture is vibrantly healthy in Cape Breton.

Not so, says Ronnie MacEachen, Frances' brother and partner.

"Fifty years ago the discussion of a Gaelic revival was taking place *in Gaelic,*" Ronnie notes. "Today it's being discussed in English. And this is the last Gaelic-speaking area in all of North America. It's a major, major asset – but it's an asset that's dying as we sit here drinking our tea."

"Yes," says Frances. "There's a danger of losing it before we can share it."

"The Scots have a certain arrogance towards other cultures," says Hector MacNeil thoughtfully, sitting in an office at the University College of Cape Breton, where he teaches Gaelic. Hector is tall, slim, fortyish, with a quick smile and a full red beard. He would look at once natural and terrifying wearing a shield and brandishing a claymore, the huge two-handed Scottish sword.

Hector lives in Castle Bay on the Bras d'Or Lakes, a hamlet named for the ancestral seat of the MacNeil chiefs on the Isle of Barra. Castle Bay (Cape Breton) is not far from Barra Strait, where a pride of emigrant MacNeils took up residence in 1817. The MacNeils were always a leonine clan; in their heyday, a servant would stride onto the parapet in Castle Bay (Barra) every evening and bellow, "The MacNeil has eaten! The lesser princes of the earth may now dine!" Hector recalls the claim that the MacNeils originated in the Garden of Eden, where – many Gaels maintain – the language spoken was Gaelic. When asked why the name "MacNeil" does not appear on the passenger list of Noah's Ark, one clansmember loftily replied that the MacNeils had their own boat.

"The Scots have a certain arrogance towards other cultures," says Hector now. "And rightly so. The Celts were the first out of the Dark Ages, and we're in the direct line of descent."

And of course (said the arrogant Scottish author) Hector Mac-Neil is quite correct: Gaelic was the third literary language of Europe, after Greek and Latin, and it boasts an impressively hoary tradition of poems, stories, and scholarship. The Celtic legend of King Arthur and the Round Table has become part of world literature, but the most deeply cherished of the Celtic story cycles are the "Fenian tales" which tell of the great Irish chief Finn MacCumhaill (or MacCool) and his band of warriors and hunters, the Fianna Eireann. The Fenian tales celebrate events of the third century AD, and they were not even written down until about 1200 AD. In the meantime, while the rest of Europe groped through the Dark Ages, monks in Ireland were keeping the flame of learning alight.

"As early as the eighth century there were Christian schools run by scribes all over Ireland," explains Hector MacNeil. "There was a system of schools in Ireland before Christianity, actually, but the learning was oral, not written. The Celts have an oral tradition as old as Europe itself."

Indeed they do. The Celts emerged in northern France and southern Germany and expanded for a thousand years until – five centuries before Christ – they dominated northern Europe from Spain to Poland, from Ireland to Turkey. The Gauls of

215

France, the Galatians of Asia Minor, the Gaels of Scotland and Ireland: these were all Celts, as is the wonderful comic-book hero, Asterix the Gaul.

But the Celts were never a well-organized imperial people, and eventually the Romans, the Germans, and others pushed them to the western fringes of Europe – into Brittany, Cornwall, Wales, the Isle of Man, and Ireland, whence they later migrated into Scotland. Against this background, the fierce resistance of the Scots and the Irish against the English – the Anglo-Saxons – is simply another skirmish in a centuries-long contest between the Celts and the Germans.

For Cape Breton's Scots, the crucial year in that contest was 1745, when the Scots invaded England under Bonnie Prince Charlie, only to be crushed the next summer at the Battle of Culloden. Their leaders were hanged or exiled, and the clan lands became sheep farms. Their people were forcibly evicted and their houses were demolished. The Gaels scattered to the far corners of the world – to Australia, to South America, to France and Russia, to the United States, to every part of Canada. By 1840 more than 20,000 emigrant Scots had poured into Cape Breton alone.

In Canada, the Scots quickly became prominent in exploration, in politics, in business. More of Canada's early prime ministers had Gaelic as a first language than either English or French. In 1886, a bill in the Senate proposed that Gaelic be given official language status. At Confederation, Gaelic was the third most-common Canadian language, and there were Gaelic-speaking communities in every province.

"Eighty years ago," says Hector MacNeil, "a man might meet a stranger on the road in Cape Breton and ask, Do you have a story on the Fenians? And then the traveller would tell a tale, and the first fellow would tell one – and if the traveller was a worthwhile story-teller they might stay there for 12 hours exchanging stories." He laughs. "I don't suppose their wives would have been too pleased."

But they would probably not have been surprised, since the Gaelic sense of time was broad and general. A Highlander did not say he would meet you at 8:00; he said he would see you "in the evening," which could be any time after supper. Gaelic does not readily express possession either; it has no verb equivalent to the English "to have." Instead of "my wife" or "my woodland," a Gaelic speaker says "the woman who is with me" or "the forest which is at me."

Like the Greek of Homer, Gaelic is a heroic language – pre-industrial, pre-commercial. It is proverbial, bardic, and mystical on the one hand, blunt and homespun on the other. It describes a world of crofters and fishers who are also warriors and prophets – an ancient world of charms and herbs, of fables and prophecies, of witches and fairies called *sithichean*. Like the Greeks, the Celts found supernatural beings in the world, intimately (and not always nobly) involved with human beings.

The repertoire of Gaelic stories ranges from short anecdotes to "wonder tales" about the Fenians to *sgeulachd*, which Hector describes as "the great stories, the big stories, which take hours to tell. Some of them can take as much as three evenings. They're very formulaic, and they rely on repetition, which makes them easier to memorize. For example, a story might be about a hero who has five or six feats to perform, and each one involves a supernatural encounter. Well, the opening of each episode echoes the others, and my version of the story would be amazingly close to yours."

Sgeulachd, Hector says, "don't deal with small people. They're on a grander scale. The women are all white-skinned, and the men are all gentry. They're followers of a loftier ideal, a noble code of conduct. The instruction manual on how to live properly and prosperously is contained within the stories."

That Celtic ideal has to do with honour and courage, with music and poetry, with hospitality, with loyal pride in family and ancestry. Until the early 1800s, surnames were uncommon in the Hebrides, for example; Highlanders traditionally identified themselves by the *sloinneadh* or pedigree, and Cape Bretoners still do. "John Willie Jim Sandy" may have been christened John MacDonald – one of a dozen John MacDonalds in the village – but this particular John is the son of Willie, the grandson of Jim, and the great-grandson of Sandy.

Applied to women, the *sloinneadh* produces some odd results, like "Bessie Archie Dan," though it can as easily include a man's mother, as in "Malcolm Effie." Often the *sloinneadh* is enriched by a family "by-name" based on a family's hair colour; or trade, or place of residence, as in Peggy Iain Gobha – Margaret of John the Blacksmith. In 1816 Alexander MacDonald settled with his family on South West Mabou Ridge, and the family has ever since been so universally known as "the Ridges" that one descendant recently had to have a paycheque altered: his last name appeared on it as "Ridge" instead of "MacDonald." The Ridges were a family of poets from Lochaber, and they continued so. Allan the Ridge in particular was the author of several well-loved lyrics.

If Gaelic flows naturally into lyrical song and epic story, it runs equally naturally to teasing humour and scathing denunciation. *Fal il e lug 's o bo e lug*, cries the song leader at a "milling frolic," where a group of neighbours have gathered to raise the nap on a homespun blanket.

Co an te og a tha seo gun chiele?
Fal il e lug 's o bo e lug, he sings out again.

The first and third lines are gibberish, but the second line asks What young girl is here without a husband?

Someone else sings the next chorus, with the same refrain, answering *Gur e Mairi tha gun chiele:* It's Mary that has no husband.

"What young man shall I choose for you?" asks the leader, and now Mary replies, "Won't you give me my sweetheart?"

"It's Malcolm that I'll give you," sings the leader, and Mary may dismiss Malcolm as *Luideanach odhar a theid fodha, nach eirich:* "A dirty sloven who'd fall down and not rise." And so it goes, with Mary rejecting the various choices in pungent language: Neil is a weakling, James is fickle, and so forth. But when the leader names Mary's sweetheart, she replies with a phrase of dazzling beauty.

Cridhe glan soluisd am broilleach a leine, she sings: "A pure heart of light in the bosom of his shirt."

In Canada, the technology of highways, radio, phonographs, and newspapers pushed Gaelic to fringe areas once more. Gaelic became a quaint anachronism, a language spoken by grandparents. Children were punished for speaking it even in the playgrounds. Like the other heritage languages of Cape Breton, Acadian French and Mi'kmaq – indeed, like most minority languages in Canada before the advent of multiculturalism – Gaelic marked its speakers as primitives and bumpkins. Donald and Mary Rankin operate a bed-and-breakfast on Mabou Harbour, and both "have the Gaelic," but even today they feel shy about using it. Frances and Ronnie MacEachen are the first generation in their family to speak English as a first language.

"The health of a language can be measured by how easily you can raise a child in it," says Rosemary MacCormack, a native of South Uist in the Hebrides who hosts a weekly Gaelic show on a Port Hawkesbury radio station. She and her husband Brian were among ten couples who for some years supported a Gaelic immersion pre-school progam in Iona – the only one, apparently, outside Scotland itself. But the project seemed forlorn: if their children did grow up knowing Gaelic, who would they speak with? In this generation, only one family has raised a family in Gaelic: Ronald and Maureen Mackenzie in Mabou Harbour. Ronald, who is Rosemary's cousin, is also from South Uist. Maureen is from Mabou.

"Our children," said Maureen fiercely, "will be able to speak to their father in his own language." But they will be the only ones who can do so.

"So far as official support is concerned, Gaelic is at the bottom of the pile," says Frances MacEachen. "French is an official language. Mi'kmaq is an aboriginal language. Other languages are supported because of multiculturalism. But when someone applied for support for Gaelic, they were told Gaelic wasn't eligible because it was a founding language. There's no support for Gaelic, none at all."

And so *Am Braighe* has a subtext of urgency, almost of despair. The music is thriving, yes, but at its moment of triumph – Juno Awards, TV specials, international tours, profiles in national magazines – the language and the culture are fading.

Frances and Ronnie have both spent time in Scotland, where Gaelic learning/tourism programs are flourishing. They see Cape Breton's Gaelic residue as a great opportunity, tragically ignored.

"People are learning Gaelic in all the big American cities," says Frances. "They call here all the time to buy books and tapes. We had a call from Florida, from a man in the Celtic Buddhist Society who wanted a text translated into Gaelic. Cape Breton is the only place in North America where people could come to hear Gaelic."

"But when you cross the Canso Causeway, how do you find it?" asks Ronnie. "How do you touch it? It isn't there for you. You have to seek it out."

You can touch it at the Gaelic College in Saint Ann's, which during the summer offers instruction in the language, the music, the dancing, the weaving. You can touch it at the Highland Village in Iona, on Barra Strait, where historic Scottish houses have been moved from all over Cape Breton along with a store, a blacksmith shop, and other buildings to form a complete panorama of the Scottish built heritage. You can touch it at the innumerable summer festivals and Scottish concerts.

But these are only fragments of the powerful Gaelic presence which the MacEachens envisage. They want to see Gaelic in the schools again; they want it given prominence in the tourism literature, the universities, and in the history books. They want

Gaelic broadcasting, Gaelic seminars and day-camps, bed-and-breakfasts with bilingual signs that say "Gaelic spoken here." Despite the romanticism of Gaelic, possession of the language has to become not just a cultural asset but an economic one as well.

But even the optimists hardly expect that Gaelic will ever again be the working language even of the smallest Cape Breton villages, says Jim St.Clair, an author, activist, and historian. What it can be is "an academic study for a small group, and a performance for a much larger group." To achieve even that, the Scottish community will have to set aside some deep divisions – "true believers" versus compromisers, the Protestant North Shore (with its Gaelic College) versus the Catholics of central Cape Breton (with their Highland Village Society, of which St.Clair, a Protestant, is a former president.)

"The dissensions are so deep, and the wounds are so painful, that there's no unity of approach," says St.Clair. A few years ago, an attempt to establish an island-wide Gaelic Council "ended with great hostility over issues like whether the meetings should be conducted in Gaelic. These conflicts keep good people away. We need to name the divisions among the Celts, and set them aside."

Is iomadh duine laghach a mhill an creideamh, says a caustic Gaelic proverb: "There's many a delightful person has been spoiled by religion."

Meanwhile, Frances MacEachen is preparing her next issue, laying out the ancient words on a computer screen, manipulating the language of the Garden with Pagemaker software. The New York Times published an article on *Am Braighe* which attracted letters from Florida to Alaska. The contributions are coming in from down the road and across the world; recent issues have contained letters to the editor – in Gaelic – from Horst Woll in Germany and Jeff Chambers in Tasmania. There is a Gaelic newsgroup on the Internet with more than 700 members worldwide, firing poems and proverbs around the globe.

Gaelic survived Julius Caesar and Attila the Hun. With such devoted moles among the microchips, it may even survive the global village.

Wine, Health, and Sociability:
An Italian Family Experience in Cape Breton

SAM MIGLIORE

> One glass of wine makes you strong like a lion,
> Two glasses make you happy like a monkey,
> While three glasses can change you into a pig.

The term *culture* can be both a useful and a potentially dangerous concept. On the positive side, it allows us to make generalizations that transcend individual experience and help us understand a people's way of life. In the process, however, these ideas can simplify and distort the very way of life we are attempting to understand (Pirandello 1974; Wittgenstein 1968). Generalizations are potentially dangerous phenomena, because they can represent people's thoughts and experiences in stereotypical terms that construct an image of a particular group as some exotic, uniform, and/or static "other" (Abu-Lughod 1991).

To avoid this problem, I suggest that it is necessary to ground discussions of *culture* in the words, thoughts, and actions of the people themselves. This entails a change in focus from the search for generalizations to an examination of how people make use of cultural knowledge in the process of their everyday life experiences. This change of direction, I believe, gives us an insight into how people perceive and make use of *meanings* that have significance for them. It is this conception of culture that informs my study of wine and winemaking among Italian-Canadians in Cape Breton.

From Folktale to Family Experience

Growing up in an Italian household, I heard many old proverbs, stories, and folktales. My father used these devices to entertain me, my brother, and my many cousins. He also used them to teach us lessons about life, and how we should live our lives. One of the stories he told was of *Noah* and the *invention of wine*. The story, as I recall it, proceeds as follows:

> *'Na vota* (once upon a time) Noah, his family, and an ark full of animals sailed high above the flood waters. During what appeared to be an endless voyage, Noah, by chance, discovered winemaking. He sampled the wine, and it was good.
>
> After one glass of wine, Noah found that he had become as strong as a lion. He had so much energy that he was able to run around and around the ark without tiring. He had so much power that he could pick up the elephants without effort.
>
> Impressed with the energy and power he had gained after just one glass of wine, Noah decided to have another drink. The second glass, however, caused Noah to act differently; he began to act like a monkey. He started to jump up and down, to chatter loudly, and to laugh at everything he heard.
>
> Since the second glass had made him so happy, Noah decided to have a third drink. This third glass of wine changed everything. He lost his strength, and he was no longer happy. The wine had made Noah sick. His pain was so great that he could only moan and groan as he fell to the floor and began to roll back and forth just like a pig.
>
> That's why we say that one glass of wine makes you as strong as a lion, two glasses make you happy like a monkey, but three glasses can change you into a pig.

When I began to work with Italian community members in Cape Breton, I was surprised to hear an elderly gentleman tell virtually the same story during a small get-together at his home. I

Gabriele Dimiche and Friends "Salute!"

was surprised because he and I are from very different regions of Italy. This makes me suspect that the story has a long history in Italy, southern Europe, and areas influenced by southern Europeans.[1] At any rate, the story is significant for the present discussion because it reveals a central feature of Italian philosophy concerning wine. More specifically, wine, consumed in moderation, can be a source of both "physical power" and "health." The importance of wine for an Italian family, however, extends well beyond health; it can represent, for instance, a source of pride, a symbol of ethnic identity, a religious symbol (i.e., wine as a component of the Roman Catholic sacrament of communion), as well as an essential ingredient in the tradition of hospitality and sociability.

Among Italians, then, wine tends to serve many purposes. My goal is to address this issue by giving "voice" to some of the thoughts and experiences of three particular Italian-Canadians from Sydney, Nova Scotia – Gabriele, Anna, and their son Gian Carlo DiMichele.[2] What follows is part description and part transcription of ideas expressed during an interview I conducted with the DiMichele family for a video production about Italians and winemaking in Cape Breton (Migliore 1994). My aim in providing extended quotes is to allow these three individuals to discuss winemaking, the relationship between wine and health, and the place of wine in the family tradition, in their own words.[3]

223

Truth in Wine: Sharing a Family Tradition

Production for the "winemaking" video with the DiMichele family began in October of 1993. Late one evening, I received an excited phone call from Gabriele letting me know that the grapes had just arrived from Halifax. Margaret, my wife, and I quickly loaded up the necessary equipment and rushed to the designated location. For the next four or five hours we observed, participated, and recorded as Gabriele, with the help of family and friends, unloaded the various cases of grapes, prepared the winemaking tools, and began the process of making wine. You could feel the excitement in the air: it was a happy moment; it was a family moment; and, it was an expression of a family tradition. This is very clear in the interview statement Gabriele provided some time later:

> When I was three years, four to five years old, I remember my parents making wine every year in the fall, and it was a big, big, big, . . I say, culture. My parents, they were very excited to make wine. The wine was . . . a big part of the family. Without wine on the table, it was like having a table with food, with almost like nothing. You have got to have that glass of wine in the old country to be set on the table and everybody to be happy. Without wine, it was something missing.
>
> So, when I came over to Canada, and I started making this wine, I was very impressed to continue the culture. . . . I can't wait to the month of October when these grapes arrive from California to Halifax, and I can't wait to get the grapes from Halifax to Sydney. For me it's a very special day when I make this wine. . . .

It was Gian Carlo, however, who described the actual winemaking activity for that evening in this way:

> Well, that particular evening . . . was a very interesting evening. We started off with the grapes that were imported from California. . . . I would say, approximately, we ordered in maybe 200 cases of

> grapes, and they were distributed in Sydney amongst the Italians that wanted to buy 10, 15, 20 cases of grapes each. And, that evening, we were getting ready to make the wine and we, our family, probably bought 50 cases. We started out . . . opening up the cases, dumping them into a crusher . . . we crushed it by hand, all the juices came out into a big, long tub, approximately 6 feet long. Then from there it fell into a bucket, and as the bucket was getting full we would empty it into a demijohn it's called.

Once a demijohn is filled, it is stored for a period of time to allow the juice to ferment. It is this fermentation process that eventually transforms the juice into wine. The wine can be tested or sampled at various points during the fermentation process but, as Gabriele indicates below, the aim is to give the wine sufficient time to mature.

> A demijohn is about 12 gallons . . . and you let the wine ferment . . . . In a range of about 45 days to 50 days, we start testing the wine. But, it doesn't mean the wine is already mature to drink. It's good, it tastes as wine, but it's not . . . old enough. To have a good result, a good taste, the wine at least has to be anywhere 6 months to a year, to have a really good drinking wine.
>
> The mature wine becomes a central component in family meals.

It represents not only a tasty beverage, but also an ingredient for cooking, and something that can be transformed into vinegar to add flavour to salads and other dishes.

> In our family, same as a lot of Italian families, when you set the table, wine is one of the first things that goes on . . . we enjoy having it with the food, and you can also cook with wine, which I do. I do a lot of cooking with wine. Just about every meal there's a little bit of wine that goes into it somewhere along the line . . . it's just a very important part of an Italian family. (Anna)

225

> We make a good vinegar out of the wine. We make our own vinegar, we don't buy vinegar. My sister came from Toronto with my niece, and they took my vinegar back because there is nothing that compares to homemade vinegar from the wine. (Gabriele)[4]

The DiMichele family produces both red and white wine. As someone who has sampled this wine, I can say that it adds a special quality to the enjoyment of a meal.

Wine, Tradition, and Well-Being

Wine is a nutritious drink that can have positive effects on one's health. According to Anna, for example, "it seems that it gives you more strength and . . . it's very healthy for you." From an Italian point of view, however, well-being is linked to conceptions of equilibrium or balance. The interrelationship between wine consumption and health is based precisely on this principle. Moderation is the key to wine consumption. This is the point Anna and Gabriele stressed repeatedly; it is also the message my father tried to teach me and others through the story of *Noah* and the *invention of wine*. Alcohol is not something to be abused. Excessive wine consumption can have a negative effect on an individual's health and, although not mentioned explicitly in the transcript, it can disrupt family relations.

Gabriele addressed the interrelationship among wine, tradition, and well-being in the following statement:

> I like to put this wine on the table, and show my family, to my kids, the tradition, to our family, come from background, from grandparents making wine, my parents making wine, I'm making wine, and I would like to see my children make wine in the future. The wine is very important to have on the table. Only, I recommend with a meal. Not with abusing and get drunk. That's what I teach my kids to drink the wine with. And drinking a glass of wine on the table with the meals it's more like health. It's like a prescription. Helps the

blood circulate better. And, all this makes me happy to make wine.

He then went on to elaborate the potential role of wine in promoting health. This discussion focused on two issues: the link between wine consumption and blood circulation; and, more specifically, the power of wine to reduce the level of cholesterol in one's system. Although part of the discussion reflects the knowledge Gabriele has gained from a medical doctor, it is obvious that this knowledge has been adapted and incorporated into his own cultural conception of wine and well-being.

> The doctor ask me, said 'Gabriel you must be doing something different than somebody else is doing.' He said 'your cholesterol level is right on borderline, I don't know what you're doing different than somebody else, but keep doing what you're doing because you're doing right.' And I told the doctor, I said 'doctor, the only thing I'm doing different than I used to do, I have two glasses of wine with my meals every night.' And he said to me 'Gabriel, that's your answer.' I said, 'what do you mean?' He said, 'Wine has a certain alcohol there which helps thin the blood.' And he said, 'that's why you are doing very good . . . by having that couple glasses of wine every night.'
>
> But I started without knowing this. I just [thought in] my own way. I said, 'I don't think a couple glasses of wine with meals is going to hurt me,' because my father used to tell me that, my mother, you know, since I was a kid, 5 years old, the old people used to tell me 'have a glass of wine, its . . . good for you.' And I believe it all along. But nobody was telling me before, said 'drink a couple glasses of wine that it's good,' but I did this from tradition to have a couple glasses of wine on my table. But I feel great. You know, today, I just, I didn't think I have a heart attack. I didn't think I have an operation. And, you know, I really believe this wine helps the health by drinking moderately.

SAM MIGLIORE

The younger generation of Italian-Canadians does not necessarily share the same conception of wine and health as that of
their parents. Although they may be brought up in an Italian
household, they are exposed to outside influences from friends,
various popular media, and other sources, right from an early
age. In addition, the age difference itself has exposed them to different life experiences. As a result, then, their ideas sometimes
overlap and sometimes differ from those of their elders. What follows is an extended dialogue between father and son that
addresses this issue and provides an insight into their conceptions
of the role of wine in well-being.

> Gian Carlo (the son): I think wine and health, in
> my particular case as opposed to my father with
> cholesterol . . . . I'm a hard working man, at least I
> like to think I am anyway, and I work 10-12 hours
> a day, and a pretty hard 10 hours too sometimes.
> So when I come home from a hard day's work, I
> kick off my shoes, and my mother will have sup-
> per ready on the table, and the first thing I'll grab
> is a nice glass of wine. I'll chug a glass of wine
> back, and I tell ya it gives me a whole new spirit.
> And, I feel, I feel refreshed again, and I feel like I
> can go work another 10 hours . . . . I think a glass
> of wine or two at the supper table or even before a
> meal really revives you, and gives you a better . . .
> outlook for the hours left in the evening. The most
> important thing, I think [is to avoid] abusing the
> wine . . . one or two glasses at the supper table
> would be plenty.
>
> Gabriele: . . . you say . . . what happened to my
> father is . . . not the same case [as] yours. But if
> wine helps me . . . in the cholesterol level, it has to
> be good for you too, because it makes your blood
> circulate much better . . . . So you're looking to not
> get the same problem I have.
>
> Gian Carlo: No, you have a point there, but I
> don't mean to bring the age difference here . . . but
> there is a little bit of an age difference . . . . My fa-

ther has a point, and also I have a point. He has
to drink the wine at his particular age,
because he doesn't get the exercise and the
moving around that I do . . . where I play
hockey, soccer, and sometimes I ride a bike. I do
a lot of different things; I don't need the wine to
thin my blood or for cholesterol problems . . . .

Gabriele: . . . when we're young . . . we think we
don't need this and we don't need that . . . when
I started to drink wine, it was not . . . because of
the cholesterol. It's because when I was drinking
that glass of wine, it made me feel different, even
when I was young . . . . You can be a young man
and have a cholesterol problem without knowing . . . . So, for you to have this two glasses of
wine every night, *definitely* will do you good . . . .

Gian Carlo: Oh, I'm not saying it won't do me
good! . . . . I'm just saying . . . I am younger and
I do get more exercise in a run of a day.

Gabriele: We talk about what the wine is doing.
The wine is good for your health; it gives you
the strength back, because it has certain amount
of alcohol and sugar. The sugar produces power
into the body, and the alcohol, the wine alcohol,
which is different alcohol than the rest of the alcohol, it helps the cholesterol level . . . even if
you don't have that cholesterol, and it makes
your blood go faster, and by the blood circulate
faster you will have more power . . . .

Gian Carlo: A big thing too that we have to take
into consideration here is the homemade wine.
There is a big difference between the homemade wine and the wine that you would buy in
the story. I think the homemade wine, there is
no preservatives, there's no added chemicals,
no, you know . . . these kind of things to keep the
wine longer. And I think the wines that you buy
today in the stores, quite a few of them, have these

added chemicals and, well, things that are not really good for you . . .

Gabriele: And you know it's made from the grapes.

Gian Carlo: Ya, it's all natural.

At this point in the conversation Gabriele and Gian Carlo reached agreement. They began with different views about the importance of wine in their lives and gradually brought the discussion to a point where they could end the conversation on common note. Gian Carlo, in his twenties, is not concerned with cholesterol. At the same time, however, he recognizes the important role wine can play in both personal well-being and family tradition.

Gabriele's statements, in contrast, are more in line with the Italian theme of *balance* as a key to *health*. His following remark reinforces this point.

> The wine . . . gives you appetite, like an appertif . . .
> it is very good for helping for digesting the meal,
> providing [you] drink one glass and two, because
> if you abuse [it] too much acid in the wine will stop
> your digestion. See we need certain amount of
> acid in the body . . . which you got in wine, but if
> you put too much it wouldn't be any good. . . . [It]
> will make you sick instead of good.

The discussion in this paper may shift from the interrelationship between wine and strength, or cholesterol, or digestion, but the central theme remains the same. Moderation is at the heart of Gabriele's philosophy concerning wine and its consumption.

Wine, Hospitality, and Sociability

Well-being extends beyond physical and mental health. Family, friendship, and other social relationships can have a significant effect on a person's quality of life. In the Italian tradition, hospitality and sociability are important factors in promoting positive social interactions, and, more specifically, in allowing people to express both closeness and respect for others. Wine plays a vital role in this process.

> In our tradition, Sam, I remember since I was a kid, a little young fellow, my parents, the first thing they put on the table when they had a friend in the house was the bottle of wine. And, I keep this tradition going since I left my parents. Today, I realize that when an Italian family comes to visit, if you don't offer them a glass of wine they are not very well welcomed. They think about it that way, and I feel the same way too . . . .
>
> Other people, when they have guests, they present a bottle of beer or liquor, rum, but in the Italian tradition, we've got to have wine on the table . . . . Without wine, I don't think it would be the same evening to be happy, as much as the wine makes you happy. So the wine serves a purpose for a lot of different reasons. (Gabriele)

For a host to offer a guest a glass of wine, and the guest to accept the offer, goes a long way towards fulfilling certain social and cultural expectations concerning hospitality and sociability. Furthermore, as Gabriele indicates, wine, in moderation, can add life to a social gathering. Well-being may not depend on wine, but it is linked to people's social experiences. If wine can contribute to people's experience of a positive and enjoyable social encounter, than it has contributed to their sense of well-being. As Anna emphatically states, winemaking and wine drinking are part of an old tradition that "goes on and on and on. And it seems that if you don't have wine, you don't have anything."

A Concluding Remark

Members of the Italian-Canadian community do not necessarily share precisely the same conception of "wine." The ideas Gabriele, Anna, and Gian Carlo DiMichele express are their own. Their statements, however, do provide us with an insight into the Italian *culture* of winemaking and the position of wine in their family tradition. Wine is intimately linked to notions of health, what constitutes a well prepared and desirable meal, the etiquette of hospitality and sociability, ethnic identity, as well as what it means to be a part of an Italian family. For the DiMicheles, and many other Italian families, wine is something special; it can, because of its significance at both the individual and the cultural level, add substance to a person's and a family's quality of life.

What I have tried to do in this paper is to avoid, at least as much as possible, the presentation of the Italian winemaking and wine drinking tradition in terms of some uniform and static phenomenon we can call *culture*. Culture, in my view, is not a concrete entity that can be isolated, identified, and examined as if it had a life of its own; instead, it represents a set of meanings that people continuously construct, deconstruct, and reconstruct in the process of their everyday life experiences. As people's experiences vary, both from person to person and from situation to situation, so to do their cultural constructions. This is why I have concentrated on one Cape Breton family's conception of wine, and why I have relied to a great extent on allowing these individuals to present the material in their own "voice." I believe that this technique gives us an insight into how specific people make use of the cultural knowledge they have developed to express their thoughts and to give meaning to their actions.

Notes

1. There are similarities, for example, between the moral contained in my father's story and Zapotec views of wine consumption in Ixtepeji, Mexico (see Kearney 1972: 96).

2. Anna's statements are relatively short, and her "voice" is heard less frequently, partly because winemaking tends to be a male activity and partly because it is easier for a male ethnographer to interview male informants.

3. Although the quotes contained in the paper represent the actual words and feelings of these three family members, the reader should be aware that I have played a role in the editing process. I selected the excerpts from the original interview tape for inclusion here, and I chose the order in which to present these excerpts.

4. This quote has been taken from a subsequent interview with Gabriele DiMichele conducted by Jan Gentile in August of 1994.

References

Abu-Lughod, Lila. 1993. *Writing Women's Worlds: Bedouin Stories.* Berkeley: University of California Press.

Kearney, Michael. 1972. *The Winds of Ixtepeji: World View and Society in a Zapotec Town.* New York: Holt, Rinehart and Winston, Inc.

Migliore, Sam. 1994. *Truth in Wine: Well-Being Among Italians in Cape Breton.* Video. Sydney: University College of Cape Breton.

Pirandello, Luigi. 1974. *On Humor.* Studies in Comparative Literature, no. 58. Chapel Hill, N.C.: University of North Carolina Press.

Wittgenstein, Ludwig. 1968. *Philosophical Investigations.* Third Edition. Oxford: Basil Blackwell.

I would like to thank the DiMichele family and the Cape Breton Italian Cultural Association. Without their help this paper would not have been possible.

Cape Bretoners as Canadians

CELESTE SULLIMAN MacPHERSON & CAROL CORBIN

In 1992 Canadians wrestled with revising the constitution, and this exercise in nation-building elicited many definitions of what it means to be a Canadian. In fact, Canadian identity was one of the defining issues of the constitutional debates. The media were charged with rhetoric designed to convince Canadians to keep the country hanging together. And it gave "ordinary Canadians" a chance to reconsider just what being Canadian means.

Debating Canadian identity is a regular pastime for those living north of the longest unguarded border in the world. How, sitting next to a colossal film-making nation that churns out mesmerizing images from Hollywood that hypnotize our children and lure us into cross-border shopping, can Canada retain a sense of its own identity? And yet we do, somehow. The heart-warming images on television about Canadian heritage teach us who we are. We are acculturated through educational, community, family, and religious institutions to be good Canadian citizens who know most of the words to the national anthem and can name most of the provinces. Yet, the identity of a people is a tricky thing.

A key word in the answer to how Canadians maintain their identity is "diversity." Every region of the country has a distinct identity, and thus a distinct notion of what being Canadian means. While constituting a nation requires that individual communities sacrifice some of their unique identities and accept a portion of a common identity, an important part of Canada's common identity nevertheless celebrates the uniqueness of one's ethnicity, culture, heritage, community, and family.

To gain an understanding of how Cape Bretoners think of themselves as Canadians, we asked 70 of them to answer a written survey that included questions like: How would you describe Canada?; What does it mean to be a Canadian?; What do you think people from other countries think of Canadians?; What symbols represent Canada?; Describe a typical Canadian; Describe a typical Cape Bretoner; and What are Canada's best features? After they completed the survey, we interviewed many of the participants to obtain further information about what it means to Cape Bretoners to be Canadian.

In examining these oral and written narratives, we discovered four themes that demonstrate how Cape Bretoners think of themselves as Canadian. They tend to have: a close connection to the geographical space and a love of the land; an appreciation for a free and peaceful country; a pride in the varied cultural backgrounds of both Cape Bretoners and Canadians; and a recognition of Canada's distinctiveness from the United States. Further, Cape Bretoners expressed their preferences for certain Canadian symbols such as the maple leaf and the beaver that act to unite the country in a common culture and solidify the national character.

Reverence for the Land

With its vast expanse of land and huge pristine tracts of wilderness, Canada is above all big and wild. Many Cape Bretoners feel close links with their natural surroundings and often described the landscape as one of Canada's best features. Their responses included statements like: "wide spacious land," "nature's beauty," "natural parks and wildlife preserves," and "pride in Canada's clean natural environment." The United States on the other hand is seen by Cape Bretoners as an industrial giant of a country in which the wilderness has been tamed. Canadians feel strength in the natural abundance of their land, although their answers ignored many of the local environmental tragedies such as Sydney's tar ponds, Cape Breton's expanding deforestation, and the near-extinction of cod.

Nevertheless, the islanders' close emotional ties to the land and sea are apparent in the clusters of answers they gave. Nearly every respondent cited some aspect of the environment as a defining characteristic of Canada, and their answers included statements about Canada's beautiful scenery (47%), our vast and diverse country (29%), our natural resources (19%), and various other natural attractions like the Rocky Mountains, Niagara Falls, and the Bay of Fundy (9%).[1]

These answers may be explained in part by the great natural beauty of the Cape Breton Island. Ranked as the fourth most beautiful island in the world by *Traveler* magazine,[2] Cape Breton is an important destination point in Atlantic Canada and the environmental beauty is one feature that is exploited by tour operators and promoters. Cape Breton is, according to Enterprise Cape Breton Corporation's logo, "Nova Scotia's Masterpiece." And as Cape Bretoners we have agreed with this slogan. We are proud of the unsullied natural beauty of this island, and our pride is evident, by extension, in considering the natural environment to be one of Canada's defining characteristics.

Grateful to Live in a Free and Peaceful Land

The second most important theme for Cape Bretoners is related to the notion of freedom. Word clusters such as "freedom," "democracy," "independence," "freedom of expression," and "freedom of religion" were used by 91% of respondents. But the word that overwhelmingly prevailed was "freedom," and it was often expressed in conjunction with either the term peace or the ideal of free expression. Forty-four percent of the respondents were proud of Canada's "peace-keeping," "peace-loving," or "peaceful" existence. Included as well in the concept of freedom was Canada's quality of being a safe place to live, with low crime and little violence. This quality was often contrasted with images of the United States's violent streets, a form of definition by negation, or what Canada is not. Freedom of expression was more important to Cape Bretoners than democracy or freedom of religion, and Cape Bretoners felt some pride in their high level of political involvement and freedom to voice their opinions.

Related to Canada's peacefulness was the national characteristic of "niceness." The picture that emerged from Cape Bretoners' descriptions of Canadians may be as much a self definition as it is a reflection of what they think of Canadians at large. Words like "friendly," "nice," "helpful," "caring," "warm," "kind," and "generous" were used by 50% of respondents to describe Canadians. But the niceness of Canadians sometimes leads to a passivity and complacency that some respondents noted as a weakness. Twenty-nine percent stated that Canadians were quiet, humble, passive, or modest. While sometimes these characteristics were noted as positive when contrasted with the loud brashness of Canada's southern neighbours, there seemed to be uncertainty about just how good it is to be so nice all the time.

Several respondents noted a certain lack of backbone among Canadians in dealing with government-imposed regulations. The GST, for example, was noted as a national symbol that had been crammed down the throats of Canadians. With some chagrin, respondents noted that Americans probably wouldn't have stood for it. Yet Cape Breton respondents consistently stated that we are a kind people who care for our neighbours, families, and friends. We do not wish to emulate the American style of corporate individualism in which success, particularly financial success, is the primary measure of human worth. Instead we wish to remain in a mutually dependent relationship with the federal government in order to guarantee a decent life for every Canadian even at the cost of a little less reward for personal achievement.

In a 1995 year-end portrait of the Canadian national character, a compilation of surveys suggested that some of Canada's optimism and even its niceness were eroding. After thinking of ourselves as peaceful people for several generations, Canadians have been confronted with images of violence in the past several months.[3] A Canadian soldier holding a gun to the bloody head of a Somali teen, the Paul Bernardo murders, priests in jail for sexual abuse, and Cape Breton's McDonald's murders have all created what Maude Barlow of the Council of Canadians calls a "loss of innocence."[4] Even though murder rates in Canada actually have been dropping, Canadians believe that violence is creeping in across the border, probably because of the cable news programs Canadians watch from Detroit and other American cities.[5]

Survey respondents also noted that they were, for the most part, middle-income earners, who enjoy an enviable standard of living but work hard for it. Canada's social programs, particularly health care, were additional defining characteristics, although there is some concern about losing them under the strain of the national deficit. According to Canadian author, Pierre Berton, "this has become a very mean-spirited country."[6] Middle-income Canadians worry about being dragged down by the deficit, unemployment insurance, and loss of social programs. Cape Bretoners already feel the pinch of necessity as more and more live on unemployment insurance or fisheries package payments.

In spite of these problems, Canadians are still proud to be Canadian, and proud that the United Nations ranks Canada as one of the best countries in which to live.

The Multicultural Mosaic

One of the discoveries of our investigation into what it means to be Canadian is that the people of Cape Breton generally are unable to describe an "ordinary" Canadian. Responses included statements like: "I cannot define a typical Canadian. I can only really think of myself as a Cape Bretoner;" "There are no typical Canadians. Canadians come from various backgrounds and strive to keep their cultural heritages." This finding supports the notion that diversity remains one of the foundations of Canadian identity. Seventy-one percent of respondents mentioned multiculturalism as part of what it means to be Canadian.

Cape Bretoners' strong connections to local cultures, heritages, and even individual families supersede commitment to the nation. This suggests that the country is a body of fragments held loosely together by an often invisible order. The nation-builders are, in a sense, trying to do what chaos scientists are doing: they are trying to find threads of order within the disorder to discover what holds the fragments or fractals together. Therefore, this indicates not surprisingly that any survey into the constitution of a people in one particular location or one particular culture may not hold true for all of the country. The way Cape Bretoners think of themselves as Canadians, for example, may be quite different than the way Albertans or Algonquins think of themselves as Canadians.

Close neighbours to the south

Canadian identity is intimately entwined with American identity because of the power of American cultural influence.[7] A 1990 Canadian survey of American and Canadian broadcasting found very little evidence of Canada on major United States networks but great evidence of the United States on Canadian networks. Yet most Cape Bretoners consistently prefer American cable TV to Canadian programming because, they state bluntly, "it's better."[8] The United States's close proximity, aggressive cable marketing, and similar ethnic, linguistic, and historic composition make it very natural for Cape Bretoners to assimilate American cultural icons, idioms, and slang, and to identify with American culture.

Some Cape Bretoners defined themselves as Canadians either by emphatically stating that they were not American, while conversely others said that they were probably thought of as an extension of the United States. Canadians may be like Americans, respondents noted, but they are quieter and less intrusive. Survey responses included the following: "I think we're perceived as fairly insignificant compared to our American neighbours;" "I feel that the most accurate way to describe how Canadians feel about being Canadian is not being American;" "We're thought of as an extension of the United States but with a more compromising attitude towards international topics;" "[We are] a much smaller version of the United States;" "I would describe Canada as a mirror image of the United States with the exception of the French-speaking people of Quebec."

Although these qualities provide some debatable distinction for Canadians from their American neighbours, they also reflect a timid and obsequious relationship with the powerful images and mass culture of the United States.[9] Cape Bretoners noted Canada's inability to take a uniquely Canadian stand on many issues or resist American international policy. Survey respondents made statements such as: "I think that, basically, Canadians are much more subdued than, say for instance, Americans;" "Canadians seem to be more apathetic and less patriotic than countries resembling the U.S.A.;" "Canada follows the lead of the United States too much. Canada has become very Americanized." Canada's leaders exacerbate this impression by reluctantly following the United States into a war with Iraq and kowtowing to American economic pressure. Yet many Cape Bretoners prefer to maintain their less aggressive and more compassionate qualities in the face of increased pressure to adopt American principles and systems in a new, more competitive, and colder world. In Cape Breton it isn't considered weak to be a pacifist, as it might be in the United States.

The relationship that Canada has with the United States is, in many respects, a love/hate relationship. Canadians adore the seductiveness of American media and American goods, while detesting the American qualities that make them possible. As

Canada's character becomes more entwined with America's, we see the United States that Canadians love to hate taking on the role of an idealized enemy. It is an enemy that is both within and without Canada. The external enemy is the image of the United States with its perceived heartless competitive spirit and its archaic social systems. And the internal one is the United States within Canada: it is Brian Mulroney as he affiliated himself more and more with American-style government; it is the American spectacle on TV every night that displays that nation's problems like a soap opera that Canadians cannot turn off; it is the United States economic system that seems to insinuate across the border and into the homes of most Canadians; it is Walmart and McDonalds. When a nation both hates and loves a large portion of its own identity, it exists in a continual identity crisis, and we believe that this may be one of Canada's most difficult problems in constituting its national character.

National Symbols and Cape Breton Characteristics

The Cape Bretoners we surveyed described the Canadian symbols that came most readily to their minds. The maple leaf was the first one, with 67% naming it as a significant Canadian symbol. The others included the beaver (39%), hockey (30%), and the flag (29%). In addition, respondents noted other images that were distinctive symbols of Canada. These included historical sites, Canadian stories, the Bluenose, "anything Scottish," the RCMP, various wildlife such as eagle and moose, the National Film Board, and the Trans-Canada Highway. Another serious symbol of Canada is beer. The film Canadian Bacon parodies Canadian love of Canadian beer when an American at a hockey game states that "Canadian beer sucks." The hockey game stops, the spectators are silenced, and all turn on the Americans in a free-for-all brawl about the quality of Canadian beer.

The most cited characteristics of Cape Bretoners, according to Cape Bretoners, are that they are friendly, unemployed, hard-working party animals, who are proud of Cape Breton. Less often-cited qualities were polite, generous, hospitable, happy, family-oriented, and big beer drinkers. Portions of Cape Bretoners' images of themselves may be reflected back to them in some of the less than admirable descriptions in Cape Breton jokes, put downs, and cultural representations. But we Cape Bretoners seem to take these jokes pretty well, laughing at ourselves more than anyone.

In 1992, official unemployment figures for the island of Cape Breton hovered between 17% and 22%,[10] but unofficial calculations indicate that the figure is much higher – something closer to 50%.[11] Sydney's median income was $5,000 below the national average.[12] The 1990s are uncomfortable times: food banks are running short and unemployment insurance benefits are being cut back. And while Cape Bretoners' attention was focused on their stomachs and their pocketbooks, the government was asking the citizens of Canada to forget their personal problems – their jobless spouses and their hungry children – and instead imagine an ideal Canada built through a new constitution. The politicians were asking the people to self-actualize when their basic needs were not being met.

As the recession deepened across North America in 1992, Canadians began to see the constitutional issue as a way for the government to divert national attention from the "real" problems they face on a daily basis. At every constitutional conference that included ordinary citizens, questions about jobs came up. Finally in Quebec the participants insisted upon the inclusion of a social charter within the constitution.[13] A social charter would, in effect, address the material and monetary needs of the people and thus begin to bridge the gap between the vision of Canada – the dream – and the day-to-day lives of ordinary Canadians – the reality. In addition to assurance of a minimum standard of living, it would guarantee the security of Canada's health care system. As former Health Minister Benoit Bouchard noted, "While Canadians are hard put to identify the symbols that hold us together, our health system, with its key principles applicable to every region of the country, constitutes . . . one of the institutions which makes the greatest contribution to Canada's distinctiveness."[14]

Conclusion

As we spoke with Cape Bretoners about what it means to be Canadian, we discovered some of the primary images that the islanders believe represent them. First, Cape Bretoners are most clearly proud of their little piece of geography, and this one trait may be the major defining point for them – many Cape Bretoners leave the island only when they have to and come back as soon as possible. Second, Cape Bretoners are proud to live in a free country where they can voice their opinions without restraint. Third, multiculturalism is surely as much a statement of the nation's soul as it is a reflection of the Cape Breton way of life. Finally, Canada's status as a peace-loving nation distinguishes the country from the United States. Canadian traits such as tolerance, friendliness, and compassion in world affairs and toward one's neighbours are typical of Canadian outlook and indicate a sentiment that appears to be counter to many United States worldviews.

The process of reconstituting the nation that began in 1992 and was repeated with the 1995 referendum is one without a definitive conclusion. Fears exist within Canada that the nation is falling apart.[15] Yet, the strength of Canada's symbols and character will prevail with or without a final resolution to the questions raised. Canada may live in constant tension between the ideal and the practical, between multiculturalism and nationalism, between atrophy and renaissance. It is in these dialectical tensions that Canada will find its strength, resilience, and adaptability. Can we not imagine an eternal national discussion much like the conversations among people about who they are and who they want to become? As esoteric ideas are batted around and visions and dreams are imagined, they are often interrupted by the baby's cry, by the telephone, and by the demands to put food on the table. Like a living constitution, Cape Bretoners' lives are never settled and thus never fixed.

As long as Cape Bretoners continue to state their pride in being Canadian, and as long as Canada can continue to discuss its future, it cannot fall apart. Any attempt to create a permanent identity or an imperishable document must ultimately fail. What is generated may be a new kind of state, one that is flexible enough to exist in the postmodern condition and one in which every individual, every community, and every region is valued in the collective whole.

Notes

1. Note that total percentages will exceed 100% because many respondents mentioned qualities or characteristics more than once in their answers.

2. Condé Nast *Traveller.* "Readers' Choice 1994 Awards." November 1994: 222. See also *Islands* magazine, October 1995, for a 12-page spread about the island.

3. Galloway, Gloria. "Down in the dumps." *Chronicle-Herald.* December 28, 1995: A2.

4. Galloway.

5. Galloway.

6. Quoted in Galloway.

7. In "Selling our innocence abroad" (*Harper's,* December 1991, p. 38), Pico Iyer explains the global phenomenon of American cultural influence: "Pop culture makes the world go round, and America makes the best pop culture. . . . The capital of the world, as Gore Vidal has said, is not Washington but Hollywood. And however much America suffers an internal loss of faith, it will continue to enjoy, abroad, some of the immunity that attaches to all things in the realm of myth. As much as we – and everyone else – assume that the French make the best perfumes and the Swiss the finest watches, the suspicion will continue that Americans make the best dreams."

8. In conversations about Canadian and American television, Canadians stated that American television programs have better colour, better actors, better sets, and the shows are more creative.

9. *The Economist* described Canada's lack of identity this way: "The question of government is central because it is central to Canadians' sense of identity. Many might deny this, but few would deny that they define themselves by reference to the United States. It is Canada's misfortune to find itself sitting next to the richest, most powerful country on Earth, whose citizens are the most intellectually, artistically and politically effervescent of nations. By comparison with that, any country might seem dull. There are many more similarities than differences between Canada and the United States, so in order to justify their separate existence as a nation, the 27 million Canadians find it necessary to stress the things that separate them from their 252 million culturally assertive neighbours." ("Canada may not have the constitution to tough it out." *Globe and Mail.* July 19, 1991, p. A7.)

10. MacKinnon, Doyle. "Island unemployment rate stuck." *Cape Breton Post.* February 8, 1992, p. 3.

11. The official unemployment figures are based upon the number of people filing for unemployment insurance. But the unofficial ones take into account as well the people who no longer qualify for assistance, who have now shifted to welfare, or who simply have given up on the system altogether.

12. "Sydney's median income below national average." *Cape Breton Post.* September 13, 1995: 6.

13. Parsons, Vic. "Ottawa's economic proposals trounced." *Cape Breton Post.* February 5, 1992, p. 4.

14. "What others are saying." *Cape Breton Post.* January 9, 1992, p. 5.

15. Galloway.

Contributors

SILVER DONALD CAMERON is the author of 14 books, 50-odd dramas for radio, TV and the stage, and numerous other writings. He is currently Dean of the School of Community Studies at the University College of Cape Breton.

CAROL CORBIN received her Ph.D. in communication from the University of Iowa. Originally from Silver Spring, Maryland, she teaches communication and media studies at the University College of Cape Breton and lives in Louisbourg.

WILLIAM DAVEY, a member of the Department of Languages and Letters at the University College of Cape Breton, teaches medieval English literature and the history of the English language. His research interests are in these teaching areas and in the language and culture of Cape Breton.

JOANNE KENNEDY graduated from the University College of Cape Breton in 1991. She resides in Bras d'Or with her husband Michael.

RON KEOUGH is a freelance journalist and playwright. He is a resident of Sydney.

HUGH MacDONALD lives in Sydney Mines with his wife Joanne and son Keith. He is a graduate of the University College of Cape Breton. Hugh has played in several bands in the industrial area and is employed with the Department of Community Services.

MICHAEL MacDONALD teaches communication at the University College of Cape Breton and coaches the successful UCCB Debating Team. He lives in Bras d'Or with his wife Joanne.

SHELDON MacINNES acquired an appreciation of Cape Breton music and dance from his father, Dan Joe MacInnes (1922-1991), who was a well known Cape Breton fiddler. Sheldon is a program director and part-time lecturer at the University College of Cape Breton.

RICHARD MacKINNON is originally from New Waterford and is now living in Sydney. He received a Ph.D. in Folklore Studies from Memorial University of Newfoundland. He is chair of the Department of Culture, Heritage, and Leisure Studies at the University College of Cape Breton.

ERNA MacLEOD, a resident of Sydney, Nova Scotia, is a communication student at the University College of Cape Breton. She has worked nine summers at the Fortress of Louisbourg as an interpreter.

CELESTE SULLIMAN MacPHERSON is an assistant professor at the University College of Cape Breton where she teaches interpersonal communication and performance studies. She lives in Sydney with her husband, two sons, and their new dog.

DAVE MAHALIK is a graduate of the University College of Cape Breton's Bachelor of Arts Community Studies program. He lives in Sydney River where he publishes *What's Goin' On,* a magazine dealing with Cape Breton's arts and entertainment.

JEANNINE McNEIL, a resident of Sydney, graduated from the University College of Cape Breton with a Bachelor of Arts Community Studies. She has recently been accepted into the Environmental Studies graduate program at York University in Toronto.

SAM MIGLIORE is an associate professor of anthropology at the University College of Cape Breton. He has conducted research among Italian-Canadians in both industrial Cape Breton and southern Ontario. More recently he has begun to work with Italians in British Columbia.

COLLEEN MOORE-HAYES is the assistant registrar at the University College of Cape Breton. A graduate of St. Francis Xavier University's Diploma in Adult Education program and a BACS student at UCCB, Colleen has worked as a manager in the field of adult education for the past fifteen years.

KEVIN O'SHEA, a resident of Lousibourg, is a communication major at the University College of Cape Breton. He has worked for six summers at the Fortress of Louisbourg as an interpreter and a drummer.

BARBARA RENDALL is a poet and fiction writer living in East Bay. She recently moved to Cape Breton Island from Saskatchewan.

ELLISON ROBERTSON is a Cape Breton writer and painter whose work has focused on labour history and the culture and social history of Cape Breton Gaels.

JUDITH A. ROLLS is an associate professor of communication at the University College of Cape Breton. Her research interests lie in the areas of gender, communication competence, and experiential learning. She is also active as a communication workshop facilitator/trainer.

MOIRA ROSS is a recent graduate of the University College of Cape Breton.

DAVID L. SCHMIDT is a linguistic anthropologist and member of the University College of Cape Breton's Department of Culture, Heritage, and Leisure Studies. His research interests include Mi'kmaq language and culture, heritage, tourism, and East Asian societies.

GERALD TAYLOR, born and bred in Cape Breton, is an avid traveller and former teacher. He left the classroom stage fifteen years ago to work behind the scenes in the entertainment field.

MARIE WESTHAVER lives in Howie Centre and teaches in the Department of Communication. Her research interests include health promotion, communication and disability.